LABRADOR ODYSSEY

McGill-Queen's/Hannah Institute Studies in the
History of Medicine, Health, and Society
Series Editors: S.O. Freedman and J.T.H. Connor

Volumes in this series have been supported by the
Hannah Institute for the History of Medicine.

Labrador Odyssey

The Journal and Photographs of Eliot Curwen
on the Second Voyage of Wilfred Grenfell, 1893

EDITED BY RONALD ROMPKEY

McGill-Queen's University Press   MONTREAL & KINGSTON • LONDON • ITHACA

© McGill-Queen's University Press 1996
ISBN 0-7735-1366-3 (cloth)
ISBN 0-7735-1870-3 (paper)

Legal deposit second quarter 1996
Bibliothèque nationale du Québec

Printed in Canada on acid-free paper

Funding for this book has been received from the Department of Canadian Heritage, Multiculturalism Programs.

McGill-Queen's University Press acknowledges the financial support of the Government of Canada through the Book Publishing Industry Development Program for its activities. We also acknowledge the support of the Canada Council for the Arts for our publishing program.

Canadian Cataloguing in Publication Data

Curwen, Eliot
  Labrador odyssey: the journal and photographs of Eliot Curwen on the second
  voyage of Wilfred Grenfell, 1893
  (McGill-Queen's/Hannah Institute Studies in the history of medicine,
  health and society, ISSN 1198-4503: 3)
  Includes bibliographical references and index.
  ISBN 0-7735-1366-3 (bnd)
  ISBN 0-7735-1870-3 (pbk)
  1. Grenfell, Wilfred Thomason, Sir, 1865–1940. 2. Curwen, Eliot. 3. Labrador (Nfld.) –
  History. 4. Labrador (Nfld.) – Social conditions. 5. Missions, Medical –
  Newfoundland – Labrador – History. 6. Missions, English – Newfoundland –
  Labrador – History. I. Rompkey, Ronald II. Title III. Series
  FC2193.3.C87 1996   971.8'202   C95-900796-2
  F1137.C87 1996

This book was typeset by Typo Litho Composition Inc.
in 10.5/13 Palatino.

For Bill and Carolyn

CONTENTS

ILLUSTRATIONS

FIGURES

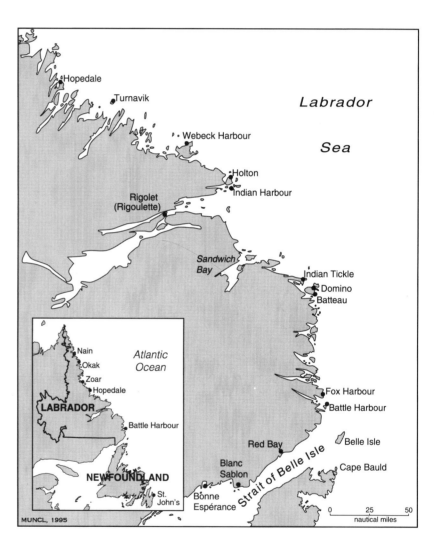

Map of Labrador

Labrador

Sea

Hopedale
Turnavik
Webeck Harbour
Holton
Indian Harbour
Rigolet
(Rigoulette)

Sandwich
Bay

Indian Tickle
Domino
Batteau

Nain
Okak
Zoar
Hopedale

Atlantic
Ocean

LABRADOR

Battle Harbour

NEWFOUNDLAND

St.
John's

Fox Harbour
Battle Harbour

Belle Isle

Red Bay

Blanc
Sablon

Cape Bauld

Strait of Belle Isle

Bonne
Espérance

0   25   50
nautical miles

MUNCL, 1995

ACKNOWLEDGMENTS

This book provides a glimpse of Labrador a century ago through the eyes of Eliot Curwen, a young medical missionary attracted to the region for a few months in 1893 by Wilfred Grenfell. Grenfell, who was laying the foundation for what would become a complex experiment in northern medicine, could not have foreseen at that point the full possibility for cultural and medical intervention. What would eventually become known as the Grenfell Mission was still in its infancy, and Grenfell himself still needed to learn more about the Labrador coast and its mixed population. The events recounted here during his second voyage to Labrador, shaped by Eliot Curwen in his journal and photographs, reveal the gradual dawning of that possibility.

Whereas Grenfell devoted the rest of his life to improving conditions in Labrador, Curwen ultimately settled in Sussex, England, where he practised medicine and took up the serious study of archaeology. A busy digger as well as a collector and a writer on archaeological matters, he dated his preoccupation with ancient culture from 1909, when he attended a lecture that Hilaire Belloc gave about Stane Street, the 57-mile Roman highway linking London and Chichester. Belloc's lecture, together with his subsequent book, *The Stane Street* (1913), aroused wide popular interest, and Curwen was one of its casualties. He joined the Sussex Archaeological Society forthwith and with his young son Cecil began to survey sections of the highway's Sussex alignments, publishing his findings in 1915 in the *Sussex Archaeological Collections*. Throughout the next three decades, he produced numerous articles, notes, and reports, which he published in the *Collections* and elsewhere. To these he added collaborations with his son (whom he bred both to medicine and to archaeology), expanding their mutual interest to lynchets, barrows, sepulchral mounds and other earthworks, early flint and stone implements, mines, roads, forts, and prehistoric pottery.

Curwen's investigations have been associated principally with the Sussex Downs. But in fact his interest in early culture had begun much earlier and had surfaced in 1893, when he joined the medical expedition to Newfoundland and Labrador fitted out by the Mission to Deep Sea Fishermen and led by Grenfell. On that occasion, he searched for ancient artifacts and implements while he was scrutinizing the colonial society he encountered and keeping detailed notes of the birds and fishes, the flora and fauna, the weather, the icebergs, and other local phenomena. His records were especially extensive during his time in Labrador, where he absorbed the technology of fishing, the living conditions of resident fishermen, the work of the Moravian missionaries, and the customs of the Labrador Inuit. Already introduced to archaeological practice, he went digging in Hopedale and speculated about the provenance of the copper, iron, and stone implements he found there. Taken together, all these observations range widely over life in Newfoundland and what was then its northern fishing and trapping territory.

The journal, notebook, and photographs of Eliot Curwen rest in the hands of his granddaughter, Ruth Eliot (Curwen) Gimlette. The journal is reproduced here with minor corrections for spelling and punctuation, supplemented with letters and reports from other members of the expedition (particularly from Grenfell) as they appeared in the journal of the Mission to Deep Sea Fishermen, *Toilers of the Deep*. The photographs are selected from two separate albums, which contain mostly Curwen's photographs but also include a few of Grenfell's. I am grateful to Mrs Gimlette for permission to publish these and for her assistance in their duplication.

I am indebted to Geoffrey Place for generously bringing the Curwen collection to my attention. I thank Melvin Baker, John Crellin, Jim Hiller, Peter Neary, Kenneth Roberts, Hans Rollmann, and

Acknowledgments

Philip Smith for assistance with historical and archaeological details, and John Hewson for advice on the transliteration of Inuktitut. I also thank Bruce Shawyer for eliminating a menacing computer bug. And I acknowledge the assistance of the following who provided archival information: Malcolm G. Underwood (Archivist, St John's College, Cambridge), Bernard Nurse (Librarian, Society of Antiquaries), Dr E.S. Leedham-Green (Assistant Keeper, Cambridge University Archives), Jonathan Evans (District Archivist, Royal London Hospital Archives), and K.W. Dickins (Archivist, Sussex Archaeological Society).

Research assistance was provided by Paula Hayden, map reproduction by the Cartography Laboratory at Memorial University, and photographic reproduction by the Salisbury Studio, Salisbury, Wiltshire. I acknowledge with gratitude Dr Michael Staveley, former Dean of Arts, Memorial University, for a grant in aid of map reproduction, and I also acknowledge with thanks the Vice-President's Research Fund and the Hannah Institute for the History of Medicine, Toronto, for the awarding of travel grants.

R.G.R.
Department of English
Memorial University

INTRODUCTION

In *Newfoundland As It Is in 1894: A Hand-book and Tourists' Guide* (1894), Moses Harvey, a relentless propagandist and promoter, casts a web over the Newfoundland past for the interest of the prospective traveller. In these pages, Harvey represents Newfoundland as an Arcadia with its doors flung open: a moral, law-abiding society of God-fearing, humble people. "Quiet, orderly, church-going, attached to their religious faith, the people live peaceably among themselves," he declares, "and outbreaks of bigotry or fanaticism are now almost unknown" (Harvey, 196). In his zeal for capturing Newfoundland as a pastoral society, he constructs what is now recognized as a familiar "founding fiction" to explain how it got that way, gliding over troublesome details that might alter the pastoral image and avoiding any challenge to the motives of the middlemen, engrossers, and regraters who made up the merchant class. The reader is thus presented with a picture of an imagined community that has somehow risen above itself – a polemical reformulation of national character and purpose.

Harvey may have seen his task partly as the smoothing over of antagonisms brought out by the general election of 1893, when what Judge D.W. Prowse called "the old leaven of prejudice against the mercantile monopolists of a former time" (Prowse, 530) still carried influence. In former days, noted Harvey, the fishery was monopolized by absentee merchants, who "cruelly wronged" the resident fishermen. "The conflict was long and bitter," he continued, "and it is not wonderful that the fishermen regarded merchants as tyrants and oppressors and reckoned them, for generations, as their natural enemies" (Harvey, 198). Then a new race of merchants "sprang up," men of superior energy, skill, and perseverance, who reinvested their capital in the fishery, operating through the credit or "supplying" system by which they advanced goods to fisherman and at the close of the fishing season received the fisherman's catch for export. This system was fraught with evils for the poor fisherman, Harvey conceded, but he cautioned that the capitalists had risks to run too and could eliminate the system only gradually. "In fact," he added generously, "the merchants have done much in recent years to curtail the 'credit system' and keep it within the narrowest possible bounds" (Harvey, 199).

According to Harvey, the attitudes of the merchant class with headquarters in Britain had undergone a profound change. More of them now took up permanent residence in the colony than ever before, opening up new industries. In time, class antagonisms would disappear, he predicted, and friendly relations would be restored, especially if the affluent took an interest in the welfare of the fishermen. "They are naturally a warm-hearted people, who will respond to kindness," he insisted. "Their faults of character, it must be remembered, are chiefly the results of their surroundings and the hard and harsh struggles through which they have been obliged to pass" (Harvey, 201). But contrary to Harvey's expectations, social conditions remained virtually unaltered and so, presumably, did the perceived faults of character. A few years later, a visitor observed, "Local capital is rarely invested here: the great field for local philanthropy in the way of public charities, public institutions, and public churches is unoccupied" (Willson, 28).

One philanthropic scheme, however, did attract the merchants to social reform: namely, the important initiative in imperial medicine taken to improve the lives of fishermen and their families, especially the 25,000 who migrated to Labrador each spring. In 1891, the Mission to Deep Sea Fishermen (MDSF), a nondenominational London charity operating principally in the North Sea, sent one of its councillors, Francis Hopwood, to investigate complaints about working conditions in the bank fishery. In the course of his inquiries, Hopwood gathered considerable information, including some surprising details about the annual migration to Labrador and what he termed the "really scandalous state of things" there (Hopwood, 12). Hopwood was referring to a number of specific "evils and scandals" he had inadvertently uncovered: the improper transportation of women and children to Labrador and their employment there, the lack of civil administration, the shortage of food and clothing, and of course the absence of adequate medical services. In the spring of 1892, after he had carefully reported these matters in London, the mission sent a crew in the 155-ton hospital ship *Albert* to cruise the Labrador coast, distributing clothing, holding prayer meetings, and treating sick and disabled fishermen. It was the beginning of what would become known fondly for the next century as the Grenfell Mission.

The expedition to Labrador was led by the mission's superintendent, Wilfred Grenfell, a vigorous, athletic young doctor of twenty-seven with strong evangelical leanings. At the end of the summer of 1892, Grenfell found himself profoundly moved both by the sordid social conditions he had encountered and by the opportunity placed before him to do so much good. He decided there and then to devote his energies to social reform in the North. When his report of the voyage of 1892 was made public in St John's, a group of fish merchants and politicians immediately undertook to raise the money for small hospitals at two strategic locations, Battle Harbour and Indian Harbour, and with the promise of local support in hand Grenfell next convinced the mission to outfit a second voyage in 1893. For this voyage, he brought with him a medical staff of four from the London Hospital and a hand-picked crew from the mission staff. There were two doctors: Eliot Curwen, a recent graduate, and Alfred O. Bobardt of Melbourne, Australia, who had been sailing with the mission in the North Sea. There were also two nurses: Sister Cecilia Williams, who was to assist Curwen in Indian Harbour, and Sister Ada Carwardine, who would assist Bobardt in Battle Harbour. The *Albert* was for the second time commanded by Captain Joseph F. Trezise, an experienced master mariner but not a member of the mission staff. The crew, however, were all (except the sailmaker) evangelical Protestants: W.H. Hewer, mate; J. Rogers, second mate (boatswain); J.H. Dobey, steward; and with these a carpenter to assist with hospital construction, a sailmaker, and three able-bodied seamen.

Despite Grenfell's careful preparations, however, the operation unfolded only partly as planned. The Battle Harbour hospital was duly accommodated in a house donated by one of the principal St John's merchants, W. Baine Grieve, who was at that time engaged in a vicious electoral battle with the prime minister, Sir William Whiteway. Constructed in the style of a Newfoundland dwelling, the house was well finished by Labrador standards, though still unfit for winter occupation. While the house was being fitted up for their purposes, Bobardt and Sister Carwardine continued to receive patients, and by early autumn they had occupied it fully. But Curwen was not so fortunate. The mail boat, failing to land the precious building materials on the first attempt, carried its cargo up the coast of Labrador and back for the next month. Thus, even though its foundation had been laid as early as 3 August, the second hospital was not completed until October. Curwen writes in his journal on 14 August, "We are very disappointed not to be able to get into the hospital this year, and it is not easy to settle how we can best spread our influence."

Grenfell now ordered Curwen to remain on board the *Albert* and use it as a floating hospital to cruise from one harbour to another while Sister Williams returned to Battle Harbour. He himself ranged up and down the coast freely with a series of short trips in the steam launch *Princess May*. This change of strategy did not sit well with Curwen, for although the *Albert* was well equipped for hospital work, it was ill suited to manoeuvring in and out of tight Labrador harbours. In the end, he made only thirteen visits, thereby leaving more time to get about in small boats and observe life at first hand – more than he would have done if he had stayed in Indian Harbour. His observations shaped the contents of his journal.

Fuller examinations of Newfoundland and Labrador life exist from this time, such as Wilfred Grenfell's *Vikings of To-day* (1895), and more specialized studies of the Labrador peninsula, including those of A.P. Low and Alphaeus Packard. But Curwen's interpretations of the summer's events, made with a readership no wider than his widowed mother and nine brothers and sisters in mind, allow us private insights into the culture of Labrador. They are presented here side by side with the more narrativized, more tendentious reports of Grenfell, which were intended for the wider readership of the mission council and the mission supporters who read the missionary journal *Toilers of the Deep*. Now, a century later, both texts are all the more poignant since the collapse of the cod fishery. Curwen writes, "The colony lives by the codfish caught, but the colony in no wise recognizes that the codfish catchers are human." In one of his reports to the mission, Grenfell writes, "Certainly some will be obliged to leave this winter and seek pastures new." A century ago, observers were concerned about the preservation of fishermen. Today, they are concerned about the preservation of fish.

Curwen's reports took in as wide a range of the small population as possible. To begin with, there were the natives, consisting of the itinerant Innu and the coastal Inuit, the latter under the social guardianship of the Moravian Brethren. Distributed along the coast as well there was a thin line of permanent white settlers (livyers), descendants of British servants, sailors, and artisans of the fur-trading companies who had intermarried with the native population. And finally there was the migratory throng of about 25,000 Newfoundlanders, divided into two groups: the "floaters" (permanent crews of fishing schooners) and "stationers" (fishermen and their families domiciled ashore in temporary huts). The health of this migratory group concerned the St John's merchants (and therefore the mission) the most. Curwen's comments touch mostly on their living and working conditions, following upon the comments of Hopwood in his first report.

As in the reports of other medical practitioners set in colonial societies, the language of medical objectivity and sanitation in Curwen's journal embodies the social and cultural prejudices of his age. With some sense of astonishment, for example, Curwen comments on the rudimentary hygiene and crude household effects of the temporary dwellings. Landing in Battle Harbour, he and Sister Williams go house to house like parish visitors to inquire into living conditions, and there they discover an "extraordinary" state of affairs. In elemental dwellings of one room, which they sometimes refer to as "hovels," they find people sleeping together and dressed in rags. In one such domicile, they find a family sleeping on "shelves," one above the other, and in another parents and children occupying the same bed. While some of these temporary shelters, heated with an open fire vented through a hole in the roof, were sometimes rented for a few dollars, others were kept permanently in the families of summer fishermen. At the end of the season, the inhabitants abandoned them temporarily to return home aboard the fishing schooners, taking with them their precious window frames and leaving the doors wide open to facilitate thawing the accumulated snow in the spring (9 October journal entry). For the migratory families, such a style of habitation was not unusual (Smith, 10), but to Curwen it constituted the source of medical and social problems.

The transportation of fishing families aboard schooners Curwen found equally scandalous, and he comments extensively on the arrangements (6 October). "I am not surprised the owners & skippers try to keep us from visiting these places where the people are stowed," he writes. Then he adds the next day, "Women certainly ought not to be allowed to travel in this way; in England they would not be allowed." The employment of women in the fishery, first reported by Hopwood, provoked considerable speculation. Throughout the journal, Curwen takes careful note of the availability of suitable women's clothing and the living arrangements in the one-room dwellings. He also deplores the presence of girls aboard the fishing vessels, an arrangement corroborated by Bobardt in Battle Harbour. "It seems a great pity that such a system of employing young girls on board these smacks should exist," Bobardt writes in his final report. "Their environment is by no means always of the purest, and they have had a very hard time of it, struggling for the few dollars they earn and an existence." Such practices did not change overnight. A law limiting the number of passengers aboard schooners and requiring separate accommodation for females had existed only since 1892 (*Consolidated Statutes*, 878–9), and another ten years would pass before the Government of Newfoundland would enforce it, partly as a result of persistent complaints from Grenfell.

As an agent of the Mission to Deep Sea Fishermen, which had campaigned against drinking in Britain, Curwen took a special interest in the availability of spirits in Labrador. Since the 1880s, the mission had as a matter of policy given attention to the floating grog ships ("copers") that sold tobacco and spirits openly to fishermen in the North Sea and off the coast of Ireland. For this reason, the *Albert* carried a large cargo of tobacco to trade with fishing vessels in British waters (4 June). But Labrador remained a virtual free trade zone for spirits and historically an open market for smugglers and unlicensed vendors. Despite tighter licensing regulations, which confined the sale of liquor to the period between May and the end of the fishing season (*Consolidated Statutes*, 941), Curwen seemed amazed that spirits were sold openly and freely. He took pains, for instance, to record in his notebook (11 July) the presence of an American "coper" in Battle Harbour that had exchanged Baine Grieve's fish for liquor. "What a pity we had no powers!" he wrote. In Batteau, he was outraged by a house that sold unlicensed rum and by another selling unlicensed gin. He was especially incensed by Edward Burgess, the government revenue officer, whom he accused of ignoring the liquor trade and looking after his own interests (20 and 26 July). Writing from Indian Harbour (12 August), he again castigated Burgess for avoiding harbours where shebeens were located and for smuggling in his own supply from England.

Next to drinking, barratry aroused Curwen's indignation the most. In Labrador, outside the reach of the law and Lloyd's surveyor, a vessel could simply be declared unseaworthy and then resold after the insurance had been collected. The specific steps required by law (*Consolidated Statutes*, 903–12) could easily be avoided, and a number of cases involving the declared wreckage and swift salvage of Labrador vessels reached Curwen's ears. In one instance, a local captain took two vessels, one of them his own, and sold one to himself while he put the other up for auction (18 September). Curwen cited in detail two other cases of barratry reported to him (7 and 16 October) and concluded, "Dishonesty is certainly the best policy on the Labrador if money making is the end & object of life." In Turnavik, when the *Albert* narrowly avoided going on the rocks, he predicted that the enemies of Captain William Bartlett, who was acting as pilot, would accuse Bartlett of deliberately threatening the vessel so that he could salvage it himself.

Finally, a commentary on the credit or "truck" system runs throughout the journal. Curwen was intrigued at first by the system by which goods were advanced to fishermen at Battle Harbour and subsequently paid for with fish. But he was equally intrigued by the apparent ignorance of the fishermen and the manipulation of their finances by the fish merchants' local agents. He cites the case of the Dyson brothers of Black Tickle (10 October), who could not read their own accounts and could not have realized the exorbitant prices charged them for food, prices that changed from day to day. "The merchants seem determined not to allow the people to make money, in fact to get as much out of the people as they can," Curwen writes (12 October); "they take their salmon, cod, herring & fur at a price they name & give in return what provision they like, always arranging prices so that there is nothing on the credit side; it makes little or no difference to the settler if he makes a good fishery during a season."

Curwen was also baffled by the Newfoundlanders' taciturnity, perhaps a form of defence against interventionists such as Curwen whom they could not "read." In small societies such as this one, great importance was attached to mutual giving, unrestrained hospitality, and egalitariansim. But in Curwen's view, the Nova Scotian schoonermen possessed more "independence and character" and were more apt to pay for medical treatment or to assist the hospital ship in getting about. He found it strange that Labradormen would leave the *Albert* after treatment with no sense of gratitude. "I cannot make the N.F. fishermen out," he wrote (10 September); "they are unlike any other class of men I have seen; as often as not I have to ask for 'thank you' from a patient, & they will receive books, woollens & even coals &c. without showing gratitude; should I hail any of them in a boat with 'Good Morning' or 'What Cheer, Old Skipper?' I have learned to expect stares and not words or signs in reply" (9 September).

Curwen's carefully indexed notebook, a source of detail for his journal, further reveals the extent of his curiosity: his inquiries into the operation of the fishing industry but also the folklore, government, and history of the colony; the animals, birds, and plants; the food, the medical services, and arrangements for the relief of the population. He lists the composition of Labrador settlers' families and their general state of health. To satisfy his curiosity about the Inuit population, he made extensive notes from two authoritative works: *Life with the Esquimaux* (1864), the study of Arctic natives by Captain Charles F. Hall, who had set out in 1860 to unravel the mystery of the Franklin expedition; and the more recent *Eskimo Life* (1893), a study of their Greenland counterparts by Fridtjof Nansen. Clearly, Curwen was intrigued by the experience of meeting natives, and his journal takes on a more respectful tone throughout the proceedings at Hopedale.

The photographs, too numerous for all to be reproduced here, present another systematic record of life as he found it. They are primarily documentary, illustrating the techniques of catching and curing fish, the construction of commercial premises, and the state of private dwellings. Although Curwen never says as much, he and Grenfell were probably gathering a collection of images for the fund-raising activities that followed in St John's and later in Canada and the United Kingdom. Curwen was the principal photographer, but he did not take the photographs illustrating the Strait of Belle Isle and the far north of Labrador. These were taken by Grenfell during side trips in the *Princess May*. Indeed, some of the photographs turned up later in Grenfell's *Vikings of To-day*, where Grenfell revealed in the preface that they were captured on "Barnet plates" donated to the MDSF by the photographic firm of Elliot & Fry.

Curwen transported the plates and his unwieldy camera from place to place and developed his photographs aboard the *Albert*. Even though he was not a professional photographer, he had mastered the dry-plate process, sparing himself further the drudgery of carrying a dark tent and a load of chemicals. Instead, he could take the plates on board the *Albert* and develop directly onto printing-out paper. Through this process, the paper was exposed when brought into contact with the negative until the image was wholly visible, then made sharper by washing and toning. While the process allowed for shorter exposure times and permitted Curwen to eliminate the tripod occasionally, it took more time in the washing stage and brought forth uneven results (29 September).

Eliot Curwen's journal and photographs are the work of a bright, religious young English doctor who had already worked among fishermen in the North Sea. He was born at Laura Place, Clapton, on 6 April 1865, one of ten children of stockbroker Thomas Taylor Curwen and Mary Elizabeth Curwen. Raised as a Congregationalist, he entered the Mill Hill School in 1877. But two years later his father died, leaving his mother with sole responsibility for the care and education of a large family (John Curwen, 196–7). Eliot did not disappoint her. When he left school in 1883, he passed the London University matriculation examination in the first division and was

Eliot Curwen, 1893

admitted as a pensioner at St John's College, Cambridge, graduating in 1886 with a second in the Natural Sciences tripos. He then proceeded to the London Hospital Medical College in September 1887 as a composition student and received the MRCS and LRCP in 1889. He was awarded the MB, B CHIR, and MA degrees by Cambridge University in 1890. For a year or more, he remained at the hospital for further training, first as house physician, then as receiving room officer, and finally as house surgeon. His instructors' reports assessed him as "very good" or "excellent," and by the time he had finished early in 1893 he was a competent and well-trained medical practitioner, ready to strike out on his own. At this point, he wanted to go to China as a medical missionary, but his mother was ill, and he did not wish to venture too far afield. As one of the leaders of the Christian Association at the London Hospital, he had already met Wilfred Grenfell, and when Grenfell offered him the opportunity for a shorter venture of a few months, he took it.

Although Curwen sent home his journal in instalments for the entertainment of his family, he brought to it a critical eye and an intelligent curiosity. Writing privately for a selection of family readers, he reveals many sides of Newfoundland and Labrador life that he could not have revealed publicly: the political and social mores, the sectarianism, the problems of the fishing industry, the language, the poverty, the economy. And, of course, he did not ignore the medical activities of the staff of five. Throughout the summer and early autumn, Bobardt and the two nursing sisters treated 33 in-patients and 647 out-patients at the new Battle Harbour hospital. Grenfell treated one in-patient and 794 out-patients in the steam launch *Princess May*. As for Curwen himself, despite the disappointments of the Indian Harbour hospital, he treated three in-patients and 1,052 out-patients aboard the *Albert*.

Keeping in mind the readers at home, he did not enter into an analysis of the illnesses he treated. He merely identified them in passing. But Grenfell's statistics, published in *Toilers of the Deep*, suggested in the medical language of the day something of the general pattern of work accomplished by the staff. There were the normal accident cases Grenfell associated with the physical and sometimes dangerous life of the fisherman, such as water boils, night blindness, strained back, sore muscles, broken limbs, dental caries, inflamed nerves, mouth ulcers, rheumatism, conjunctivitis, urine retention, strangulated hernia, and arthritis. There were also untreated cases resulting from influenza, pneumonia, pleurisy, and diphtheria. The repetitive diet of salt fish, tea, flour, and game, together with hurried eating, was seen as the cause of prolonged constipation, indigestion, haemorrhoids, xerophthalmia, peritonitis, scurvy, pellagra, beri-beri, edema, and rickets. Overall, the preponderance of medical cases lay in diseases of the digestive system (633) and the respiratory and circulatory systems (194) as well as afflictions of the eye, including thirty-four cases of night blindness. Of surgical cases, Grenfell reported frequent interventions of the upper and lower limbs, perhaps for minor ailments such as boils, and cases of the "glands," bones, and "special agues," as well as rickets, tumours, and fistula. There were sixty-four cases of "women's" complaints reported but no childbirths. Seventeen operations were performed under chloroform.

During Curwen's ten days in St John's, he found that he had arrived at a pivotal point in Newfoundland political history. Overwhelmed by the hospitality of the merchant community, he came to realize that 1893 was an election year and that a political battle was being fought for control of economic policy. A Liberal government under Sir William Whiteway was struggling to maintain office with a program to increase local industry and develop the railway system. The Conservatives, under Walter Baine Grieve and Moses Monroe, advocated confederation with Canada. The campaign was marked by excessive scurrility, and Curwen would remark later in November, on the day of the election, "Polling day: much mud thrown about, & much underfoot, both very adhesive." Thus, both sides wanted to be associated with the highly publicized philanthropic activities to be conducted on the Labrador coast, and the hospitality provided by the allied families of the mercantile class was relentless. The churches, however, showed more caution. Grenfell's group could feel before the end of the summer a rising sectarian resentment over the perceived encroachments of the MDSF into an established mission territory.

The restriction of the journal to family readers also permitted Curwen to express some small dissatisfaction with the young Wilfred Grenfell. While Curwen was excited by the opportunity to do good, he was sceptical about Grenfell's qualities of leadership at this early stage of his long career and was reluctant to admire Grenfell's tendency to dash about in all directions. During the summer of 1893, Grenfell slowly realized that he would adopt Labrador as a way to fulfil his own sense of identity. His report (appendix) shows how he and Bobardt later proceeded to establish fund-raising branches of the MDSF in Canada. But Curwen himself chose not to participate in this extension of the summer's activities. Despite the excitement of his venture overseas, he leaves the impression that he was not completely satisfied with Grenfell as a colleague.

Curwen did not appear comfortable with what he represented as Grenfell's impulsiveness, whether Grenfell was leaping over the ship's railing after a cricket ball or chugging off on a side trip to Nain. And he did not suffer gladly Grenfell's organizational decisions. The two disagreed on 19 August about whether to keep a patient on board the *Albert* or send her to Battle Harbour, and when Curwen wanted to use the *Albert* as a substitute for the northern hospital, Grenfell overruled him. Again, on 19 September, Curwen records his reluctance to return to Turnavik in view of the danger to navigation, but again he was overruled. He comments more explicitly on 5 October, when the *Albert* loses track of Grenfell's whereabouts, "He is a great anxiety to us." Finally, on the return trip to St John's, Grenfell set off on his own and lost touch with the *Albert*, "but whether he was going down [the] Straits of Belle Isle or across to the 'French Shore' I do not think he knew himself," Curwen commented ruefully. For his part, Grenfell may have resented the extra leisure granted Curwen by the loss of the hospital. When Grenfell was reported lost during the subsequent passage to St John's in October and Curwen telegraphed to inform Grenfell's mother, Grenfell later wrote to relieve her worries about his safety. "It is all very well for Curwen to write long letters. I haven't nearly the time he has," he noted (Grenfell Papers, 24 October 1893).

At the conclusion of the 1893 expedition, Bobardt and Grenfell set off together to raise money and stir up interest in Halifax, Montreal, and Ottawa. They then continued on holiday as far as Victoria, British Columbia, with the help of a rail pass from Donald Smith, president of the Canadian Pacific Railway and a former Labrador agent of the Hudson's Bay Company. When Bobardt requested reimbursement for this further mission work, he was refused by the MDSF, which pointed out that his formal connection with the mission had closed when he left Labrador and that, anyway, Grenfell had written to say that they were travelling at their own expense (RNMDSF Finance Committee minutes, 20 April 1894). It was the first of many such clashes between the mission council and Grenfell over policy and funding. Over the years to come, Grenfell would often act first and settle the details later. For the moment, Bobardt returned to England and subsequently entered the Royal Navy. Grenfell went back to his job as superintendent of the mission's affairs and planned his next voyage overseas.

The two nurses returned to England in the autumn of 1893. But as evangelical Christians they were now committed to the work in Labrador, and during the next few years, as the mission's buildings were improved and upgraded for cold weather, they wintered over. Sister Williams assisted the doctors at Indian Harbour until 1898. Sister Carwardine married her Battle Harbour colleague, Dr Graham Aspland, in 1897 and remained until 1900. The two women were thus the mainstays of Grenfell's enterprise in the early years, and they became more accustomed to Labrador life than Grenfell himself. When Grenfell told a fisherman in Rigolet that he was spending the winter in the United States, perhaps to recruit staff, the fisherman replied, "In America? You show me the American that can travel on snow shoes in winter with Sister Aspland or Sister Williams. I've seen them," he added, "going round the corner of the harbour (opposite his door) when it warn't fit for a dog to stir, and that just for visiting someone who was sick" (*Toilers* 15 [1900]: 244).

As for Curwen himself, that winter he lectured in Britain to raise money for the Labrador mission, but he never returned to Labrador. On 8 January 1894 his mother died, and he was again presented with a chance to go to China under the auspices of the London Missionary Society. This time he did not hesitate. He was appointed surgeon at the Peking Hospital, where he served from 1894 to 1900, and was physician for Imperial Maritime Customs, 1898–99, returning to England at the onset of the Boxer Rebellion. He settled at Hove, Sussex, in 1901 with his wife Ann, whom he had married in 1894, and their son Eliot Cecil Curwen, born in 1895. There he installed himself in a medical practice and began his preoccupation with the Sussex Downs.

From this point, archaeology became Curwen's avocation. After joining the Sussex Archaeological Society in 1909, he began a surface survey of the minor earthworks of the Downs, amassing a large collection of flint implements. The description and preservation of early implements thus became the obsession of his leisure hours and those of his son Cecil, whom he introduced to the study of archaeology at an early age. Cecil published his first paper while still a boy at Rugby School in 1912 and two years later began a series of collaborations with his father. In particular, the two wrote regularly for the society's *Collections*, running up an astonishing range of studies at a time when archaeology had not yet become the preserve of professional scholars. Their work found its fullest expression in Cecil Curwen's *Prehistoric Sussex* (1929). In this way, the two advanced the study of neolithic culture, isolating varying groups of continental artifacts (Evans, 405).

Not content with the mere description and analysis of early arti-facts, Curwen *père* also turned his attention to their administration. He was elected to the council of the Sussex Archaeological Society in 1917 and stood successively, year by year, until his death in 1950, serving as its chairman, 1942–47. He was also elected a fellow of the Society of Antiquaries in 1922 and contributed reports to the *Antiquaries Journal*. He was a member of that society's council in 1932. His greatest contribution to the Sussex society, however, is said to have been the reorganization of its museum at Lewes, whose committee he chaired from 1929 to 1949. Largely because of his labours in later life, this institution was transformed into a first-rate regional museum.

Meanwhile, chiefly through his own personal magnetism and energy, Wilfred Grenfell had built an extensive medical service in northern Newfoundland and Labrador with its headquarters in St Anthony. An indefatigable fund raiser with an eye for new ideas in community and rural development, he virtually took over health care and social reform in the northern part of the colony, with the grudging acknowledgment of the colonial government. Here, high morbidity and mortality rates interfered with efficiency and profit-ability in the fishing industry, just as they did in the mines, planta-tions, and factories elsewhere in the British Empire (Arnold, 15). With Grenfell, the Newfoundland government had acquired the luxury of a professional medical service staffed by volunteers from Britain and the United States, even though it sometimes suffered the embarrassment of Grenfell's fund-raising lectures with their star-tling images of poverty and disease. In 1927, with the completion of a modern hospital in St Anthony, Grenfell was created a knight com-mander of the Order of St Michael and St George, and widely acknowledged as a hero by those familiar with his achievements.

Grenfell at first kept in touch with Curwen's work in China, and he announced Curwen's engagement in *Toilers of the Deep* in 1895. But Curwen did not remain in close touch with Grenfell during the busy years to follow. By 1929, the Royal National Mission to Deep

Wilfred Grenfell, 1893

Introduction

Sea Fishermen transferred all its Newfoundland properties to the International Grenfell Association, the organization Grenfell had founded in the United States. Thenceforth, Grenfell raised money in Britain through an association of his own creation, but Curwen rarely participated in its activities with the exception of the first alumni meeting of Grenfell workers at St Ermin's Hotel, Westminster, in 1932. Grenfell himself died in 1940, and Curwen last appeared at the reunion in 1948, two years before his own death.

SELECTED ARCHAEOLOGICAL WRITINGS AND COLLABORATIONS OF ELIOT CURWEN

Curwen, Eliot, and E. Cecil Curwen. "Ancient Trackways Near Saddlescombe." *Brighton & Hove Archaeologist* 1 (1914): 36–42.

Curwen, Eliot. "On Stane Street in Its Passage over the South Downs." *Sussex Arch. Coll.* 57 (1915): 136–47.

– "A Note on Stane Street on Halnaker Hill." *Sussex Arch. Coll.* 58 (1916): 132–7.

Curwen, Eliot, and E. Cecil Curwen. "Covered Ways on the Sussex Downs." *Sussex Arch. Coll.* 59 (1918): 35–75.

– "The Earthworks of Rewell Hill, Near Arundell." *Sussex Arch. Coll.* 61 (1920): 20–30.

– "Notes on the Archaeology of Burpham and the Neighbouring Downs." *Sussex Arch. Coll.* 63 (1922): 1–53.

– "Sussex Lynchets and Their Associated Field-ways." *Sussex Arch. Coll.* 64 (1923): 1–65.

Curwen, Eliot, C. H. Goodman, Marian Frost, and E. Cecil Curwen. "Blackpatch Flint-mine Excavation, 1922." *Sussex Arch. Coll.* 65 (1924): 69–111.

Curwen, Eliot, and E. Cecil Curwen, "The Hove Tumulus." *Brighton & Hove Archaeologist* 2 (1924): 21–8.

– "Earthworks and Celtic Road, Binderton." *Sussex Arch. Coll.* 66 (1925): 163–71.

– "Harrow Hill Flint-mine Excavation, 1924–5." *Sussex Arch. Coll.* 67 (1926): 102–38.

- "A Thirteenth Century Steelyard Weight." *Sussex Arch. Coll.* 67 (1926): 189–95.
- "Excavations in the Caburn, Near Lewes." *Sussex Arch. Coll.* 68 (1927): 1–56.
- "Ancient Cultivations at Grassington, Yorkshire." *Antiquity* 2 (1928): 168–72.
- "Notes on Some Uncommon Types of Stone Implements Found in Sussex." *Sussex Arch. Coll.* 69 (1928): 77–91.
- "Port's Road, the Ancient Road of Portslade." *Brighton & Hove Archaeologist* 3 (1928): 28–42.
- "Prehistoric Remains from Kingston Buci." *Sussex Arch. Coll.* 72 (1931): 185–217.
- "Rackham Bank and Earthwork." *Sussex Arch. Coll.* 73 (1932): 169–86.
- "A Flint Sickle from Salveston, Sussex." *Antiquaries Journal* 14 (1934): 389–92.
- "On Sussex Flint Arrow-heads." *Sussex Arch. Coll.* 77 (1936): 15–25.
- "Two Bronzes and a Flint from Sussex." *Trans. Carmarthenshire Antiquarian Soc. and Field Club* 64 (1937): 50–1.
- "Late Bronze Age Ditches at Selmuston." *Sussex Arch. Coll.* 79 (1938): 195–8.
- "Blunted Axe-like Implements." *Proc. of the Prehistoric Soc.* 5 (1939): 196–201.
- "An Egg-shaped Mace-head." *Antiquaries Journal* 21 (1941): 337–41.
- "An Unusual Bone Implement." *Sussex Arch. Coll.* 84 (1945): 108–13.

REFERENCES

MANUSCRIPTS

Catalogus der Missionare. Moravian Archives, Bethlehem, Pennsylvania. Microfilm copies at the Centre for Newfoundland Studies, Memorial University of Newfoundland, and at the National Archives of Canada, Ottawa.

Curwen Papers. Sussex Archaeological Society, Barbican House, Lewes, Sussex.

Dienerblatt. Unitaetsarchiv Herrnhut, Germany. Microfilm copies at the Centre for Newfoundland Studies, Memorial University of Newfoundland, and at the National Archives of Canada, Ottawa.

Grenfell Papers. Stirling Library, Yale University, New Haven, Connecticut.

RNMDSF Committee Minutes and Records. Royal National Mission to Deep Sea Fishermen, London.

PRINTED BOOKS

Arnold, David, ed. *Imperial Medicine and Indigenous Societies*. Manchester and New York: Manchester University Press 1988.

Boileau, Lambert de. *Recollections of Labrador Life*. London: Saunders, Otley, and Co. 1861.

Consolidated Statutes of Newfoundland ... 1892. St John's: Queen's Printer 1896.

Curwen, E. Cecil. *Prehistoric Sussex*. London: Homeland Association 1929.

– *The Archaeology of Sussex*. London: Methuen 1937.

Curwen, John F. *A History of the Ancient House of Curwen of Workington in Cumberland*. Kendal: Titus Wilson & Son 1928.

Evans, Joan. *A History of the Society of Antiquaries*. Oxford: Oxford University Press 1956.

Grenfell, Wilfred T. *Vikings of To-day, or, Life and Work among the Fishermen of Labrador*. London: Marshall Bros; New York: Fleming H. Revell 1895.

Hall, Capt. Charles Francis. *Life with the Esquimaux: A Narrative of Arctic Experience in Search of Survivors of Sir John Franklin's Expedition*. 2 vols. London: Sampson, Low, Son, and Marston 1864.

Harvey, Rev. M. *Newfoundland As It Is in 1894: A Hand-book and Tourists' Guide*. St John's: Queen's Printer 1894.

Hopwood, Francis J.S. *Newfoundland Fisheries and Fishermen*. London: Mission to Deep Sea Fishermen [1891].

Levine, Philippa. *The Amateur and the Professional: Antiquarians, Historians and Archaeologists in Victorian England, 1838–1886*. Cambridge: Cambridge University Press 1986.

Low, A.P. *Report on Explorations in the Labrador Peninsula along the East Main, Koksoak, Hamilton, Menicuagan and Portions of Other Rivers in 1892–93–94–95*. Ottawa: Queen's Printer 1896.

Mott, Henry Youmans, ed. *Newfoundland Men: A Collection of Biographical Sketches*. Concord, N.H.: T.W. and J.F. Cragg 1894.

Nansen, Fridtjof. *Eskimo Life*. London: Longmans, Green 1893.

Packard, Alphaeus Spring. *The Labrador Coast: A Journal of Two Summer Cruises to That Region*. New York: N.D.C. Hodges; London: Kegan, Paul, Trench, Trübner 1891.

Prowse, D.W. *A History of Newfoundland from the English, Colonial and Foreign Records*. London: Macmillan 1895.

Rompkey, Ronald. *Grenfell of Labrador: A Biography*. Toronto: University of Toronto Press 1991.

Salzman, L.F. "A History of the Sussex Archaeological Society." *Sussex Arch. Coll.* 85 (1946): 3–76.

Smith, Philip E.L. "In Winter Quarters." *Newfoundland Studies* 3 (1987): 1–36.

[Stevens, Frank Bentham]. Obituary of Eliot Curwen. *Sussex Notes and Queries* 13 (1950–53): 70–1.

Toilers of the Deep: A Monthly Record of Mission Work amongst Them. London: Royal National Mission to Deep Sea Fishermen, vols. 1-[in progress] (1885-   ).

Trigger, Bruce G. *A History of Archaeological Thought.* Cambridge: Cambridge University Press 1989.

Willson, Beckles. *The Tenth Island: Being Some Account of Newfoundland, Its People, Its Politics, Its Problems, and Its Peculiarities.* London: Grant Richards 1897.

Winbolt, S.E. "Romano-British Sussex." In L.F. Salzman, ed., *The Victoria History of the County of Sussex*, vol. 3. London: Institute of Historical Research 1935.

THE JOURNAL OF ELIOT CURWEN

The Journal of Eliot Curwen

Saturday, May 27th. Left home 5.15 with 27 boxes & parcels and [brother] Harry. [Brother] Edwd. saw us off at Paddington 6.20. Bristol 9.20. Sent goods to boat in cab; followed with Skipper White [of the Mission to Deep Sea Fishermen (MDSF)] who met us at train.

Sunday, May 28th. Called on Geo: Leonard. Highbury Chapel, Mr. Arnold Thomas: dinner, tea & supper with H.B. Evans. In afternoon visited Broad Plain Working Men's Club & schools. After evening service walk over downs & suspension bridge.

Monday, May 29th. Up anchor 3 a.m. did not reach basin till abt. 6.30. Tow down river Avon. No wind, so tow on to Nash Head. Off Mumbles about midnight, & drop anchor as tide began to take us back. Put dredge over late in evening in hope of oysters, but nothing.

Tuesday, May 30th. Tow into Swansea. At quay by about 7.30 a.m. After breakfast visit post office; letters from [sister] Etta & [brother] E.S.C. Call on Mr. F. Rocke & Rev. Owen. Dine with Miss [Mary] Grenfell. [Prayer] Meeting on board 3.30, again 7 p.m. deck crowded both times. £17.10.0 collected including 6d. for tea. Dr. Bobardt arrived at midnight.

Wednesday, May 31st. Steam train to the Mumbles; fine coast; very sleepy. Shopping in afternoon. 7.30 Service on board. 9.0 Magic lantern views of Labrador. £1.11.0 collected.

Thursday, June lst. Went over steel & tin works (Dyffins). In afternoon shopped. Bought new boat for £12.6.6. Miss Grenfell gave £8 & we subscribed the remainder; Miss G. came down to "Christen" her with soda water; named the "Mary Grenfell." Left quay abt. 6.30 & got out of harbour abt. 7.45 – no wind. Towed till we were off Mumbles.

Friday, June 2nd. Calm all day. Shot birds (guillemot, puffin & seagull) & skinned; shot one with rifle from deck. Painted boat. Bathed. By evening were abt. 30 miles from Swansea.

Saturday, June 3rd. Before we got up six trawlers boarded us & brought fish for tobacco. Dobby [Dobey] was disappointed because 4 of us did not eat 9 soles, so he eat 2 after he had finished his breakfast! Nice breeze so we sail well. A bit off colour during afternoon & evening.

Sunday, June 4th. Off Irish coast – head wind. Tack, tack, tack, all day. Stiff breeze. Lie to off Ballycotton for service; are taken for coper;[1] two boats come off, are followed & sent back by coastguards who come on; we sail off: are asked next day by customs officers at Queenstown if we have seen copers about. Lie to off Q. harbour mouth at midnight.

Monday, June 5th. Called at 5. Pilot on board. Sail into harbour. Anchor at 6.30 having taken 81 hours to do 140 miles! After breakfast go ashore. Find letters from [sisters] M[ary] & Etta. Meet Grenfell: all go to Cork; buy strawberries &c, back to dinner. In afternoon go on shore & moon about; very hot.

TRANSIT TO NEWFOUNDLAND

Tuesday, June 6th. Up at 7. Go ashore 8.15 with Capt., Bobardt & [brother] Harry; no letters. Say goodbye to [brother] H.B.C. at station, he going to Cork for packet to Bristol. Buy more oatmeal, lime juice &c. Heave anchor 9.15. Slowly sail out of harbour with very light breeze. Signal "Newfoundland." Winds very light all day, so that at nightfall we are still within sight of Queenstown! At first wet & misty, but later sun came out warmly, but no more wind. Saw Harry's steamer

Labrador Odyssey

leave harbour, but too far off to signal or photograph. General regret at his leaving.

Played ball on deck; ball went over; Grenfell off with his clothes & overboard at once; a long & good swim. After lunch bore hole through ball & tether it with a long cord; play cricket with broom-handle & pail for bat & stumps.

Rearrange goods in hospital; great job; opened tobacco cupboard but do not break seal on case as we may have to touch land again.[2]

In afternoon more cricket & read. Lose dredge, the rope bought in Queenstown proving rotten. Bathe. Quoits at night. At prayers started life of Paul; preliminary.[3] Beautiful night; "wouldn't your brother have enjoyed this!" The question is, shall we go to Crook-haven tomorrow for eggs & rabbits? Opinions vary but are decided; everything will depend on the wind; without more wind than we have at present we shall not get anywhere, unless it is further East; drifted with the tide.

Wednesday, June 7th. Calm all night. About 15 miles from Queenstown when we got up! Still E. of Kinsale Old Head. Day very fine and the wind *very* light. In morning sailed through a fleet of luggers out of Kinsale, mostly Scotch or Manx boats; rowed to one boat; Skipper from Murray Firth, 6 miles from Lossiemouth, says Wm. Campbell of Lossie-mouth who took Etta & me for a sail is now in Kinsale; mate hales from Dunvegan in Skye; we exchange tobacco for mackerel. Read Saunders "Manual of British Birds" – an excellent book,[4] & list of birds found in Labrador, making notes.

Bathe in afternoon. Sail within 70 yards of a fine three-mast ship in full rigging bound in to Queenstown; speak her; alongside her was the boat of a Q. tailor who had sailed out in order to be first in asking for orders; Capt. says that the crew altogether will leave over £100 behind them in Queenstown tailor's hands, so that there is great competition among the tailors to be first on board a vessel home from a long voyage; if the vessel's Capt. gets many orders for the tailor he will probably get his clothes made for nothing!

Very few birds seen today, and very little fish spawn netted. Very few herring the last 3 days; mackerel fetch 3/6 a 100 in Queenstown.

On coming on deck at 8 p.m. after prayers the Mission smack "Edward Birkbeck" sighted in the distance; she is stationed at Crookhaven and is coming to meet us in response to a wire we sent her from Queenstown; this means letters home, and fresh fish.

Beautiful sunset over Irish land behind Galley Head; a long line of coast in view, from Kinsale, which now shuts off view of Queenstown in the E. towards Cape Clear in the W.

Since 7 a.m. when we were off Kinsale Head we have sailed to Galley Head (now 9 p.m.), a distance of 17 miles; by daylight we hope to be off Fastnet Rock.

Thursday, June 8th. Skipper Budd of the "Birkbeck" boarded us at supper time & stayed till after midnight. He left Yarmouth 9 wks ago for Crookhaven and was so favoured by the wind that he did not touch a single rope or alter his canvas from the time he left Y. till he reached Land's End; at Land's End he drew in his sheets a bit & sailed straight for Kinsale without needing to touch the sails or ropes again! He is busy working at Crookhaven among the Manxmen & the local Irish, but these seem neither to fish, cultivate the land, except for potato, or catch the thousands of rabbits which abound there.

Just before Budd boarded us a long open boat came alongside with 5 Irishmen; they told us they often spent the night at sea – 10 or 12 miles out – in this boat and that they never carried a compass. We invited them aboard in their tatters and gave them tea & biscuits; as a fog was coming on Grenfell offered them a pocket compass and carefully explained to them what it was and how it was to be used; it was curious to watch their expressionless faces as they looked at it, and curious to watch the faces of our crew when the chief of the Irish said, pushing the compass a little from him, "If you'll give me a compass, now, Sirs, I can tell you which is the North." At last we made him understand that it was a veritable compass that he was looking at, and after further instruction he was able to use it fairly. But will he ever make use of it? [New] Testaments all round, some papers and a pair of trousers to the owner of the most tattered pair completed the entertainment.

When Skipper Budd left he took letters for the post; one for Mother.

We passed Cape Clear & Fastnet Rock between 3 & 4 this morning, a fair wind having risen. This fair wind lasted till early afternoon & we made 5 knots an hour. At breakfast time we were off the Bull Rock, & the s.w. coast of Old Ireland was becoming more & more indistinct. Regular observations of sun, clouds, wind, temp: & sp. gr. of water &c. every 4 hours have commenced, and we now feel that we have started; started at last. 1640 miles to Newfoundland. We go off w.n.w. ½ n. Saw a large scolter jumping; crew says it is very common in the N. Sea following the herring; they think it is a kind of very large porpoise, and is sometimes called a "blower."

Tonight sunset n.n.w. at 8.17.

9.15 p.m. a "Dominion" liner passes going w. Only 3 vessels seen all day, a smack, 4-mast ship, & a liner.

Friday, June 9th. Another calm day! From noon yesterday to noon today 61 miles. At noon today 51°34′ Lat. 12°29′ Long. Temp. of water 60°F., i.e. higher than on 7th because we are in the Gulf Stream.

Have seen only one vessel – a 4-masted one, black funneled boat going e.

Three or four "black fish" passed us to the s. this morning; Capt. says it is a kind of whale, of some size & black and always travels slowly; the movement was very like that of a porpoise in character, but very much slower and the dorsal fin & part of back we saw was very black.

We were reminded of the outside world by the company of a martin; it joined us in the early morning & did not leave till midday. Scarcely any sea birds have been seen, a kittiwake & two young seagulls only.

During the afternoon & evening the sea has been full of myriads of small brown jellyfish; bell up to 2½ in. in diam. of a uniform rich brown, the larger ones only having a pink centre – a colour which did not contrast with the brown well. The tentacles were abt. 3 in. long & brown, but the larger ones had in addition to these about 8 thin white cotton-like tentacles nearly a foot in length. A very large quantity of a unicellular algae has been present in the surface water; the cell wall is well marked … and chlorophyll is present in a no. of spots, not uniformly distributed.

Dobby, our "pie crust," made some bread this morning which got very heavy when cold, so he tried his hand again before dinner & sent up a loaf still hot; we slipped some discs of lead into the loaf & sending for him told him it was really too bad of him & that he must try & make some lighter bread. He took it to heart poor chap & said he really could not understand it, so brought us another loaf of the same bake & hoped we should find that better; we told him we should prefer the first loaf cut & toasted, and he went to obey. Later in the day the discs of lead were found in the Capt's pocket, and our cigar tins, which we hang from the ceiling of the crew's cabin for dryness sake, were found to contain rope twist! However the cigars were all right. Only 4 of our crew of 9 smoke, & the Capt. gave it up last year.

Our Capt. is a fine fellow; he has knocked about a great deal, and "done no good" during the 25 years he has been on the sea – running rum into Africa &c. Rum he says is invoiced to the merchants on the African coast at 2/- the doz. quart bottles! Notwithstanding this a considerable profit is made by the original merchants (mostly German) although all dues, freight & insurance charges are paid before the coast merchants receive it. What can such stuff be made of? Capt. says you can buy good 3 star brandy for 1s/3d on the coast.

Saturday, June 10th. Run up to noon 52 knots. True course w. Compass course NW x w½w. Bar. 30.42 to 30.30. Therm: dry 57–60°, wet 57–58.5°. Early morning wet fog, mid-day dry fog, later very fine. Wind E. Sea very smooth. Surface temp. 58–59°. Sp. gr. 1029. Dead reckoning Lat. 51°34′. Long. 14°55′. Mist of this morning due probably to our being near edge of the Gulf Stream.

Am surprised at amount of dew tonight; sails wet & dripping. Another calm day; spent reading, looking out for fish & talking. I opened a packing case from the *bottom* and at once laid my hand on what I wanted!

During morning fog-horn blown frequently: one blast means on starboard tack, two on port tack & three running. Heard horn of large steamer going w.

Capt. saw large "devil fish" [manta] about 50 yrds from ship; I cannot make out description; he seems familiar with it. The great event of the day was the endeavour to catch a sunfish (*Mola rotunda*) about 5 ft. 6 in. long which I saw just under our stern 10 yds. off as we were sailing 2 knots; we brought ship about & got dinghy out as soon as possible, armed ourselves with grain & rifle & put a lookout on rigging, but we had gone too far & failed to find the fish again. Disappointment was great; we ought to have thrown a float overboard to mark the spot we saw it; this was easy to think of afterwards. I saw it lying on the surface & did not know what it was till Capt. told us, and then it turned on its side & showed us one great fin. It was basking in the sun in the same place for hours.

The only bird we have seen all day was a stormy petrel, or one of "Mother Carey's Chickens" as they are called.

Surface net brought up the same algae as yesterday, and a number of copopods, which are minute crustacean of the eutromostica group. The same Medusa appeared again tonight in great numbers.

At prayers we take Life of Paul; tonight the work at Antioch Acts XI. Very good.

Sunday, June 11th.   Distance of run for day 113 knots. Wind moderate, later fresh, then strong. East. Bar. 30.24–30.13. Therm. dry 59.5–60.5°. Wet bulb 58–58.5°. Sea "smooth" at 2 a.m., "rather rough" since noon. Sea temp. 59°, sp. gr. 27–29. Lat. 51° 28′N. Long. 17°6′ at noon.

Began the day under buckets of seawater on deck. During morning we sailed "wing and wing," that is with main boom well out on the port side, and mizzen boom out on starboard side; one tow foresail has been boomed out on both sides for some days.

The martin seen on 9th. flew round the vessel again this morning; its flight was weak; unfortunately we have no suitable food on board for it. The only other birds we have seen are 1. one we do not know; it is like the description of a fulmar – the largest of the petrels – and was probably a young one, and 2. another stormy petrel; this bird flew by us & then settled on the water; it did not sit in the water like a gull but as it were paddled, keeping itself in position by constant motion of its wings; some say this bird never rests on the water; it is hard to believe this so I must watch.

Service 6.30 to 8.0; subject parable of talents (5.2 & 1); much singing; followed by prayer meeting. All on board are Christians except sails [sailmaker]. After service I gave a Revised New Test[ament] to each of the crew.

Monday, June 12th. Ran 168 knots yesterday. (See "Meteor. Register.") Up at 6. Buckets on deck. Read Stalker till breakfast. Passed a sunken vessel; did not see her till we were nearly broadside, about 50 yds. off; would have been terrible to have run into wreck; being so near the water we have very little chance of seeing anything in the water far ahead of us. Sighted a vessel on horizon at 7 a.m. going w.; we caught her up at 2 p.m. going 4½ knots; an old barque "Silentia" of Svelvig from Liverpool to Nova Scotia. She was 12 days out of Liverpool, while we were 4 from Fastnet Rock. Capt. suggests she is an old English barque condemned by Board of Trade & consequently sold to ?Swedes; this is a very usual practice; just before we left Bristol a 1500-ton vessel which had been condemned by B. of T. was sold to a Norwegian at 7/6 a ton!

No birds or fish seen. Read meteorology. Cricket.

Tuesday, June 13th. Morning very calm; wind sprang up at mid-day and by night blew ½ a gale. 83 knots.

Labrador Odyssey

Wednesday, June 14th.	A gale! One end of the vessel thrown up at the same time as the other was thrown down; went on all day. The *only* excitement all day was our aftercabin lamp falling, the fastening being partly worn & partly snapped; as the lamp was out at the time the "safety" qualities were not exhibited. 140 knots.
Thursday, June 15th.	Gale continued; wind from the West and sea very great; we only made 25 knots as the sea was so great & pounding into it stopped the way on the ship and threw us all about to such an extent that we "lay to" most of the day. It is a little consoling to me to see everyone a bit shy of feeding. We try to be cheerful but fail; cricket falls very flat; as the ball takes the wicket you are probably more concerned with the position of your legs than the bat. Capt. Trezise says he is always off colour in a sailing vessel in a breeze though he is as right as possible on a steamer, and this morning said that for safety & seaworthiness he would rather cross the Atlantic in the "Albert," but for comfort in a liner or large merchant vessel.
Friday, June 16th.	65. When will the wind & sea go down? Can neither think, read nor write; cold strong wind and rain. 65 knots.
Saturday, June 17th.	Late last evening a sudden calm; hopes rise high; at 3 a.m. strong wind suddenly arises in s. & sea gets up *very* quickly. Can we have passed through centre of cyclone? Waves 20 ft. from trough to crest. To avoid sailing in trough we sail 3 points s. of our course. Dinner laid at 12; fortunately a meagre repast, for just before sitting down the ship gives a bigger lurch than usual, iron rings break, spun yarn is burst and the table is on its side with the tinned beef, potatoes, pickles & contents of cruet either adhering to the cabin panels or on the floor; 10 minutes later Drs. G. & B., who sit to leeward, would have had 24 stone of Capt. & Dr. C. in their laps in addition.
Sunday, June 18th.	Such a change! After 5 days of storms, a really lovely day. Moderate breeze from s.s.e. and a quiet sea; warm sun & very few clouds. "Slinking along" at from 7 to 8 knots an hour; by noon had left

1000 miles behind us, hurrah! Only 600 odd left & expectation of reaching St. John's before next Sunday. We are now requiring to look out for ice; very likely we may find miles & miles of floe ice between us & N.F.D. and have to sail South to find an opening through.

It is surprising how much one can sleep on board; this morning while sitting in the sun on deck trying to read we sighted & after a time passed a barque going E. – the first vessel seen since Tuesday – and while wondering what they would be making of us & our little craft I nodded – and lo! the morning was gone. This evening at service Ps. XL and Parable of Sower.

Monday, June 19th.   Sailing 7 or 8 knots all day. Made 170 for the day. A fine day with a steady E.S.E. breeze. Spent 2½ hours at helm in morning; afternoon spent in reading & cricket.

Tuesday, June 20th.   The day the Allan Liner should leave Liverpool carrying our steam launch, two nurses, and let me hope letters for me. How glad I shall be to hear; I am not accustomed to spend between 2 & 3 weeks without *any* news, and before the s.s. arrives it will be more than 3 weeks! I do not find it so desolate & lonely on the Atlantic as I had expected to, though surely we are far enough away from our nearest neighbours; a vessel seen today & not another for 5 days perhaps; with blue sky or clouds above and between 2 & 3 miles of water below surely ought to make one feel a bit alone, but we are 13 and get on well with one another and are moreover busy the whole day long.

As the light was beginning to fail lookout in the bows saw a bottle with the cork covered over with canvas – a "message from the sea" probably – our bows hit it as we were running 8 knots, and by the time Hewer was told of it we were too far past to give us a chance of finding it if we had put about. Was it a message from the s.s. "Naronic"?[5] or tidings of a more recent wreck? Capt. Trezise never leaves the deck night or day but he scans the horizon carefully all round; he was once 3 days & 3 nights in an open boat in winter on the edge of N.Foundland Bank – one of 3 of the crew of a barque saved – and his memory of the terror of that time is very keen.

Wednesday, June 21st. Running 8 knots an hour till late afternoon – 190 for the day. In afternoon we got into the fog, almost constant on the great Bank where the Arctic & Gulf Currents meet. The water has got very cold; yesterday it was 55.5° at 4 p.m., oddly enough shot up to 61° at 6 p.m. – equal to the highest temp. we have met with – but dropped to 53° an hour later! This afternoon it was 43°.

I am looking forward to seeing the icebergs, but the presence of a fog takes the edge off the pleasure of knowing they are near; our watch at the bows is doubled and a keen lookout is kept; tonight the fog has lifted & the wind dropped, otherwise we should be hove to for the night. We are within 200 miles of St. John's, but if we have fogs & much ice we may be long before getting there.

s.s. "Naronic" is supposed to have run into a berg; in 1880 s.s. "Arizona" (Guion Line) ran straight into a berg between 7 & 8 p.m.; Capt. had gone below half an hour thinking a fog bank only was ahead, & 2nd. officer in charge was talking on the bridge; 35 ft. of bows completely smashed in, & tons of ice fell on deck.

Thursday, June 22nd. Today our latitude is a little s. of Paris, and yet at the end of June the temp. is down to 44°! A cold damp day for we have been enveloped in fog, lying to most of the time fearing to sail ahead.

This morning early I presented a queer spectacle on deck – seaboots, flannel nightshirt, sweater & waistcoat – being called up to see our first iceberg; unfortunately it was too thick for us to see it well at ½ mile distance, but it seemed about 100 ft. high, pure white with grey in the shadows; its shape somewhat resembled that of the "Dent du Chat" opposite Aix.

Friday, June 23rd. Another cold & wet day in a fog! The presence of icebergs makes us very careful so we have been lying to all day although the wind has been favourable. During the 24 hrs. we made 45 knots only. The fog has been so thick that we have seen nothing all day; in the early hours of the morning as we were drifting to leeward we went close by a berg, for although it could not be seen the watch heard the sea breaking on it as if it had been on the seashore. This afternoon we took the temp. of the water at various depths, e.g. 10, 30, 60 & 100 fathom, and found the reading to vary between 30° & 31.5°F.

Saturday, June 24th. Another day lying to because of fog, drifting with the Arctic Current. The only excitement of the day, indeed of the last three days, was the sudden announcement that we were drifting straight into a berg 100 ft. high … we were within 50 yds., or less than two ship's lengths of it, before it was seen, and even then it was taken in the fog for a schooner; helm put up & mizzensheet let out at once and we passed to leeward of it just in time. When to leeward we could hear the "moderately rough" sea roaring as it broke against the ice and could see the spray thrown up half its height. The wind was very cold as it came to us past it, but the sea was warmer than it had been earlier in the morning (42° agst. 41°F).

No prospect of fog lifting; we must stop out here – within about 100 miles of land – till it lifts for in addition to the danger of running into ice there is the difficulty of making port as we cannot be sure of our position within a few miles, not having seen the sun since Tuesday.

Sunday, June 25th. Fog cleared 3.30 a.m. & we began running at 8½ knots keeping it up till fog settled down again about 8 p.m., when we calculated we were about 20 miles from the coast. By 10 p.m. the fog had lifted somewhat but Cape Spear light had not been made out. Day spent for the most part in reading, writing & talking with crew.

ST JOHN'S

Monday, June 26th. Fog did not lift sufficiently for us to see land till 7.30 a.m. when we were about 10 miles off, but in a calm. Navigation a marvel to me, for notwithstanding the 90 hours continuous fog when the mist

Labrador Odyssey

cleared we were the calculated distance from land and heading *straight* for port! After some hours calm a stiff breeze sprang up from N. and we entered the Narrows just before noon.

Remembering kindness shown last year the "Albert" saluted the city with a gun rocket; this brought Dr. and Mrs. [Moses] Harvey[6] & handkerchiefs to their window. Customs saluted us & refused to board. Landed at once & made for post; letters from Mother & [sisters] Etta, Mary, [nieces] Gladys & Elsie; *most* refreshing after 3 weeks' absence of news. Dr. Harvey met us at post office, a very courteous & quietly enthusiastic old gentleman; being Reuters' agent he wired our arrival home; we learnt from him of the terrible disaster to H.M.S. "Victoria" & death of Admiral Tryon.[7] After dinner wrote letters; then walked through town & explored ruins of Anglican cathedral; to tea with Dr. H. at his house; there we met Dr. & Mrs. H. (Junr.), a Mrs. H., and Mr. [T.C.] Chapman, City Engineer, son of the Head of Western College, Plymouth.

Tuesday, June 27th.   Called on His Excellency the Governor – Sir Terence O'Brien[8] – a hearty, blunt but very friendly & portly gentleman; spent an hour talking to him, learning many strange things about N.F. & its inhabitants; he is a photographer so we have borrowed his darkroom for our developing. In morning we heard Princess May had permitted steam launch to be named after her, so we asked the Gov. if Lady O'Brien would "Christen" it; the idea of a ceremony pleased him immensely; he must be very dull, poor man, for very little goes on here & he has no hobby but photography – and it would never do for the Gov. of Britain's oldest colony to be seen much with his head under a black cloth! – and avoids politics, wishing to keep his hands clean. We left him for an hour & returned to lunch at 2; while there message came that H.M.S. "Blake" had arrived in harbour 12 hours before she was expected but instead of being put in a flurry he made a very good lunch and would not let us leave till 4. He had heard from London that Vice Adm. Hopkins of "Blake" was to succeed Adm. Tryon [as commander on the Mediterranean station], so he sent Mr. Melville,[9] his aide-de-camp, to inform the V.A. Among other things he told us that though he is "Commander in Chief" and "Vice-Admiral" he has not a soldier or a gun to command, so that should a boat with 200 men lay off harbour & demand a large sum of money, threatening to burn the town on refusal, they would be *obliged* to pay; he says the people think of nothing but fish. By "fish" is meant cod, and nothing but cod, so that at dinner you will be asked whether you will take "fish or salmon"; oddly enough there is no fishmonger's in the place.

Sectarianism seems to be the root of the miserable want of honesty and all the quarrels & bitterness here; Catholics, Anglicans, & Wesleyans (including Congl. & Presby.) are about equal in number throughout the Island but in St. John's the R.C.s preponderate greatly; there is a truce between the parties, the terms being that what one has the others have too; consequently there are 3 boards of education, 3 school inspectors, 3 everything where possible, and where it is not possible to have three men in one post – e.g. head clerkship of post office – when a R.C. resigns he must be succeeded by a Wesleyan & he again by an Anglican; the result is that promotion by merit is unknown. E.g. since last year the R.C. head clerkship of P.O. died & was succeeded by a Wesleyan grocer who knew nothing of the work, the other clerks of the P.O. not having a chance as they were R.C.s or A. Separate gov. grants are made to the three different sets of schools; a village is either without a school altogether or has to have three – three bad ones with teachers who scarcely know more than A.B.C. instead of one good one. This is only one example of the system.

In politics corruption & sharp practice are studied as fine arts; no one hides it, for what's the good as everyone knows it. The Governor tells us he has frequently to write home and ask if an explanation can be offered for the fact that men lose the honesty which Englishmen pride themselves on directly they cross the Atlantic; he has never found an answer, but no one even here denies the truth of the statement.

How to catch votes. There is a general election in November so they are all hard at it; I wonder if this fact has anything to do with the fact that all the leaders of both government & opposition are on our local committee; the Labrador fishermen's vote is a large one; last year the reporter of our meeting here got into very hot water because while he reported all the speeches by [the] gov's supporters he did not that of Sir Robert Thorburn,[10] who leads the opposition.

Sir Wm. Whiteway[11] has 28 supporters in the present House of Assembly of 36 members, and the Governor tells us 26 out of the 28 have already received some appointment or large govt. grant! Sir Wm. W. makes politics pay; last autumn a man asked him to induce the government to make him a grant of a particular tract of land as it was the only one in the island that would answer the purpose he had in view; Sir Wm. asked the House to make the grant, but to himself and then proceeded to *sell* the land granted to him to the man who wanted & had asked for it!

The Governor is going to visit the N. of the island in 2 or 3 weeks' time in his yacht, s.s. "Phiona" [*Faiona*] and will probably cross to Blanc Sablon; we are doing our best to induce him to visit Battle Harbour while there; it [is] only one day's steam on.

I took some photos from roof of Governor's house, and then went down by request to photo[graph] landing of Vice-Admiral Hopkins, and the police who were drawn up as a guard of honour.

Went to tea with Dr. Shea[12] who is Res. Med. Officer at hospital; had not been there ½ hour before telephone message came announcing that Allan Liner "Corean" was in the Narrows; hurried down to meet her; nurses arrived safely, good passage. Steam launch on board. Nurses go to hospital as there is no hotel in the place; there was one *before* the fire. Return on board at 11.15 and find a large mail. Letters from Mother, Etta, Harry, Cecil, Carlisle, Dr. Rudge, Eliot Reed; papers &c; sat up very late reading & then writing.

Wednesday, June 28th.   Morning spent at committee meeting in office of Postmaster General. Present Hon. A.W. Harvey[13] (in chair), Sir Wm. Whiteway (the Premier & Attorney Gen.), Sir Rob. Thorburn (Leader of Opposition), Mr. Monroe (the probable Premier after the next election),[14] Mr. [William C.] Job (merchant with station at Indian Harbour),[15] and our three selves.

They are treating us *very* well; not charging "Albert" harbour dues, customs duty, pilotage &c &c; $1400 (=£300) have been subscribed privately and house at Battle Harbour worth $900 given and government has guaranteed up to $1000 more. Sub. com. taking charge of Battle H. hosp. consists of Mr. Monroe, Mr. W.B. Grieve[16] & Mr. A.W. Harvey; and of Indian Harbour hosp. of Sir Wm. Whiteway, Capt. [Samuel] Blandford, & Mr. Job; practically matters are left in our hands; we say what we want, they provide & pay.

Battle H. hosp. is practically finished; Indian Harb. hosp. is in manufacture here & will be conveyed north in pieces in the first mail steamer leaving here on July 6th., in charge of a carpenter who will commence construction before we arrive.

Great efforts are being made to remove our launch from deck of s.s. "Corean" but at present there has been no success. There was no difficulty in putting her on board at Liverpool, but in St. John's there is no such thing as a crane; derricks have been rigged up from the yardarm, but have given way under the weight of the 10 tons they were wanted to lift. s.s. "Corean" should sail at 8 tomorrow morning, but so far *no* progress has been made in the removal of the launch though there has been much effort; her crew are very sick at the business. The Allan Line have been very generous, bringing the boat out for £50 instead of the £125 usually charged.

After dinner we drove out to Murray's Pond with Mr. Chapman and tried to catch some large Rainbow trout; a N.W. wind was blowing and we did not get a rise; no fish has been caught in that pond this year; the Rainbow trout is a Canadian fish & in Murray's Pond they run from 1–4 lbs. Coming home saw a muskrat in a swamp.

Thursday, June 29th. At 10 a.m. steamed round H.M.S. "Blake" & H.M.S. "Cleopatra" in Mr. Job's steam launch; our launch still on deck of "Corean." Spars were rigged up to strengthen yardarm & stronger derricks fixed;

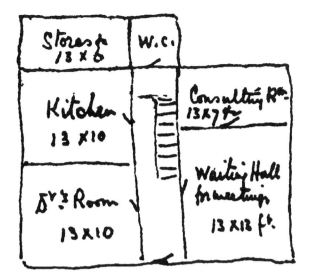
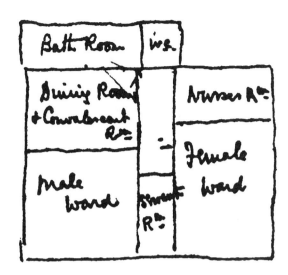

Floor plans of Indian Harbour hospital.

we could not stay to watch final effort as we had appointment to meet builder of my hospital, see wood in preparation & talk over plans.

This is rough plan of ground & 1st floor of my hospital; outside measurement will be 32 × 22 ft. with the addition of piece occupied by stores & bathroom.

Called on Lady Whiteway, & then on Dr. [Earnest H.] Kendall, who had left cards on us; he & wife had come to N.F. last autumn; very nice people; hope we may see them again; asked us in to tea on Sunday; had read of M.D.S.F. in "The Christian."

After lunch went to Mr. Steer's[17] house with G., B. & Capt.; afternoon spent in fishing large pond [Long Pond] preserved by Piscatorial Soc.; this soc. has leave to preserve this pond for 16 yrs. in return for 10,000 young trout annually for stocking ponds in district; the hatchery seems to be very successful.[18] The Piscat. Soc. has given us right to fish there; very good sport notwithstanding the cold N. wind; about 3½ doz. fish but small – "red lake trout," "salmon peal trout" & "Loch Levan trout." After tea went round Mrs. Steer's garden;[19] she has succeeded in making it very like her old Devonshire garden; I was surprised at its richness for the winters are terribly severe; she takes very great trouble herself to protect the plants; fruit blossom well out, lilac in bud, lily of valley in bloom; large Mexican poppy about to open and a few tulip still out.

Steam launch safely launched; good looking but not over strong for the work wanted of her. s.s. "Corean" delayed over 12 hours.

Friday, June 30th. St. John's looks like a town recovering from a bombardment; it has a most ramshackle & temporary appearance; last year fire which destroyed 5/6 of the city must have been fearful; the wooden houses burnt very rapidly but the stone & brick ones of which there were very few were equally destroyed. The cathedral (Anglican) was the finest building of the kind this side of the Atlantic, a really beautiful stone building; it was commenced in 1820[20] but the chancel had only just been completed; the whole had cost £100,000 and was not paid for when destroyed; the nave & crypt were filled with goods rescued from houses but they all perished when the church caught; the effect of heat on stone is well demonstrated; the nave has not been touched since; it requires some climbing to walk down it; chancel & transepts have been roofed in & will be ready for service in two years time!

The rest of the town is filled with ruins of stone houses, empty spaces dotted over with brick chimney-stacks where wooden houses used to stand, and hastily run up matchbox-like wooden structures which owing to the unevenness of the ground are often built on piles. Shops few, poor, very expensive. The expense is to a large extent due to the large duties, averaging 25%, on all introduced goods; duty on sugar is 100%.

This morning was spent at the hospital – 60 beds, clean, airy, but from a London point of view badly nursed. The matron died 7 mo. ago, & *no* effort has been made by the government to obtain another!

Met Sir Robt. Thorburn who took us to Commercial Club & entered our names as members while we are here; we are now members of every club in the place; M.D.S.F. is very popular and we are not able to accept all the invitations we receive.

After lunch sailed in harbour with Bobardt in dinghy; harbour is a very pretty one & looks especially fine now with two warships in. Found Rev. Snowdon on board when we returned, a Wesleyan minister from Old Perlican, Trinity Bay; liked him much; just now there is a w. conference in St. John's; we expect a visit tomorrow.

Nurses & Dr. Harvey came; former stayed to tea & talked over stores list &c.

Saturday, July 1st. Called on the Governor in morning; he again talked freely on the political parties of the colony and expressed his disgust of both; there is no political question save the French Shore question,[21] which is treated commercially, & the question of union with Canada, which no one dares bring forward. The fight is for power & consequent emolument, and this alone. The Gov. told me that when the present house was returned Nov. 3 yrs. ago (there are 4-year parliaments here) not one of the ministry of the preceding government had a seat, and that the then ministry refused to resign although they had a following in the House of Assembly of 8 out of 36 only; the Gov. had no power to turn them out and felt in a great fix, for as he said he was a soldier & not a lawyer and did not know what to do. He ultimately got rid of them by threatening continued sessions and they resigned in Feb. following after having given all appointments & government contracts to their own supporters.

Went to lunch with Mr. & Mrs. Job Junr., Mr. Job Senr.[22] present also; *very* nice people; they feel unable to help us enough & have arranged to send us papers by each mail.

They vouch for the truth of the following bear story: last winter a man who lives on the shore in a bay at the N. of the island was surprised to hear a noise outside his cabin, went outside & was just in time to see a small black bear jump onto a puncheon (or large barrel) and disappear as the end gave way under its weight; the poor man was so frightened that he got into his small boat at his feet, pushed off as fast & far as he could and *then* discovered his oars were on shore; the tide took him out and he was not picked up for 36 hrs.

Last winter a large polar bear was seen on floe ice off St. John's; two boats went after it and shared in the spoil; instead of selling the skin & dividing they actually halved the skin and shared in that way. I have heard from several people the story of two vessels finding a wreck in the s. of n.fd. & agreeing to share everything washed ashore, and of their sawing a piano in halves as they could not think how to share it any other way!

After lunch we all went down to an "at home" on h.m.s. "Blake,"[23] passing on our way a good specimen of the swallow-tail butterfly. The quarterdeck was covered in with flags and was used for dancing, the 50 midshipmen taking great delight in this. The senior surgeon took Grenfell & me over the whole vessel – all the decks, conning tower, gun compartments, searchlight rooms, crew's quarters, hospital, engine-room, torpedo deck, and all the cabins. What struck me most was the enormous size & space, then the order & cleanness; it is dreadful to think of this beautiful vessel as a great mankilling machine. She carries 12 big guns only, two of which (fore & aft) are [siton?] guns; on the upper decks are many quick-firing guns – up to 3 in. bore – such as Hotchkiss, Nordenfelt, Maxim. The conning tower is a tower forward, the walls of which are 18 in. of solid steel & then backed with wood; it is the brain of the vessel, or may be used as such, as from it the commander who is supposed to shelter here when he is within rifle range of the enemy is able to steer, fire the guns & torpedoes and control every part & department of the ship by means of speaking tubes, electric bells &c. &c. &c.

Great kindness was shown us by all the officers; the Capt. was very pleasant and expressed sorrow that we had not asked him to take our launch off the deck of s.s. "Corean," "as," said he, "if the 'Corean' had come alongside we could have got her off in no time with our derricks"; he asked to be introduced to the nurses as did also the Governor & Lady O'Brien.

Commodore Curzon-Howe, commander of H.M.S. "Cleopatra," a smaller vessel belonging to the N. Atlantic fleet, pressed us to let him know if there was anything he could bring up to Labrador for us when he goes North later in the summer; he has just returned from the French Shore and reports very great distress among the people there, many of the children having no clothes at all.[24]

Evening spent with Dr. Shea at the hospital.

I bought some fowls – 6 hens & a cock – from a farmer thro' Mr. Steer; this is a speculation but it is doubtful if I shall make them pay the $8 they, their corn & wire netting have cost me; however, I look forward to *some* new laid eggs and roast fowl during the latter part of my time at "Indian Harbour" if the dogs should be averse to raw cold fowl.

Sunday, July 2nd.   Grenfell had service for Boys' Brigade on board at noon – 30 present; subject "all are different." Lunch with Chapman; he tells me stonemasons receive $4 a day wages, & carpenters $2 so great is the demand for their work since the fire.

The sun is of a copper colour; this is a pathognomonic sign of a large fire somewhere; they say it is the "reflection" of the fire in the sun, but I would suggest it is due to some particles from the fire coming between us & the sun.

News has come in that the Straits of Belle Isle are blocked with ice and that so many vessels are waiting to get through that St. Anthony harbour will not hold another boat.

Was asked to speak at George St. Sunday School; two schools united & filled the building with 800 children; thought it was annual missionary meeting so spun a yarn about New Guinea and did not know till afterwards that the missy. meeting was at another church & that this was a meeting to meet the Methodist conference now sitting; was much interested in a tall, wigged minister who told me afterwards that I had done "fairly well."

Tea with Dr. & Mrs. Kendall; met Rev. Hall from Carbonear. Service at Congl. schoolroom; the new church not commenced yet; went to Rev. G.M. Siddall's afterwards and endeavoured to interest him in our work. Mr. S. used to attend Uncle Charles' church at Plymouth and has always held him up as his ideal of a minister. Mrs. S. gave me some non-fermented whort-wine & gave directions how to make it.

Monday, July 3rd. Cannot leave harbour because of E. wind & fog; ship quite ready; launch getting into condition.

Looked into Mr. Duder's[25] store to see furs; Mr. Patrick[26] tells me a black fox skin from Hudson Bay has just realised £156 in London; he not infrequently gets one worth £60 from Labrador.

In afternoon Dr. Harvey tells me of the Architeuthis Harveyi, an enormous cuttlefish with 10 arms he was the first to describe; his first specimen was 7 ft. in the body & the arms 20 ft. long, the beak the size of a large parrot & chitonous and the suckers from 1 in. in diam. downwards; the largest ever found & measured was 15 ft. in the body with arms 40 ft. long; they live in deep water & come near shore only in bad weather.

Two men & a boy were out fishing from Trinity Bay many years ago & stuck a boathook into a queer looking object on the sea; it immediately raised up its head a foot or two and threw two arms round the boat; the men were paralysed with fear as they saw their boat being drawn under the water but the boy of 10 yrs. old cut off first one arm & then the other with his knife and the enormous squid disappeared in a cloud of sepia; these two arms are in the St. John's museum and Dr. Harvey has seen & got the history from this lad, who is now a full-grown man.

Dr. Harvey gave me some specimens of globigerina or "Atlantic ooze" which had been obtained from the Atlantic at a depth of 2½ miles; they are the silica cases of a little protozoon which lives in the ocean and are rained down as they die; this ooze raised, dried, hardened &c is chalk and it is of this that our chalk cliffs are formed.

Mr. Job Senr. asked me if I knew Mr. Horton of Hampstead, & his friend Mr. Darloe, who used to be his minister in Liverpool; Mrs. Selby of Highgate is a cousin of his. This is the fifth person I have met in St. John's who knew some of our family or friends. Mr. Job remembers having met Aunt John Curwen of Manchester;[27] he was very intimate with the Cowards.

Many people are speculating on the chance of keeping our nurses in St. John's when they return from Labrador; Dr. Shea wants one as matron of the hospital, and Lady O'Brien wants the other to start private nursing; there is no one in the colony who knows anything of nursing.

Bobardt & I spent the evening with Sir Robt. Thorburn, the late premier; he is a vast improvement on Sir Wm. Whiteway, the present premier; he has retired from politics & now Mr. Monroe leads the party. Whenever we have been out to tea we have had ham or salmon, sometimes both, a little scone called a bun, some preserve of a local berry & Devonshire cream, and to these Sir Robt. added sweetbread & oatcake. I spent the whole evening learning about the various fishing industries; Sir Robt. is a great fish merchant & came here from Scotland 40 yrs. ago, but he has never been up in Labrador himself; he tells me the experienced fishermen can tell where they are on the coast at night or in a fog by what they call the "rout" (pron. rôte) of the shore, i.e. the sound of the water breaking on different rocks or harbours, each place having its own characteristic sound. Sir Robt. Thorburn got his K.C.M.G. when he was in England at the Colonial Conference, & being the representative of the oldest colony to him was given the honour of reading the address to the Queen.

Tuesday, July 4th. Had tea with Dr. Harvey; in answer to a question as to whether he had ever sat in the House of Assembly said, "Sir, am I a dog that I should do this thing?" He gave Bobardt & me copies of a book of his,[28] and lent me several scientific papers by himself & others to read; being Reuter's agent he has sent home several cablegrams about the "Albert" & today sends that on the morrow our steam launch is to be named "Princess May" by Lady O'Brien. Evening spent at his daughter-in-law's; music.

On reaching the ship found a steamer had arrived from England bringing a letter from Edward & book from Harry, both sent off on

June 19 & just too late for the last mail. Developed photos at the Governor's.

Wednesday, July 5th. The great event in St. John's today has been the "Christening" of our little steam launch; notices were put in the papers, cards of invitation sent out & our two boats decked with flags. At 12.30 the people came in crowds to inspect us – all the most important people came – merchants, "politicians" and some of the ministers of Established & Methodist Churches but the Catholics were not represented.

Dr. G. made a short speech, and then Lady O'Brien performed her duty by swinging at the launch a bottle hung from the masthead containing not champagne but fresh water coloured with cochineal which did just as well. The Governor, Sir Terence O'Brien, spoke well, one of the happiest speeches he has made I am told, and was followed by Sir Robt. Thorburn & Hon. A.W. Harvey. "God Save the Queen," two gun rockets, and "Praise God from whom all blessings flow"; and then Sir T. O'B. insisted on risking his life by going down the steep steps onto the launch & squeezing through the companion into the cabin: he was mightily pleased with himself when he reached the wharf again & his wife was relieved when he returned. Of course the photographer – there is only one in St. John's – was to the fore.

In the evening we had several visitors & talked on many things; old Dr. Harvey came again; he will be very sorry when we are gone; Mr. Steer & several others looked in, so we got out our magic lantern & Dr. G. gave a short lecture in the crew's cabin.

I showed Mr. Steer a very large lobster's claw Dr. G. has and he told me of a lobster caught a year or two back weighing 26 lbs.!

News has come in of a steamer of the Beaver Line – a cattle boat from Montreal to England – having run into an iceberg and been beached in Forteau's Bay, Labrador; what a good chance of getting fresh meat!

Today the wind is fair & the day bright but the mouth of the harbour is filled with fog; tomorrow we shall be off fog or no fog if the wind keeps fair.

Labrador Odyssey

Dr. Bobardt has decided to accompany Dr. G. in the launch; they are taking an engineer & another man & hope to start in a day or two; the two nurses are going north in the "Albert" to save time & expense and to get them to Labrador as comfortably as possible; they will have the aftercabin and I shall take the hospital.

TRANSIT TO LABRADOR

Thursday, July 6th. A lovely day; bright sun & fair wind. Public holiday for the royal wedding [between Prince George and Princess May]. Up at 6.30 for a bath. We heave anchor at 10.30 amid many farewells from folk on shore; G. & B. return to shore in the launch & dinghy taking the last of their stores & life-jackets; we try & believe all the bunting exhibited is in our honour; we salute H.M.S. "Cleopatra" as we pass, lowering our jack three times, and our salutation is returned; Dr. & Mrs. Harvey wave pocket handkerchiefs, I work the flag again, and once more in response to the salute from the signal station at the entrance to the Narrows. The tug takes us a mile out, we hoist sails, flap our wings and steer N. by E.; glad beyond measure to be on our way again; we have had a very good time in St. John's but have been oppressed by the kindness, generosity & extreme hospitality of the people; we have had *no* time to ourselves and are wanting a little quiet. The breeze was very light, but the nurses are not good sailors. Shortly after we left the harbour we saw the "Windsor Lake" leave on her way to Labrador; she is conveying much of our stores to Battle Harbour, and my hospital to Indian Harbour.

Today we have seen queer things; at noon we saw a cloud coloured red, yellow & greenish blue (colours in this order from above downwards) surrounded by perfectly natural white ones; it lasted half an hour or more & was due S. of us; Capt. had never seen or heard of such a thing before; it had certainly nothing to do with a rainbow, and we could only suggest that it was caused by the enormous forest fire now burning to the W. of St. John's which had given rise to the copper colour of the sun on Sunday; this is only a suggestion & is far from an explanation. "I'll believe it when

MDSF vessel *Albert* hoists mainsail
before leaving St John's.

I see it with my eyes"; this expression has ceased to have any meaning to me after this afternoon's experience for I have spent a long time in wonder & almost confusion. I look at an iceberg on the horizon; it looks quite small & square; in a moment like a jack-in-the-box it is 4 or 6 times taller than it was; then after a few minutes it is divided into two, and by carefully examining it with my glasses I find I am looking at a berg in the sea with another one just like it but upside down immediately over it, but this one is in the air & not in the sea at all; then while I am looking it is all small again, to alter in appearance again by & by. I look at a barque bound from Europe to Harbour Grace and she looks like any other barque, but in a minute she seems to have enormous masts and to be rapidly hoisting & lowering large flags on each mast, each flag being the size & shape of the topsails; again she seems to be like any ordinary barque and I turn away, but when I look in a few minutes she is in three pieces. I look at the land at the opening into Trinity Bay and at Baccalieu Island, and it looks low & flat like the North German & Dutch shores, but in a little time it looks high & rugged with castles dotted along on the most prominent peaks, and then all of a sudden there is movement on the tops of the hills and the castles appear lighthouses and then go and appear somewhere else, their places being taken by what look like very big men walking about, and by & by castles, men & hills have all gone and I see a low, flat coastline in the distance. This mirage is the most remarkable thing I remember to have seen and it entertained & astonished us for a long time. Hewer & I were telling Rogers the bo's'n who is laid up with sciatica about it in the evening, and Hewer could not understand my pronunciation of the word "mirage": "Why here's a blooming yarn! Here's the Dr. says m i r a g e does not spell mīrāge!"

Two eggs today. At prayers started on the Life of Moses.[29]

Friday, July 7th. A lovely day with but little fog and not much wind; we are running in our course and in 30 hours made 140 knots. At 9 a.m. heard a loud gun report at a distance; the only thing in sight was a small iceberg but I was looking at it at the time and know it did not move, and the report was not so drawn out & low as that caused by the capsizing of a berg. Later in the day we sailed near a large berg so I fired an explosive bullet at it to hear the report of the explosion & see what damage would be done; the report on contact with the ice was very great and a fairly large hole was made in its flat side.

During the morning we saw a large brown whale abt. 45 ft. long apparently and got within 30 yds. of it.

The afternoon was spent in sewing a strip of muskrat fur down the inner side of the front of a leather coat I bought in St. John's; I have ordered a leather collar for the coat & shall line it too when it arrives as the fur will help to keep the cold wind out from the openings into the jacket.

One nurse has not left her bunk all day, though it has been so calm; the other is better.

Saturday, July 8th. Six weeks since I left home. A calm day with a very light wind on our beam so that we make about 3½ knots an hour. The day spent reading; of the nurses one kept her bunk, the other was up but asleep most of the day. On going to sea as a passenger with nothing that must be done the tendency to sleep a great deal for the first week is very great, almost or quite irresistible; it is best to sleep for the disturbance of the cerebral circulation that gives rise to this sleepiness prevents one either reading or thinking; after a time one gets used to it and unless the sea is very rough one can read as well as on shore.

We passed a very beautiful iceberg after dinner but too far off to photograph; it was peaked & reminded me of photographs of the Matterhorn. A couple of hours later we were within ½ mile of another large berg that was falling to pieces; the sea s. of it was strewn with pieces of a great shelf that had fallen off so we put out in the dinghy and took enough to fill our beef tub and were very glad of it as the little we got with the fresh meat in St. John's was almost gone; we gave the berg a wide berth and hearing a roar were in time to look round and see another large piece fall off into the sea.

Tonight the "Northern Lights," or aurora borealis, are showing very well; they are steady & spread over the whole of the N. of the sky; sometimes they are like waves flashing across the sky, sometimes like broad sheets of lightning; when seen to the *South* they mean bad weather.

Sunday, July 9th.   Woken up by my cock crowing. Fog all day, but dry so I was not kept below deck. Read much. Took God's promises to Moses when he sent him to Pharoah for evening service. Reread home letters before turning in.

BATTLE HARBOUR

Monday, July 10th.   When called at 6.30 was told there was a dense fog but a quarter of an hour later went on deck to find the fog suddenly lifted, sun shining warmly, wind blowing cold from icebergs all round, and land in sight. Expecting to find fog, what a glorious view!

I climbed into the rigging and counted 117 icebergs or islands of ice on the port side; most of them were this side of the vessel as the East wind had driven them on shore, where they were stranded. The icebergs were most beautiful, looking white in the sunlight but under projecting shelves & pieces were of a beautiful starch blue but brighter & much more transparent; parts seen through a thin layer of water were of an emerald green; some of the shapes were very fantastic and as we sailed by and changed our viewpoint the shapes were continually altering. On one berg we saw a very large number of birds, sitting on it as if it was a house roof, and on firing a gun they rose in a cloud and were joined by two other clouds of birds which got up from the water.

As we approached and made our way in through numerous islands the country looked very bare, rocks covered with lichen & rockplants but never a tree. We hoisted flags, a jack and M.D.S.F. [flag], and stood by firing a gun rocket for a pilot. We learnt that the average time that it had taken schooners to reach Battle from St. John's this year had been 21 days; this was on account of the great

Battle Harbour. Left to right: MDSF hospital, George Hall's storehouse and shop, and Hall's house.

George Hall's employees, Battle Harbour.

quantity of ice on the coast & in the Straits of Belle Isle; this harbour has been open a week only, having been blocked till last Monday; we feel pleased that we have taken only 4 days by keeping well out to sea & arriving after the ice had left. The "Windsor Lake" – the mail boat which left St. John's with us – has not yet arrived, having called at several ports in the straits; she is expected tomorrow.

Battle Harbour – the Capital of Labrador – is an odd looking little place but picturesquely situated on the rock; it consists of a church without a clergyman, a schoolhouse at present without a schoolmaster, an agent's house with Mr. [George] Hall the agent, a large storehouse, the hospital not yet fully completed and several fishermen's houses and wharfs & stages for drying fish; these buildings are scattered and as far as I have seen are unconnected by roads.

Mr. Hall sent a boat's crew to help us moor our vessel, and himself met us at his wharf; a plain, rough, pleasant man of about 35; he took us up to his house and gave us some spruce beer, an unfermented beverage made from the branches of the spruce fir and used largely in this part of Labrador; it was not at all bad but tasted too strongly of the molasses with which it was sweetened. As we were returning to the ship a boat returned from visiting the salmon nets and brought in two fish, 11 lbs. & 8 lbs., which Mr. Hall gave us in return for a joint of fresh meat we had given him – a reversion to the custom pertaining in savage countries of giving & receiving presents I suppose. After dinner we visited Mr. Hall's stores – he, as Mr. W. Baine Grieve's agent, supplies all their fisherfolk 30 miles up & down the coast with what they need, giving them "tick" for the goods & expecting to be paid in fish at the end of the season: flannel, boots, string, nets, lamp glasses, buttons, rice, salt &c, a great variety & a great mixture.

The first salmon caught this year in this part of Labrador was taken on June 15, and the first fish – nothing is called "fish" but cod – on June 16th.

A small porpoise was taken in the salmon nets yesterday; they are very seldom seen so far north; I have the skull & a steak for tomorrow's breakfast, old Harry, an old man of 76 who has lived here 50 yrs., another steak and the dogs the rest.

The dogs are a snarly lot but perfectly safe; they are Newfoundlanders, the Esquimo dogs having been killed; in winter they are

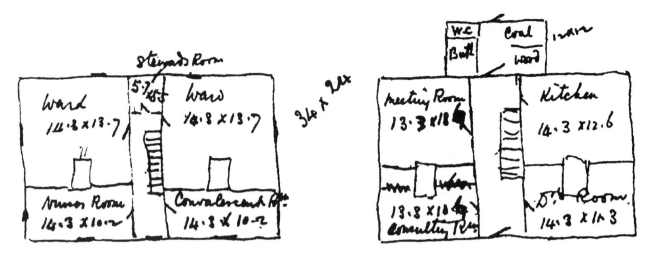

Floor plans of Battle Harbour hospital.

used in the sleighs; Mr. Hall keeps a pack of 16. Unfortunately the dogs are hungry creatures & partial to birds so I can't give my fowls an airing on shore.

Tuesday, July 11th. Morning spent opening packing cases looking for drugs which should have been put on board at St. John's; unfortunately a mistake had been made and we had brought up sugar & bacon instead of the boxes I had wanted, so we must wait till the "Windsor Lake" – the mail boat – arrives with the rest of our stores.

Afternoon spent in arranging internal arrangements of Battle Harbour hospital.

There are a large number of dogs – cross between Newfoundland & Eskimo, sulky, cowardly during day, and at night they roam about & fight and howl; the howling at night is terrific, the Bordighera[30] frogs are nowhere in comparison; our night watch marches up & down deck armed with a heavy stick, ready for any number of them.

A good many folk came to the service in evening.

Labrador Odyssey

Wednesday, July 12th.   Up at 5 – read – breakfast at 6.30 and at 7 a.m. Sister Williams and I got on board Mr. W. Baine Grieve's steam launch "Pundit" (Capt. Smith) and crossed St. Lewis Sound to Fox Harbour – a distance of about six miles; we took medicine chest, camera, gun & lunch.

Before landing we saw a black mass moving in the water & discovered it to be a shoal of caplin, a fish about 6 or 7 inches long & largely used for bait & in N.F. for manure; I put my hand among them and caught two at a time; so thick were they that they could not get away. We landed on Mr. Geo. Holley's fish stage & slimy, wet and fishy it was; met Mr. H. himself and were conducted past the tables and stack of fish in salt back across the hill to his house – a neat wooden, sod-covered building of two rooms; here he, his wife and an adopted Esquimaux boy of 1½ yrs. live and with them are lodging his two brothers & a sister who have come up from N.F. for the season. It was breakfast time and we sat talking as they eat caplin – fried by being placed on the stove without a dish or paper – and drank tea or coffee sweetened with molasses.

They are well off – much better off than Mr. Edwd. Holley who lives in a miserable one-roomed house with his wife and boy of 18 who is bad with consumption. In the winter these two families move into a smaller house consisting of one room 16 × 14 ft. and live together for greater warmth, the walls being more airtight; they have not enough windows for all three houses so when the winter comes round they take the window frames from one of the houses & put it in the winter house. We were shown some snowshoes; without them it is not possible to walk in the soft snow; they consist of a double framework of wood with sealskin net & lashes for foot in centre & cotton net before & aft. They are called "rackets," and measure 18 × 18 inches.

In visiting the 10 houses in this harbour the plan we adopted was to enter together, sit down, glean as much information as we could as to their condition, possession of nets, chance of catching fish or shooting animals, food, number of children &c. &c., then I made some excuse to draw their men out of the house while nurse enquired into the condition of the women's clothing. In this way we got a very great deal of useful information and discovered an extraordinary state of affairs. Six of the ten houses consisted of one room only, and in this room the whole family lived – one family consisting of an Esquimaux widow woman, 3 sons & 3 daughters: all lived together; they had no nets & had not caught any fish with the hook yet; during the winter the eldest boy, aet. 19, shot two otters and got $9 (i.e. 37/6) for each; the boys were clothed in patchwork of cloth but fairly warmly; the women & girls had each an old patched linsey dress and underneath one layer of cotton in rags but very clean; they had no other clothes at all and had to turn in under a wool quilt they received from the Mission last year on washing days.

Poorer than this was Chas. Mangrove, an old man of 62 but old at that; he was a widower and had 8 children; 6 of these had been taken off his hands by neighbours; he had one lad of 18 at home and a girl of 15; the boy had shot 3 lynx in the winter & got $3 for each; the girl was clothed with two layers of rags – thin cotton & linsey – and though she could keep fairly warm in this weather had nothing to fall back on when the frosts came. The house was clean inside – as they nearly all were – and on the wall was the front page of a copy of "Great Thoughts" with a portrait of Mr. Horton![31] He could not read, never having been to school, was quite blind in one eye & had commencing cataract in the other. I asked him when he last had any money and he said, "God knows when I had any money; afore I was married I had a scattered shilling."

George Brown's house looks like a mound of earth on the bare rocks; it is a one-roomed log hut 13 × 12 × 8 ft. with 3 or 4 ft. of earth on the outside to keep the cold out; there is less earth on the top and a hole had been made to let the light through the roof; in addition to this hole were others the dogs had made when they frolicked on the roof. In this hovel he lived with his two boys of 7 & 8 and two stepdaughters of 12 & 14, the elder of whom had a crippled left arm. He slept on a shelf with the boys, and the girls had two other shelves, one above the other. This poor man had two old salmon nets that would hardly hold a fish and had taken very little with them, and he would certainly starve if he was not helped very

Mrs Thoms and seven of her nine children, Fox Harbour. "She is a widow – a half-breed. They are wearing all the clothes they possess. They have no nets, only jiggers and two old guns. Last winter they lived on 5 barrels of flour, 1 cwt. hard bread, G viii molasses and lbs. iv tea."

greatly by the only other people who lived on his side of the harbour. These were Mrs. Thoms, her blind brother Pawlo, and her brother with his wife, Mr. and Mrs. Pawlo – full-blooded Esquimaux. These all lived in one large house with their four children and are a thriving family. In 7 days they had taken 95 quintals of cod – a quintal is 112 lbs. of dried fish, which corresponds to 230 lbs. of fresh; last year they got 13/- a quintal credited to them, not that they received any money for them; they sent the fish to "the firm," i.e. Baine, Johnson & Co., which is represented by Mr. Walter Baine Grieve, of Battle Harbour, and received back the fishes' worth in food & clothing. Food & clothing is very expensive here, & that's how the money is made; swanswool flannel 2/6 a yd., scotch yarn 6/- a lb. or 8 knots, linsey 15 cents (i.e. 7½d instead of 2¾ or 3¼). Mr. Hall – Mr. W.B. Grieve's agent – is very good to the poor and gives much food & clothing away to those who cannot pay.

Mr. Pawlo met us at his stage and led us up to his house, where we found Mrs. Thoms, who had gone up to prepare dinner for her household; she was a very odd figure, short, very broad, flatish dark-coloured face with black hair hidden under an ample cap; her skirt

"Mrs. Pawlo, wife of a successful fisherman at Fox Harbour. One of her grandparents was an Englishman; the other three were Esquimaux."

reached but little below her knees and displayed very substantial seaboots – she looked a fisher*man* and seemed to enjoy her dirty work on the stage, cleaning & splitting fish. She took us into a large, airy, clean room – the common living room, and immediately started washing herself, leaving us to talk to Mr. P., whose English though good was not fluent, herself turning round every now & again as she passed her soapy hand across her face or round her neck to make a remark; she was a very odd looking object, and she had not finished these operations long before Mrs. Pawlo, a younger & yet broader woman, came in and went through the same process with the same water. Their faces & those of the children were all dark & flat and the hair black, straight & very soft. Mr. Pawlo is a great hunter & showed me his guns – all muzzle loaders with 4-foot barrels so that they reached from the ground to the middle of my forehead. In the winter he told me he went "swailing (i.e., sealing) scattered times." Some of their expressions strike one from their oddity; the people address Sister as "young woman," or "woman" alone, and one woman told her adopted boy of 1½ yrs. to "heave the man a kiss," but the said lad was too busy taking me in with his eyes to heed her.

As we left the stage to row out to the steam launch, the whole household came to bid farewell (or "ethani" [*aksunai*] as it is in Esquimaux); the three women & one man stayed on the stage while 3 men & 2 boys manned the boat.

In returning we made a small detour to look for some bay seals but did not see any, and returned to the "Albert" about 4.30 p.m., passing several schooners on their way north. Some of these schooners are only 15 tons & come all the way from St. John's or Harbour Grace – a distance of 400 miles – towing their dinghys, as they have not room for them on deck.

Thursday, July 13th.

Fried caplin & porpoise chops for breakfast, the former very nice & sweet, the latter not half bad, though I could not prevail on the Capt. to try any; it was very dark meat, beautifully tender, but had an unmistakably fishy taste. I am told seal tastes much like porpoise and is eaten a good deal in the sealing season, but the people

Labrador Odyssey

here do not eat the few porpoises that are caught. Taste, after all, is largely dependent on habit; here the virtues of flat-fish are unknown & it is not at all unusual to see a number of flounders lying dead among the cod heads about a fish stage.

Today one of my fowls took ill & had to be killed; they are laying very badly and will be better on shore. I dare not put them on shore here because of the dogs, who would find them very tasty.

At 6.30 our steam launch arrived, greatly to our relief, having had a very good run of 400 miles in a week, anchoring in harbours each night; all well; the boat had gone well; G. & B. much bitten by mosquitoes when on land yesterday.

About 28 at evening prayers; fish are very plentiful just now, so all hands are busy, otherwise more would attend.

At 9.30 a.m. Capt., Sister Williams & I went in Mr. Hall's steam launch to Indian Cove on the other side of Great Caribou Island, as a message had come that a man was ill & wanted to see me. A pretty little cove, though bare. Isaac Hill had pleurisy & was bad; am sorry our hospital is not ready for him; his house had 2 rooms & a loft and was clean; visited Bertha Bradley aet. 5 ?diphtheria; Bradleys are well off & live in a large, clean house. From there went to Mrs. Mugford, who has come up from N.F. with her husband & two girls for the season; she keeps a shop and sells lb. of cloth, i.e. scraps which she sells by the lb. for patchwork dresses; we bought some Scotch yarn at 7 cents (3½[d]) a knot to send to Mrs. Thoms of Fox Harbour to darn stockings with.

From Indian Cove we went on to Cape St. Charles Harbour, a settlement of 7 or 8 families of liv'eres who do well and live in houses of two stories; they nearly all have nets of their own, and as fish is plentiful they are very busy.

Friday, July 14th. All day spent in looking over stores for the two hospitals and getting the Battle Harbour goods ashore. Visited the cemetery and saw the grave of the brother of my patient in Indian Cove, who 2 yrs. ago was lost in the snow & perished, not being able to find his way on this little island of Battle, which is only 3 or 4 miles across; he left home after a bird he saw 300 yds. behind the house; directly he had left the door it began to snow & before long it came down so thick that they could not see 10 yds. ahead; it was 48 hrs. before anyone could even leave their houses to go and look for him, & when found he was dead. On the tombstone was

IN MEMORY OF JOHN
HILL WHO DIED
DECEMBER 30. 1890
AGED 34.
WEEP.NOT.DEAR.PARENTS.
FOR.YOUR.LOST.TIS.MY.
ETERANEL.GAIN.MAY.
CRIST.YOU.ALL.TAKE.UP.
THE.CROST.THAT.WE.
SHOULD.MEAT.AGAIN.

This verse is the local rendering of

"WEEP NOT DEAR PARENTS, FOR YOUR LOSS
IS MY ETERNAL GAIN;
MAKE CHRIST YOUR ALL, TAKE UP THE CROSS
AND WE SHALL MEET AGAIN."

In the same cemetery we found this:

SARAH
COMBE
DID THE FORTH
HAGE 31   HOF
YEARS   HOGES
1881

This means "Sarah Combe died the fourth of August 1881, aged 31 years." And this:

WLLE
COMBE
1881

In the afternoon paid a few calls with the two nurses; Mrs. Ash, who has lived here 20 yrs., is the proud possessor of the only fuchsia on this part of the coast; she grows balsam, asters, & even sunflowers & chrysanthemums in her window.

Mrs. Smith gave us two kittens, one for Indian Harbour hosp. and one for the Captain; she wanted us to take the four she had; a day or two back she had 8, but 4 – well the dogs knew where they were; her old man gave me a grilse taken in his cod trap.

Saturday, July 15th. Dr. Grenfell started in steam launch to visit the harbours down the Straits of Belle Isle & hopes to be back in a week; as she can only carry 2 ton of coal a good deal of careful arrangement is needed as there are only a very few coaling stations and these are small private ones. As she was to pass Indian Cove, Capt., Sister W., Dr. B. & I went in her; found our patient mending and made a few new calls.

Robt. R[umbolt] is a lazy, thriftless man and his wife does not help him; their cottage is 10 ft. by 15 and the family consists of a girl of 13 & two boys of 6 & 4; dirty house & dirty people; the house consisted of two rooms, the bedroom measuring 10 × 5.6, in one end of which was a bed; this bed is 5 ft. 6 in. long & 3 ft. 4 in. wide, and on the bare feather bed sleep husband, wife *and* two boys, all under one wool coverlid they had from the Mission last year. The man told me he had not eaten any meat (save seal in the spring) since his nets wore out 3 yrs. ago, and that he had in the house only enough biscuit & tea for two meals.

As we were long Capt. had walked home across the island; and at 1.20 we started a hard walk along a track leading over bare hills and across moist, boggy patches; it took us 1½ hrs. to do what they call 3 miles but it is certainly longer than this, and sister was very fatigued after it. We reached the vessel at 3 – two hours late for dinner, and found the s.s. "Windsor Lake" alongside the "Albert" discharging our hospital cargoes; all our Indian [Harbour] hosp. cargo was landed too as they had not been assorted and as we did not want to delay the vessel, which was already late; the "Windsor

Lake" is carrying all our goods up from St. John's free of cost; she has the frame of my hospital on board but as she is so pressed for time perhaps she will not have time to leave it at Indian Harbour this trip, as being a mail boat she must keep good time or her connection with the "Virginia Lake" would be thrown out. Should the frame of my hospital not be landed this trip there will be a delay of a fortnight, and this will mean that the chance of getting into the house this year will be small.

In the evening a magic lantern lecture on Palestine.

Sunday, July 16th. Another fine day. Yesterday we sent word to all the harbours that our services would be at 11.0 & 6.30 for adults, and 3 for children; so in the morning boats began to arrive and by the time service commenced we had over 100 people, some of whom had walked over from Indian Cove & some sailed 6 miles from Fox Harbour. Mr. Hall lent us a large, empty storehouse approached by a steep but broad ladder, and this we fitted with seats by placing planks on herring & flour barrels; a table at the end was covered with a large flag, and other pieces of bunting had been hung up at the end of the store. I took the service and chose Mk. i. 40–45 [the cleansing of the leper].

Before dinner we went to the flagstaff at the top of the hill behind the village and had a view of the whole island and the icebergs beyond; icebergs are so numerous & we have become so used to them that now we only notice those extraordinary for size or shape.

Dr. Bobardt took the afternoon service for children in the crew's cabin & hold of the "Albert"; 87 were present but they were not all young children by any means; our Fox Harbour Esquimaux friends were over to this.

The evening service was taken by the Captain, who spoke very well and gave us some of his past history; it was a bit thrilling and will surely do good: 130 were at this service.

Monday, July 17th. The day was cold & foggy, and a sharp N. wind blew all day, so that I was glad of the occupation of unpacking and stowing ship's drugs in the morning. In the early afternoon Dr. B. & I were called to a bad case in the harbour and had some trouble in bringing our patient round. The great event of the day, however, was the arrival of the "Falcon," a sealing steamer which is carrying Lieut. [Robert E.] Peary, Mrs. P. & her maid and the 11 members of his expedition to North Greenland.[32]

As we walked back from seeing our patient we saw [Peary] a big, powerful man of about 35 standing with Mr. Hall & our captain buying dogs from some of the natives. He came on board and saw over the "Albert" and then we went off with him to the "Falcon" (Capt. [Henry B.] Bartlett),[33] which was lying to the east of the islands. She is a steam barque that for 17 yrs. has been used in the spring seal fisheries and has been engaged by Lieut. Peary at $3300 a month and will be away from 2½ to 6 months; last spring she only caught 7000 seals, and this did not pay the cost. We were very kindly received on board by the members of the expedition, who had heard of us at St. John's, & Lieut. Peary was anxious to learn as much as possible about the M.D.S.F.

The "Falcon" was steamed round into Battle Harbour, and during the hour we were on board she had as much water on her decks as we had the whole of the way across the Atlantic. She carries besides her crew of 18 & the 14 members of the expedition all the stores &c needed for 2½ years as well as a wooden house in frame. Right forward on deck were eight burros or Mexican donkeys which it is hoped may prove useful in carrying provisions up onto the central plateau of N. Greenland, but while we were on board one had to be shot, for it was dying from pneumonia, and later in the evening another was taken ill. All round the deck were dogs, some Esquimaux ones which had already drawn Mr. Peary & Mr. Ashtrup [Eivind Astrüp] 1500 miles in Greenland, and some half-breed Esquimaux & Newfoundlanders; they intend taking 100 or more altogether and will collect them as they pass up the Labrador coast; it was necessary to keep the dogs tethered, and they gave us many opportunities of examining their teeth as they snarled at the newcomers just bought on shore.

We learnt that they had been well received wherever they had called in America; 25 cents was charged for admission over the vessel, and in a fortnight they had taken $5000, Boston alone giving them $1400.

The object of the expedition is to prove that Greenland is an island. The "Falcon" will land the party at Lat. 72° abt. Aug. 8 & the crew [will] then help in the erection of the house; while the house is building Mr. Ashtrup & half the party will convey heavy provisions about 200 or 300 miles inland and then return to the house or headquarters; sun will set at end of Oct. & not appear till the middle of February again, & during this time all will live together in the house (35 ft. by 14); on March 1st. the cross-country journey is to commence & Lieut. Peary expects to reach his most N.E. point by July 1st., proving what he expects, and then retrace steps to headquarters which will be reached before the sunset in Oct.; here they must winter again and be picked up by the "Falcon" again as soon as the ice breaks in 1895.

Mr. G.H. Clark (Brooklyn, Mass.) is taxidermist; Mr. F.W. Stokes (Philadelphia) is artist; Mr. Evelyn B. Baldwin (Oswego, Kansas) meteorologist; Dr. [Edward E.] Vincent (Springfield, Illinois) surgeon. All are American, except Mr. A. Ashtrup, who was in the last Peary expedition, a Norwegian, & Mr. [George H.] Carr, a native of Devon. Our calls were repaid in the evening and several of the party came to our service in the store – the last service perhaps for 2½ years! One of the party, Mr. Stokes, had worked with Mr. [R.W.] McAll in Paris for 3 yrs.[34]

Letter from Capt. Trezise to the MDSF

Mission Hospital Ship *Albert*,
Battle Harbour, July 18, 1893
Several cases have already come under the doctor's hands, some serious ones, and even while I write Dr. Curwen is on an eight-mile tramp to a sick family, and will not return until midnight. There is no road, and the ground is rocky and boggy.

Our meetings have been largely attended, people coming from two to five miles' distance, and proving attentive and apparently appreciative audiences; and although their work is enormous on account of the short season, they appear ever ready to attend our meetings instead of resting. Dr. Grenfell is now away down the Straits of Belle Isle, and as the local agent here for W.B. Grieve, Esq. (Mr. G. Hall), has kindly offered to accommodate Dr. Bobardt and Sister Carwardine until the hospital is ready, I propose sailing north to-morrow with Dr. Curwen and Sister Williams as far as Indian Harbour. The hospital at that place will not be ready for use until September, so probably fresh arrangements will be made when Dr. Grenfell joins us again.

To give you an idea of the attendance at our meetings, I would mention that our week-night attendance averages 50; Sunday morning, Dr. Curwen, 108; afternoon, Dr. Bobardt (for children), 86; evening, myself, 134; Monday evening, myself, 50. Six members of Lieutenant Peary's second Arctic expedition were present at the Monday meeting, their vessel, the ss *Falcon*, having put in here on account of heavy weather, and also for the purpose of buying Indian dogs. They left us late at night with feelings of deep thankfulness at having met Christian brothers in a strange land.

Joseph F. Trezise, Master, *Albert*

Tuesday, July 18th.   Up early to bid "Falcon" farewell; in raising anchor she lifted one of our six, dropped it over a schooner's anchor, lifted this one in turn & finally dropped it over a mooring chain across the harbour; this occupied the attention of the whole crew for about 3 hours in the afternoon.

At 9 a.m. rowed out to salmon net & on way watched a crew haul their cod trap; the cod trap is a square bag, each side of which is from 10–15 fathom long, and to the "doors" of the trap there is a long lead; occasionally 50 or even 100 quintals of fish (a quintal is 112 lbs. of dried fish, which corresponds to 230 lbs. fresh) have been taken at one time in a trap. Salmon are never trapped here, though they are not infrequently taken in cod traps; a long fleet of nets runs straight out from the rocks and the salmon coming along get caught in the meshes in the same way as herring are. We visited three fleets of nets but only got 2 salmon; 22 had been taken from them at 6 p.m. & 4 more at 5 p.m.

Last year a sperm whale came ashore and was towed up to the wharf; part of its backbone lay nearly under our vessel in about 4 fathom of water; never had Mr. Hall known the water to be clearer; objects at the bottom such as sea urchins and fish were clearly visible in 5 fathoms of water; with the help of a jigger and an enormous boathook we got a rope round this piece of the whale's vertebral column and hauled it to the wharf and with the aid of the crane lifted it. Our crew & several of the men on the wharf tried to make me think it smelt badly, but I take it it was fancy on their part; however, now four separate vertebrae lie over the side of the wharf with spun yarn attached and I hope will be sufficiently clean to take to England in the autumn. This whale was 64 ft. long & the tail 22 ft. across, and yielded 2500 gallons of oil; most of the oil lay in pockets in the enormous head, so an opening was made into one pocket at a time & then a pump inserted.

After dinner I took photographs of Battle, and in rowing down to an island at the mouth of the harbour we came in sight of the finest iceberg I have seen; it must have been an enormous fellow at one time & now consisted of three pinnacles, the centre having gone; it was three miles away or I would have got near enough to photograph it. Icebergs are so common I am quite used to them and should be at once struck if I saw an expanse of sea without some floating ice; I only notice those which are striking from size or shape; at first I left a standing order that I was to be called whenever a berg was sighted but I have long since countermanded it; our steward, the redoubtable Dobby, counted 110 from the deck this morning (July 19).

Just as we were sitting down to tea a message came to say that a little patient of ours the other side of Great Caribou Island was much worse, and as Dr. Bobardt was unable to leave a patient he has in Battle and moreover had the meeting to take during the evening I offered to go to Indian Cove; I wanted to go for many reasons; it was a beautiful night, and then when we walked back (Dr. B., Sister Williams & I) from a visit to the cove on Saturday 15th we had taken an hour & a half to do what we were told could have been done in an hour. Could it? That was one point to be settled; besides I was anxious to see the lad again because I could not be quite sure what was the matter when I saw him on Saturday and knew that after 3 days there would be no doubt. None of the crew would volunteer to accompany me; seamen are bad walkers, and I made one trot with me one day, which has made the rest shy. I rowed across the harbour to Trap Cove where the track commenced, and then commenced a magnificent walk up hill & down valley along a badly defined track which needed much looking for in parts; I walked west by north facing the setting sun and from the hills & along the ridges had magnificent views of islands beyond islands and very large numbers of icebergs; but I did not delay, as I wanted to get on quickly, for I knew it would be dark before I could get back. In 47 minutes from starting I was at my patient's house; a lad of 7 with most severe diphtheria which must almost certainly kill him, caught from his sister of 5, who had it so slightly that, while I thought it was & treated it as diphtheria, I would not give a diagnosis to the parents. But where did she get it from? Certainly three families have come to the cove from a part of Newfoundland where there is diphtheria, but there has been absolutely no known illness in these families since they left the cove last fall, and when at home in N.F. they have had no communication with anyone who has had the disease; is it *possible* for them to have brought the germs of the disease 400 miles, a journey which took them two or three weeks, & not to have been affected themselves? If the soil in Labrador is so receptive of the diphtheria germ as this supposition would lead one to think where will the disease stop? It's frightful to think of.

Walking back was a very different thing to walking there for the sun had set and the moon was very young & low down; the "Northern Lights" however were very marked and the sky was nearly cloudless. The lad's father walked the first half of the way with me and left me at the end of a long pond, directing me to follow the track which I "could not miss" and telling me that I must cross a range at a spot he pointed to, then descend into the valley on the other side, cross it and bear away down along the hills on the other side; this seemed very clear & his directions tallied very well with what I recollected of the track; we parted and for a time I succeeded in keeping the track, crossed moist places and was led by it up the side of the bare hills, but here the path appeared to cease; the hills seen by the evening light appeared very different to those I had seen when the sun was shining, and to add to my difficulty there were three valleys and not one only; I carried out what I believed to be the directions given, stumbling over the ground as quickly as I could, & by & by I became quite certain I had not been there before; on referring to the compass Mother gave me I found I was making due N. instead of E. by S.; over another low range then and down and along another valley, and a little further on other valleys opened up, and I had no idea which I ought to take; so I climbed up a spar between two; about this time the howling of the dogs became very audible and I gripped my stick tighter as I went on. The direction was right, in a general kind of way, but which was my valley? I turned to the left and began to descend and then spontaneously and almost unconsciously turned right about and marched straight on; but I soon came to a very steep place & had to use great care in descending into a wide valley in which the coarse grass was about six inches high. Going down this valley a little way, and suddenly looking up at the skyline in front of me I was surprised at seeing a cross upright & alone, but a few steps further on I saw some other stones and recognized it as an old delapidated Roman Catholic cemetery by the side of which my track led. I was mightily glad to find the track again though I lost it half a dozen times in walking half a mile across the rough stones into Trap Cove. Most folk go to bed at 9 here so as to be up by 3 or 4 and out after the fish; so I began to question how I could get a boat to row down the harbour to the vessel; in the first house however I saw a light, though it was as late as 10.15, and the girl who opened the door took me down to the fish stage where her father, mother & two brothers were just finishing cleaning & salting their day's fish.

A short row brought me back safely; I am very glad I went though it is not advisable to walk back at night alone as the track is so very ill defined, and too because there are 60 dogs at Trap Cove; as a rule the dogs are harmless enough, but last night they killed two goats.

I went to Mr. Hall's house to supper and took my letters to finish as we must leave our mail behind us to be quite sure of catching it.

BATTEAU

Wednesday, July 19th. Wind from the s. so we up anchor, and after a hurried good-bye to Mr. Hall & Dr. B., who came on board, and the customary salute from the old cannon on the hill, which we answered with a gun rocket, three gunshots and dipping of flags, we sail away; the day was fine and the sun warm so we spent the day on deck, reading, writing and following the coastline along with the chart. In the morning I washed my seagull, a bird taken out of its egg a fortnight ago on Mercanter Island by the Capt. of one of Mr. Hall's schooners, and it was very interesting watching its movements, almost expressions, as it stood about on deck.

We passed some beautiful icebergs and noticed two with arches; one of these was like a ruined abbey with a great flying buttress as we saw it in the distance, and the other was perhaps the most remarkable I have seen. When it was N.W. of us we were more struck with the presence of the arch than anything else; but as we passed further north and it became more in the west we were struck with the resemblance of one pinnacle to a white bear's head: everything seemed to be there, eye, nostril, both ears & even a crack which did very well for a chain round the neck; here is the bear but where is the keeper? He appeared when it was s.w. of us and was on the reverse side of the same pinnacle; his resemblance to Lord Hartingdon was far greater than is shown in the picture of it, and was remarked by one of the crew though another seaman thought it was more like General Booth; so great was the resemblance to a human face that the second eyebrow appeared as we got a fuller view.

Our destination was Batteau Harbour – 60 miles from Battle – and as the entrance is very difficult and could only be made by us during daylight we were sorry to see the wind dropping about 6.30; the entrance was made the more difficult by the presence of ice in the runs where there was deep water, but by careful management, slow progress, sounding time after time as quick as a man could heave the lead & haul it in again, and by keeping a lookout on the yardarm, we succeeded in making the harbour ... and letting go our anchors at 9 p.m. Ten minutes later the wind shifted to N. and blew hard right out of the harbour so that if we had been a quarter of an hour later we should have been blown out to sea.

Thursday, July 20th. Stiff N. wind blowing all day. The morning spent in visiting the huts in one part of the harbour. There are some 40 families from N.F. and only one family of liv'eres – this family is ½ caste & very lazy. The houses or huts were very poor; the small ones consisted of one room with bunks in cupboards or partitioned off; the larger as a rule contained two families; some had the ordinary N.F. stove, but others open hearths on which wood was burnt, the smoke passing up through a barrel in the roof; a usual rent is $4 for the four months, but many of the fishermen have built their own houses. One house we visited was an unlicensed grog shop where rum is sold; this is one of the two harbours where drink is plentiful, and last year three men were drowned while drunk in the harbour; it is kept by two [Thompson] sisters who have such an unmistakable s. Ireland accent, that I was surprised to find that neither they nor their parents had ever been in Ireland; their grandparents came from Waterford.

In afternoon visited Queer Island & the folk there.

At the fall of the year when the people leave for N.F. they pack up all their goods, and take home the window frames & sometimes the stoves; the door is left wide open, for the snow is certain to come through the birch-bark covered roof and get through the plank walls where they are not covered with earth, and unless the door & window are open the sun cannot get in to melt the snow nor the water get out; not infrequently when a family arrives in the spring (this year abt. June 5) they find their house more than half full of snow and have to go at it with spades – a very cold welcome at the end of the horrors of a long journey (from 7 to 23 days) on a Labrador schooner.

The evening service was a good one, there being about 58 visitors; patients came to see me till 10.30 p.m. and including those I saw at their houses I saw 38 in all.

Friday, July 21st.   In the morning a man – Joseph Goss – came in in his jackboat[35] and asked me to go with him to Inner Sandy Island, about 5 miles s. of Batteau to see one of his crew who thought himself ill; the wind was favourable but showed signs of dropping so we took our ulsters, rugs, bag of provisions & camera and were prepared to spend the night out if necessary; a pleasant sail and a talkative skipper, so I got a good deal of information about the fishery and the way the people come up to the Labrador & return in the autumn. This man paid $30 for this passage of himself, wife & boy, a maid & two men on a schooner and for this had a space allotted to him 8 ft. wide & 6 ft. long on the top of the cargo of salt below deck; on the salt he placed his luggage, consisting of food & everything he would want for 4 months' work, including sails & nets, and when he had placed his bed on the top of this, there was only 2½ feet between it & the deck; this space – 8 ft. by 6 by 2½ – was the only space his crew of 6 had of their own to move about in; if they wanted to dress & undress they must do it lying down; washing was only possible on deck and each crew had to cook what food they wanted on deck in an open galley; there were 90 passengers in addition to the crew in this little schooner of 50 tons ("Industry") and the parties were separated from one another in the forecastle by sail partitions only; the passage was a very cold one of three weeks, there being much delay owing to ice & fog.

Joseph Goss's tilt, Inner Sandy Islands: "Newfoundland fishermen's tilts are log and plank structures banked up with earth outside, with birch bark and turf roof and often with an empty flour barrel for chimney. They consist of one room, one end of which is partitioned off and serves as bedroom for skipper and larder; the rest of the crew sleep in a bunkhouse. When the house is left in the fall the windows are taken home to Newfoundland and the door left open to allow warm air to enter in spring and melt the snow that has come through roof."

I found my patient shamming; it appears he is a great coward & fears to go in the boat when there is the least wind, and as fish is very scarce and there is very little chance of making money here this season he wants to be invalided home that he may find some more profitable work at home; he has received $20 of his pay in advance. I felt very sorry for his skipper for it was a lost day to him as he had to come & fetch me & then take me back again, and this took nearly the whole day as the journey back was longer.

In the evening after visiting several patients on shore we had our service on board & then came the usual run of patients.

Saturday, July 22nd. A quieter day; visited patients; glad to have a day of rest to work up arrears. In the afternoon there was a funeral; a neat deal coffin

Labrador Odyssey

Interior of Goss's tilt, Inner Sandy Islands: "Showing open fire, open chimney, rough boarding of interior which will let in light and wind; and one of the crew (the man on the left) who pretended to be ill that he might be sent home and thus enabled to engage in more profitable employment than the fishery on the Labrador provided this year."

with the inscription "Jenny Lind, obit. July 22nd. 1893, aged 21 days; mourned by his sorrowing owner [relation]. His (or her) merits were many." Consigned to the deep as the ship's bell was solemnly tolled.

Sunday, July 23rd. A cold, raw, misty day with E. wind. About 40 to service in morning, 56 in evening, and 25 women in afternoon at Sister's meeting. In afternoon Dobbie & I went for a walk over the hills round the end of the harbour and came across a great quantity of snow in one part; we are told that this snow seldom melts during summer.

Letter of Dr Bobardt to the MDSF

Battle Harbour, Labrador, July 23
There can be not the slightest doubt as to the necessity of a doctor at

Battle; the people here are unprovided for, their life is hard, and when ill, they must either work or die. They are rather uneducated, and there is amongst them an abundant element of faith and reliance in quack remedies, for which they pay extravagant prices.

My hospital is not finished, but will be ready within another month. It is a good house, the best on the coast, so it is said, and will be a perfect boon to the inhabitants here. The great difficulty will be to keep them out of the hospital, and to save one's drugs, as they are no sooner provided with medicine for one ailment than they request more for another ailment; and I fear, ere my term is completed, there will be very little left.

From what I have seen there will be an abundance of work for me to perform, and the nurse will also have as much as she can do; and I think the person who proposed the sending of a nurse deserves praise, as she can do much good here; it is quite one of the good institutions of this particular branch of the Mission.

Albert Bobardt

Monday, July 24th. Fog, rain, cold E. wind; even if we dare leave harbour in a fog the wind is a head one, and as three schooners going N. have put into the harbour this morning for shelter we shall not stir today. The wind increased as the day went on so we had to give up the idea of going to Black Tickle.

Last night I sat up late writing to [sister-in-law] Margaret, knowing the mail steamer was expected today and little dreaming she would come in on a foggy night; when Dobbie called me at 6 he told me the boat had come & gone, and my letter lay on the table where I had left it over night.

Have spent the greater part of today developing [photographs] – a very poor lot; this morning I washed the two kittens on deck and very nearly drowned one; however, he got over it and is now asleep with his chum wrapped up in a sheet.

In afternoon the strong wind became stronger & backed to N.E. and right glad were we we were snug & not at Black Tickle.

Tuesday, July 25th.   A gale from the N. blowing with wind of hurricane force during the squalls; even in the harbour the wind caught the tops of the waves and covered the surface of the water with spray; getting on shore was totally out of the question so we had to content ourselves with watching the effect of the wind from a distance; walking up & down deck was very difficult, for the rain was driving & the force of the wind down the harbour very strong; we saw a long open boat – value abt. £30 – break away and drive onto Queer Island to be dashed to pieces, and a little later the oars of another boat passed us; near the entrance to the harbour was another longboat still moored but sunk, showing only her stern, and one of the boats of a large Norwegian schooner which came in on Friday for a cargo of fish was also waterlogged; we saw too that the fish stages had suffered badly, the canvas or bark covering having gone from several and the sides blown in but from the ship we did not see any totally wrecked.

In the early afternoon the anchors of the large Norwegian schooner began to drag, and she drifted onto the point of rocks running out from the E. shore and turned partly on her side; fortunately the waves were not large or she would very soon have worn a hole; she signalled for help and after a time a rope was stretched from the w. side and she was got off safely – the accident will cost her $200 or 300 for the assistance rendered alone; tonight though the wind is not so strong she is dragging again.

Since 1.30 the bar. has been rising steadily – it had dropped to 29.20 – and tonight the squalls are not so frequent, so we hope for better weather tomorrow; it is feared the destruction of nets must be great and as a cod trap costs from £80-£120 this means ruin to many; not only is there danger to the nets from the waves but from the ice which must have come s.

Outside the harbour the sea must be running very high; in the mist I saw what I took for a big berg this morning lying off Queer Island but it proved to be the white spray rising from seas breaking over rocks. This will be a very trying time for the little steam launch even if she is in a harbour; she could not live 10 minutes outside.

After tea we saw three men put off from the little 19-ton schooner lying near us; they came to ask us to give them some fresh water as they had run short using their last drop at dinner; two or three days ago we gave them some coal as they had run short of wood and there is no wood to be got within a day from here; they had no barometer on board & asked Capt. how it stood; the skipper said there had been no storm like this on the coast since Oct. 1885 when 100 schooners were lost; most of these were in harbours & dragged their anchors; the loss of life was never determined as no record of the crews is kept in N.F.

Our only other visitors were the crew of the "Sea Bride," another schooner lying astern of us; we had seen them lay two more anchors in the afternoon – making 4 altogether – but so uneasy were they that they had packed up everything to take ashore, intending to leave the vessel to take its chance during the night and board her again in the morning if she were not on the rocks; before leaving however they came to ask Capt's opinion as to the weather, and returned reassured taking with them one end of our steel rope; so now they have their 4 small anchors & a steel rope on our ship, and trust more to us than to them; we have a third anchor hanging over our bow to drop at a moment's notice if we begin to drag but there is little chance of that as our anchors dig deeper the greater the strain & the bottom is mud. The "Sea Bride" is 28 tons & carries 5 men; she is the only schooner we have met or heard of in which there is no woman; she came in yesterday morning without a pilot, and none of the crew had been in this harbour before; they took their course from a boat returning from visiting a cod trap; there is a chart on board but they do not know how to make use of it, and never heaved a lead!

Wednesday, July 26th.   A lovely day; very little wind & that more easterly. We went ashore & were glad to find less damage had been done than we had expected. Mr. [Tom?] Bartlett told us he had not known so severe a storm in July for 20 yrs. The wind had got through the plank walls of his house & blown the wallpaper off! Mrs. B. got tea ready for

Sister, Capt. & me & old Mr. B. came in for his share; we talked of guns & berries; Mrs. B. took Sister & me up on the hills after & showed us several berry-plants such as "blackberry," "blueberry," "bearberry" & "bakeapple" – there are 31 berries found in N.F. & Labrador & they seem much used by the people. We tasted "crystal tea," a tea made from the leaves of a local plant [crystal berry] – very aromatic but too much sweetened; gathered some of the leaves from which the tea is made & intend making it.

Learn from Mr. Samuel Wilcox that Mr. Poor – a man with whom we have left 2½ tons of coal for the steam launch – has been burning our coal; the man keeps a gin store without a licence; the government revenue officer, Mr. Burgess,[36] passed N. in his schooner; he too is a Roman Catholic and like most government officials has feathered his nest & shut his eyes; he did not call at this harbour at all. Passing down the harbour Mr. P. hailed me & when I got near poured abuse on me & the Mission; he was semi-drunk at the time so I did not prolong the interview as Sister was in the boat, but tomorrow Capt. & I are going to call to give him a chance of explaining himself; he is doing a tremendous amount of harm here; only last year 3 men from the harbour were drowned while drunk; if we do nothing more on Labrador than make it too hot for him & for two Miss Thompsons, who also keep a gin shop illicitly, we shall have made a good voyage; we intend informing not only Mr. Burgess but the N.F. government & Governor.

After lunch Capt. went off in the dinghy & I followed with Sails, Bob & a local man in the "Mary Grenfell" to Sandy Bay looking for wild fowl & seals; we saw 8 seals, a goose, 2 ducks & a pigeon but did not get within range of anything so returned with clean guns. Gathering that it would take 2 hours or more to sail home from the bay & wanting to be back by service time I elected to walk across country & make the harbour – a very nice walk; from the top of a hill I ascended to take in the lie of the country I had to traverse. I got the best, or second best, view I have had in the country; islands innumerable with long arms of the sea – called "bays" – running into the land, and 70 or more icebergs, pure white in the sun, and schooners picking their way in & out as they went North, while nearby were men in longboats tending their cod traps. The walk took me an hour, and when I reached the ship I found the shore folk were so busy with their fish & gear that none came on board. Two of our hands have been ashore all day mending nets.

Thursday, July 27th. Another foggy morning with E. wind. Everyone tells us this foggy, cold weather is quite unprecedented at this season; we are certainly having a very great deal, & the continuance of the N. or E. wind prevents us getting out of Batteau as beating against a strong wind amongst the rocks & shoals is not to be thought of for the "Albert."

Being anxious to run over to Domino Harbour and being doubtful if a better day would present, about 12.30 we start – Sister, I, Walter Wilcox (as Capt. & pilot), Bob & Case – in "Mary Grenfell." I looked course up on chart & found it N.E., a straight run of 3 miles across Wild Bight, but Walter thought we ought to make N.N.E.; by & by coming to an island he did not recognize in the fog he thought he was outside the land altogether & told me to steer N.W. – a great error as it turned out, for when we altered we were ½ mile from Salmon Bight & by going N.W. we ran 1½ miles up the bay & had to row down.

We landed in Salmon Bight at Mr. Percy's stage & took our oilys, wraps, gun &c. to his house; they knew of our presence in Batteau & were hoping to have had a visit. With a sailing ship like the "Albert" it is impossible to do the work we could with a steamer for we are so dependent on the wind, & the harbours are very intricate for a heavy vessel. I heard of several cases of illness in Salmon Bight, so after a cup of tea we hurried across country to Domino Harbour – ¾ mile – to Mr. Isaac Bartlett's[37] house; he was out fishing but his daughter took us into a large house & immediately gave us dinner not allowing us to eat what we had brought with us. After dinner Sister visited all the houses in Domino Harbr. while I returned to Salmon Bight with my medicine chest – a very compact little chest & not too heavy – & saw a good many patients; Mr. Percy acted guide & took me over the hill to Black Tickle to see a man very bad with rheumatism, but it was too late for me to visit every house in the tickle so I contented myself with visiting Mrs. Keith, an Esquimaux, the "wise woman" of the neighbourhood, who has I believe a considerable practice. She was outside her house – short, broad, flatfaced & darkskinned as all Eskimo are – surrounded by her pack of Esquimaux dogs when we arrived, but she asked us in and it was not long before I got her to tell me about her cases & her principles of treatment. She tells me she has never had a patient she has not cured – and if her cures are like that of the man who I saw hobbling over to Domino after 3 weeks of her treatment and who let me see his leg I dare say she is right; if the Indian Harbr. hosp. had been open I should have advised him to go there, but he tells me the leg is much better than it was before its treatment with "Indian tea," flour & molasses outside, & "fir tea" internally. We had reached Domino too late in the day to think of returning that night so had asked Miss Bartlett to put us up on the floor; it was nearly 9 before I returned from Salmon Bight & Black Tickle & when I arrived I found a number of patients Sister had collected for me to see to save me the trouble & time of visiting in Domino.

Mr. B. is one of the best educated men I have seen here, a man of character, very quiet & socially far superior to the very great majority of the men; he was very pleased to see us but very disappointed we did not intend coming round with the ship. Sister was to sleep in a little room with Miss B. & the two maids, & I was told I was to share a bed with Mr. B. while the men slept on forms in the large common room downstairs; our room was a small one in the roof separated from the rest of the loft in which Mr. B.'s crew slept & where the stores were kept & salmon hung up to dry by a partial partition, and it was occupied by two beds abt. 4 ft. 6 wide with an alley between just wide enough to walk up; in one bed I found Walter & another man and into the other I crept after partly undressing & was followed by my large host; we lay shoulder to shoulder under a blanket & three thick bedcovers which rose & fell as he breathed. There was only one lamp in the house so when I had turned in Mr. B. took up a plank & let it down to the ladies in the room below. I had a fairly good night, but often woke to hear my neighbours snore or the rain falling heavily on the birchbark roof which slanted up within six inches of my head. At 3 all the men went off to haul their cod trap, and an hour later the postman from the mail steamer brought the letters for the district & took up the mail. I was called at 6 but breakfast did not come till 8 as we waited to see if the men would come back; should they have a good catch they wd. come back & go off again, but if not they would remain out all day.

The wind being N.E. we knew the "Albert" could not leave so determined to go across Domino Run to Spotted Island; we borrowed a boat & got over in half an hour & were busy for two hours visiting & seeing patients; one man I saw was quite mad. At Spotted Island there are a number of half-breed Esquimaux who live there all the year round; we found the "king" suffering from debility following an attack of influenza; his father was an Englishman and his parents refusing to allow him to marry a lady he liked he left home saying he would marry the ugliest woman he could meet; those who saw his Esquimaux wife say that he could not have found one of less prepossessing appearance; they managed to make a lot of money & drink a lot of rum & when they died left their son Sam Hallowell with a store & a schooner. He gave us some tea & cake and his third wife waited on us; his second wife died last year and he wanted to marry her sister but the minister who came down from Rigoulette refusing to marry them he chose one of the girls "out of the crowd" and married her on the spot.

Mr. Bartlett when we got back & had had dinner was very loath to let us go; he & Miss B. walked down to Salmon Bight & with Mr. & Mrs. Percy helped us off asking us to go over on Sunday should we be in Batteau still.

We returned after a capital run across the bay about 5 o'clock; and in the evening I took my fowls on shore asking Mrs. Tom Bartlett (sister-in-law of Mr. B. of Domino) to take charge of 4 for me & Mrs. Sam Wilcox of the other two; I had hoped to have had them at Indian Harbr. but as there is little chance of our settling on shore this year & as the birds do not lay on board ship I left them as we shall be glad of fresh meat when we are returning South.

Saturday, July 29th.   Another foggy day; full moon last night, but no one has seen the moon since she was born!

Did not leave board all morning; in afternoon Capt. & I visited schooners "Bessie A" & "Vinilla" from Le Havre, Nova Scotia, & stayed a long time chatting; we notice a vast difference between these men & the great majority of the Newfoundland men – much more independence & character; I wonder if the N.F. men would be as good if they were treated less vilely by the government & merchants; these men are all farmers, some owning 300 acres, & come to the Labrador every year because they make it pay, which is what no N.F. fisherman does. Several of the crews came on board in the evening & insisted on paying a small sum for every bottle of medicine I gave them – so different again; one skipper of a N.F. schooner came & asked us for some rope; we gave him 20 fathom, gave him a pail of coal as he had no fuel, a can of water as he had none, mittens & helmets for each member of the crew, and *then* he asked us what else we had to give him & did not like it when we told him we had no stockings! The skipper of one of these schoo-

Trapboats "on collar" at Bonne Espérance. Canadian revenue cutter (left) at anchor.

ners told us that at Black Island Tickle, Hamilton Inlet, he last year met two families – 10 in all – living together in a room 9 ft. square; they had come down from the end of the inlet for codfishing; one of them – consisting of father, two boys & two girls – had been supplied with only 12 lbs. of biscuits for one month! and they had scarcely a rag on; the skipper took three of the children to Nova Scotia with him, & the other girl who was daft has been sent to the asylum in St. John's; the other family – man, woman, boy & 2 girls – had lived on one rabbit for three days during the previous winter.

Dr Grenfell's Report to the MDSF, 15–29 July

s.s. *Princess May*, steaming from Battle Harbour
over to Red Bay, Labrador, July 15, 1893

… Saturday morning the *Princess May* took Dr. Curwen to Indian Cove to see a poor fisherman with pleurisy and bronchitis, and then went on up the Straits to Red Bay. We had a very foggy passage, but found the way all right, and were greeted warmly by our old friends of last year. They had just emerged from the inner harbour at the end of the bay, where they spend their winter, and had commenced the summer or cod fishery. Salmon was fairly plentiful at Battle Harbour, and many seals had been caught in places; but the dense packs of ice blocking up the Straits just while the cod are plentiful has damaged the "cod" prospects considerably. We stayed here with a fisherman friend, as the Wesleyan missionary here, the Rev. John Sidey, had packed up all his things and was leaving for England or Canada. Here we found several sick people, and some very poor – only kept from starvation by the charity of others, who could ill afford it – one woman especially with seven children, youngest two months, was in a high fever with pleurisy and bronchitis. She lay on two boards near a cracked stove in a barn-like house, draughty and dirty, with one wood partition to cut off the general bedroom. Food was only just what the neighbours gave. The children were naked to all intents and purposes, so much so that the eldest little lad was unable to go out in the boat to help his father to hook a few fish.

Here we were able to do much, but if we could have taken her to Battle, 45 miles away, it would have been better. She could not leave, however, they decided, though what help she could be at home it was impossible to see. Among several other patients here, I found more than one whose disease could be best cured by wholesome food. We had splendid gatherings on Sunday, the church being put entirely at our disposal. Our literature also was eagerly sought for after the winter's seclusion. Having no companion, I persuaded the Rev. J. Sidey to accompany me up the Straits, and on Monday we started westward. We were asked to call at a little place – West St. Modeste – to see a girl with a compound dislocation of the wrist, done some months ago. This we did, but found she had gone on to L'Anse au Loup. Accordingly we went on for the night, and were hospitably entertained by Captain Watson at L'Anse au Loup, the third largest station in the Straits. We had several patients to see, but found it impossible to get a week-night service, for as all the year's catch, or the main part of it, has to be caught in one month, everyone was working night and day, frequently having only one or two hours to sleep in the twenty-four, while many times the men will work on day and night, snatching a nap in the boat or anywhere they can. The next day, as we rounded Cape Forteau, we saw the bones of HMS *Lily*, lost here some four years back, and then we ran into a small harbour, called L'Anse Amour, to see a man with cancer of the hip.

Here we found that one of the Beaver line of steamers had been run ashore last week, having rammed into some ice, and been forced to go aground at once. Like HMS *Victoria*, the water filled her fore portions, and broke into her second. Before she was beached her head was under water almost, and her screw was lifted right out of the water. Her third set of water-tight bulkheads just saved her, and that was all. The wrecked crew had taken refuge at L'Anse Amour, and her doctor the previous Sunday had operated on an old dislocated wrist, and also removed the cancer. We were able only to dress them; not knowing of our arrival they had naturally embraced this, the only means within their reach, perhaps in a lifetime; a fact that speaks only too eloquently for the needs of medical mission work here.

Thence we steamed to L'Anse au Clair. Here we found about fifteen families of liv'eres, all very poor. One poor woman, aged twenty-five, with two children, and living in a miserable one-roomed hovel, was suffering from scurvy, just such as affected sailors on long voyages before the need of fresh vegetable food was known. Here we were able to be of some use to the people before leaving for Blanc Sablon for the night. We were kindly welcomed by Captain [Samuel] Blandford here. He is perhaps best known in Newfoundland as the most successful seal hunter, and here he has charge of the largest establishment for the summer cod fishery in the whole of Labrador.[38]

The following day we visited Greenly Island, on Canadian territory, and found several sick people, especially one poor fellow who had been landed from a schooner, and whose lungs were much affected. We were kept late here and proceeded thence to Isle de Bois, where again were several sick folk. At 11.30 p.m. we left to return for the night to Captain Blandford's house at Blanc Sablon. It was very thick with fog, and so dark we could not see a yard. We had first to thread our way among many schooners, all now invisible, and very slowly and carefully we went ahead. Unfortunately we had not calculated for the strong tide, and suddenly the bump, bump, bump of the vessel, and a nasty lurch over, announced to us that we were aground on rocks. The little boat was at once thrown out, and the heavy anchor and chain put into it. It was then used to pull her head round while we weighed the vessel down till she lay right over on one side, then her head slowly came off, and sending her full speed ahead we were soon again in deep water. Retracing our steps and guided by a fog-horn, we were soon alongside a schooner at anchor near the island. To her we fastened the *Princess May,* and at dawn of day steamed back to Blanc Sablon. Having found that beyond a dent or so in her copper no harm was done, we left for Bonne Espérance or "Bony," as it is called here.

On the way we called at Letter Island, Bradore, and Middle Bay, finding a few sick people; and by evening we were safely berthed alongside a large sealing steamer, in a landlocked tickle or run off Bonne Espérance. The agent here, Mr. Whiteley, at once made us at home. Mr. Whiteley holds a compendium of offices, being a Canadian by birth and Newfoundlander by adoption. He is a member of the Legislative Assembly of Newfoundland and overseer of Canadian fisheries here, Justice of the Peace, Postmaster-General, &c. His also is a very large fishing station, and has this year caught far more fish than any other station, probably than any two other stations.[39] After seeing the sick folk here we took a volunteer pilot, and proceeded to a few neighbouring Canadian fishing stations. Alas! our pilot was self-styled, and suddenly while going at full speed we ran up on a big reef, and were brought up all standing. We were below at tea at the time, and most fortunately the tide was off the reef, and I had the company on board of a captain of an English vessel, and the chief engineer of the largest sealing steamer. When we got on deck the launch lay on her beam ends, and we feared the worst. However, by throwing out the boat, the anchor and chain, and all our bags of coal, her head floated, and the tide drove her off the reef. We only draw 3 ft. 6 in., and were just prepared to jump overboard to lighten her, and shove her astern. She had bumped considerably before we got off, so we steamed straight home for Bonne Espérance. We were making no water, so anchored her close in shallow water for the night. Saturday morning early we lay her right over on her side, and with fish glasses in this clear water we carefully examined her bottom. Only in one place was the copper off, and the wisdom of having a splendid wood hull was apparent, for again we found her practically uninjured. This day, therefore, we again steamed all day, visiting many poor settlers, Mr. Whiteley himself piloting us. We had several sick folk, one being a similar case to one I have mentioned previously, being a poor woman with true scurvy.

We find everywhere the terrible lack of fresh food severely telling on the resident population. The fish, and occasional fowl, stave off partially the worst dangers, but an almost entire lack of any vegetables whatever is severely felt. Very short summers, and all hands then busy at the fishing, is against gardening, yet in places already I have seen a Labrador-grown potato. The extent of the Newfoundland fishery in the Straits of Belle Isle will be partially estimated by the statement of the Canadian Revenue officer for this shore. He tells me he has 2,500 schooners this spring in his district alone, besides American and Nova Scotia men. Besides these are those working on the coast both sides, belonging to Newfoundland and all those on the east coast of Labrador. There are no statistics kept, so it is impossible to say how many there are. We found in one place that they had just lost a lad of 15, who had driven accidentally a nail into his knee-joint; he had died untreated in twelve days in terrible agony.

To-morrow is Sunday, and we expect to meet the mail steamer. We have announced two services in the little building set aside for Divine worship, and are looking for God's blessing on the gatherings of the people from the Islands.

Wilfred Grenfell

Sunday, July 30th.   Foggy in the harbour but it looked like clearing so at 9 a.m. Walter Wilcox, Case & I set off for Domino Harbr. in a trapboat lent by one of the Nova Scotia schooners, & took with us two half-breed Esquimaux who wanted a passage; it took us an hour to reach Salmon Bight, where of course I had to wait for tea at Mr. Percy's; walk to Domino Harbr. & a few visits; send message of service to 17 schooners in the harbr.; dinner, & at 2 nail a red pocket handkerchief to a pole by way of a flag; I was surprised at the number of people – about 130 inside & out the house – but unfortunately we have but few hymn-books & the singing was not over grand; this is the first service that has been held in Domino for months. After tea we started back and had to beat against a headwind (s.); she behaved beautifully & took us back in 2 hrs., just as the service on the "Albert" was over. Today has been one of our best days: three services with attendances of 130, 127 & 98 & a service for women. The wind being s. we intend leaving early in the morning in company of our Nova Scotian friends who will act as guides.

SANDWICH BAY

Monday, July 31st.

Awoken by the bustle of heaving anchor & setting sail & go on deck in light attire; 4.15 a.m. *very* light s. wind & only a little mist; our friends are ready & waiting for us. I turn in again but get out in a hurry a little later to enquire the meaning of a curious little thump, thump, thump & find our bows are on the rocks; tacking out of the harbour just as we were putting about the wind left us & we went on, but fortunately there was no swell so we did not bump much; we take a steel rope across the harbour, our friends help us hauling and we are off in a very little time with no damage done – another illustration of the fact that a sailing vessel is not a fit craft for the work *we* have to do here; nothing but a steamer will do.

All day we have been sailing with our friends; when the wind is light they go ahead but lower their main peak or foresail to keep in touch with us; when a breeze comes we draw away & lower sail till they approach again; our course has lain between islands and as they know the track to take we have carefully followed their leading; for the most part the day has been fine & when the sun has shone the islands have looked beautiful although absolutely devoid of trees – nothing but bare rocks covered with mosses, lichens & low-growing, berry-bearing plants.

We reached "Independent Harbour" about 8.30 and anchored in the wide part of the tickle; I went on shore to the largest house (Dawson) & found there were only 8 families in this large harbour & that there was very little sickness; behind the house I saw fir & dwarf spruce trees 3 ft. high – the highest growth I have seen here; on returning I found several patients on board from schooners lying in the harbour; our crew had been up since 3 a.m. so we did not have a service. Returning to the ship at 10 p.m. after a visit to another house to which I had been taken (Mr. Mesher) I heard a small piece of ice fall from a berg and looked around just in time to see it turn over.

Tuesday, August 1st. Fog again & no wind so after breakfast go on shore with Capt. & capts. of the two Nova Scotia schooners; I borrow a cast net and catch a good many caplin – a fish which the cod follows into the bays. At noon there was a little wind so we weigh anchor with our friends & leave; fog clears as we clear the harbour and till 3.30 the sun shone brightly & so warmly that we sit on deck working; it was not easy to read for we passed between islands & down narrow tickles & found much to look at; at the back of Newfoundland Island we were joined by two other Nova Scotia vessels and for the rest of the day all 5 of us kept together; we were particularly glad of their experience when the fog came up again at 3.30, and by means of foghorns & a gun were able to keep in touch with one another.

We saw the Mealy Mountains for the first time today – a high, rugged-looking range, high that is for this part of Labrador, 1000 ft.

Pardy family, Huntingdon Island. *Back*, l. to r., Levi Pardy, Martha (Davis) Campbell (sister of Sarah), Alvina and Thomas. *Front*, l. to r., Manuel, Harriet, Sarah (Davis) Pardy (holding Eliza), Edward, James, and William. "These people live in a one-roomed house, and when visited by the lay reader from Cartwright during the winter of 1892 were in a starving condition. The eldest girl wore a man's waistcoat and trousers, while the seven youngest children had a blanket between them."

Labrador Odyssey

only, but then they look higher than many mts. seen from shore, for the 1000 ft. is *above* us.

Huntingdon Island was covered with tall, thin fir trees; there is much wood in Sandwich Bay & many natives, also mosquitoes we are told.

The fog continued so we kept close together and sailed *very* slowly and reached Tub Harbour at 8.30; we had scarcely dropped anchor before we were boarded by 19 men from the two N.S. vessels who insisted on stowing our sails for us; these vessels carry 17 men each & as their sails set very easily they have scarcely anything to do when not fishing; the "Albert" was not intended for work of this kind and her canvas, blocks & ropes are suited for North Sea work where the sails are set & not touched for 2 months; and being *very* heavy our friends took pity on us & our small crew and several times flocked on board & insisted on doing all the work; in the morning when they had set their sails they boarded us and told our men to go down below while they set ours!

A few patients from the 17 schooners in the harbour but there was only one man who was really ill.

INDIAN HARBOUR

Wednesday, August 2nd. Up at 5.30 to find our numerous friends aboard setting our sails; it's not often we can expect to come across such men as these – so different from the New Foundlanders, who would stand & watch and never think of helping. The morning was clear & the sun shining brightly so we were able to see the remarkable island-hill that gives the name to the harbour; it looked very like an inverted tub rising out of the sea, and one view showed what I took for a raised beach on each side. There was but little wind to take us out; this time we got along quickest and five miles out waited for the N.S. men; there they branched off west to Black Island Tickle and we E. to Indian Island after much cheering, dipping of flags & firing of gun rocket.

Becalmed for an hour under lee of George Island, and then sailed slowly & carefully across the wide opening to Hamilton Inlet (or Groswater Bay) to Indian Island: sun warm and views of the tall Mealy Mountains & hills on Rodney Mundy & Ice Tickle Island very fine; those on White Bear Islands more rugged than any I have seen, the cause being – as we saw afterwards on entering the harbour – great masses of black trap-rock which had burst up through & lay spread out over & capping the white gneiss; this sudden change from black trap to white gneiss was most marked in the rocks we passed entering the harbour from the west; the surface had been well smoothed by ice in the ancient glacial times here – long, long ago, and gave very little footing for any vegetation, even moss.

I went into harbour at w. entrance & sent off a pilot who took vessel in through the East Tickle, a narrow & for a heavy vessel like ours dangerous passage; before the vessel was in I had examined site of hospital which had been changed from the totally unsuitable spot chosen at Paine's Cove – an exposed, raised beach ¼ mile away on land separated from Indian Island at high water & 500 yds. from any fresh water – to a really good situation on dry ground 150 yds. behind Mr. Simms' (Mr. Job's agent's) house & store near fresh water and where drainage would be very simple. Afternoon spent on shore at Mr. Simms' house & in seeing patients. In evening Sister & I returned to tea with Mr. Simms, son & carpenter of the hospital.

Letter of Capt. Trezise to the MDSF

Albert, Indian Harbour, August 3, 1893
I last wrote you on the 18th ult., since which we have managed to reach this place. Our progress has been considerably retarded owing to strong head winds and fog, and in addition to which we have experienced only three fine days since leaving St. John's. According to all reports, such a summer has not been experienced for many years on the Labrador. We have encountered one very severe storm, and it was so violent for thirty hours that I deemed it necessary to lower the topmasts. Our good ship rode well, and,

with our Heavenly Father's help, we were enabled to prevent a schooner from being lost, by making him fast to us when his anchors were dragging. The fishermen all state that such a severe storm has not been experienced in July for over twenty years. The hospital at this place will hardly be tenable this year, consequently Dr. Curwen and Sister Williams are still on board here, and we are awaiting Dr. Grenfell's arrival in the *Princess May* before proceeding north; we have not seen him for three weeks, but hope to see him soon. Dr. Curwen, who is medical officer in charge during Dr. Grenfell's absence, has alone treated 196 patients, exclusive of Battle Harbour and district and the Straits; and I feel assured that could we move without regard to wind and tide the number would have been doubled. Owing to the heavy weather experienced in July eighteen meetings only were attended, with a total of 1,260 people, and should the weather prove finer, the attendance will soon increase.

We fell in with two Nova Scotia fishing schooners, of a much superior type to the Newfoundlanders; being better acquainted than me with the coast, they escorted us for some days, piloting us into safe harbours at night, and assisting us in getting under weigh in the morning. They evinced great interest in the work, and the captains state that if this vessel went to Halifax in the autumn much financial aid would be obtained.

Joseph F. Trezise

Letter of Dr Bobardt to the MDSF

Mission Hospital, Battle Harbour, August 3
I have been very busy, and during the week have been assisting to complete the hospital, and I am pleased to be able to announce that the rooms are now ready for the reception of patients, and already there have been two in-patients. Last week I visited numerous places in the steam launch *Pundit*, which goes round collecting fish and distributing stores, with my bags. I find I can do quite a lot of work. Dr. Grenfell has left for the North; he departed August 2. He

may return here next week with various articles of furniture that were left on the *Albert*.

Albert Bobardt

Dr Grenfell's Report to the MDSF, 29 July to 3 August

I wrote you last from Bonne Espérance in Canada. Now I write from Venison Tickle, some fifty miles north of Battle Harbour. We have had day after day of fog, and progress has been difficult. Tonight a north-easterly gale is howling outside the harbour, and making the s.s. *Princess May* tug and strain at her moorings. For some years ice has not been so plentiful on the coast as it is this year; countless icebergs fill the bays and line the coast, while many entrances even now are blocked up with these huge masses, and prevent anything but small boats entering. The late ice has considerably impeded the fishing, and done much damage, not only to nets, but also to craft. I have just been looking at a schooner with a very nasty smash in her bows from over-friendly relationship with a mass of it. The master told me while he was crossing the Straits of Belle Isle he saw several vessels with holes stove in them. The crews had to land on large pans of ice, careen their craft as in old days, and patch the holes with tin, boarding, felt, or anything they had convenient. One he saw abandoned off the French Shore.

A strong gale kept us in Bonne Espérance till last Wednesday [26 July], and also some screws broke in our piston. This might have been troublesome, but the chief engineer of the sealing steamer *Neptune* most kindly made us four new screws, and generally put everything into good order again. He strongly advised that we should have a condenser fitted next winter, as now we use all salt water in the boiler. We have now been steaming a month, and today I inspected the inside of our boiler. I am glad to say, to the credit of our engineer, that there was no visible deposit of salt. We have on occasions been able to use the fire hose lent us, and bringing the launch right up to perpendicular rocks fill our boiler with fresh water from small waterfalls. Leaving Bonne Espérance, by request I carried Dr. MacDonnel, Roman Catholic Bishop of Harbour Grace, and his chaplain, Father Lynch, as far as Blanc Sablon. The Rev. John Sidey, Wesleyan Missionary, who is leaving this circuit, also accompanied me from Red Bay to Bonne Espérance and back again. His knowledge of the coast and people was most useful to me, and his help in the many services we have been able to hold was most welcome.

At Blanc Sablon I had two very severe cases to treat – one in a poor Newfoundland fisherman with a large abscess in the armpit, treated with white paint and herb poultice till I saw him; the other in a French Canadian with disease in the back. The latter is now in Battle Harbour Hospital under Dr. Bobardt. Also I carried up from the Isle de Bois a Newfoundland fisherman landed there from a fishing schooner, with inflammation of the lungs and pleurisy. I carried him on the *Princess May* 80 miles to Battle Harbour Hospital. He was put into, I think, the "Harris" bed, and is now in a fair way to recovery. Three poor people died while I was up the Straits from lung affections.

From Blanc Sablon I went to L'Anse au Loup, and visited Riverhead; also I visited Long Point and Greenly Island, in Canadian territory. At all these places I find many poor folk, and I must beg you to ask for more clothing for me, especially for children. Anything would be useful. Please, also, if you can, send out at the same time some old mats and carpeting for use at the hospitals. The bare boards are not warm-looking in these Arctic regions. I should, however, prefer *good oilcloth*, as more suited for hospitals, being less likely to collect dirt. We sorely need, also, more old linen and more woollens, and Nurse Carwardine especially asks me to appeal for extra sheets and blankets. She says my supply is inadequate. I feel sure, if you could make these needs known in the *Toilers*, many of our friends would be only too glad to help. They would be cheaper and better probably in England, could be sent by steamer to us, care of Messrs. Job Brothers, St. John's, for Labrador, and would be forwarded free of carriage and duty thence, direct to Battle Harbour.

I am more and more convinced that if Battle Harbour hospital could be kept open during the winter, at least this year, as an experiment, magnificent work could be done. At L'Anse au Loup we found people who had themselves come out direct from Devonshire and Somerset, from Chard, Dartmouth, Torquay, &c., and some at one place from Bude in Cornwall. Thence we journeyed to Red Bay. Here some of the people also are desperately poor, as I think I told you. The fisheries for the last two or three years have been bad there, and this year promise no better. Certainly some will be obliged to leave this winter and seek pastures new. The Newfoundland Government will no doubt give them passages free to the Island, and they may there get work on the railway lines or roads. After seeing several patients I left Red Bay the same day, and at 8.30 at night, Saturday [29 July], the *Princess May* once more brought up safely in Battle Harbour. Here we found the doctor and nurse already with plenty of work. The hospital was not yet inhabited, for no stoves had been put in, but they had several patients in huts on the island and in neighbouring coves, which they visited either on foot or in Mr. W. Baine Grieve's little launch *Pundit*, when she could be spared from her usual work of fetching fish, or more often when her usual course of work took her near those harbours. Sunday [30 July], Dr. Bobardt left for a neighbouring cove, whence a boat came to fetch him to a dying man. There he stayed till tea, holding services and talking with the people. After the service in the little wooden church we held a prayer meeting in the school, Dr. Bobardt, our musician, having returned. The place was crowded to suffocation, and the singing bade fair to outrival a North Sea meeting.

Monday [31 July] was spent in getting the furniture, &c., into the hospital. The building is square, with four windows each side, five in front, and a door. A large adjunct for bath-room, &c., is also in course of erection. The walls are wood inside, then two inches of sawdust, then tongued and grooved wood again, then felt, and outside clap-board again, like a clinker-built boat. As soon as possible, but probably next spring, we shall cover the inside walls with canvas and paint them. The house is raised up on stones, and we shall double-floor it when possible. At present in the two front rooms, most to be used, we have just a thick flooring, then feltine, then a thin layer of straw then sacking (from old packing-cases), and lastly oilcloth. Thus this building is really one of the very best on the whole coast. The hospital to be raised at Indian Harbour will only possibly be this year a shed compared with this building. The Society [the MDSF] and the people here owe a sincere debt of gratitude to Mr. W. Baine Grieve for his most seasonable gift.

Tuesday [1 August] we were called to some out-harbours, and I took Dr. Bobardt round in the *Princess May*. Nurse Carwardine had been obliged to be up all the last two nights with the pneumonia patient.

This morning we heard of the death of the sick man visited on Sunday, a man of thirty-eight, leaving five children up to seven years of age and a young widow. In the absence of anyone else, I was asked to conduct the burial service, and on Wednesday morning [2 August] the funeral took place. The arrival of the large rowing boat, manned by six oarsmen, was announced by the lowering of all flags to half-mast and the tolling of the only bell. We read the Church service. The burial-ground is a cleft in between three rugged hills and the stormy ocean – a most appropriate resting-place for those who might almost be called "sons of the ocean." It was a sad occasion, though as a lesson to the little value of living for earthly ends it spoke deeply to everyone present. Immediately after the service we left in the *Princess May*, in dense fog, for the north, and at night found our way into Cape St. Francis Harbour. We came, in our course, across numberless islands of ice, and managed to overshoot our harbour. This we discovered at last, and retraced our way. The fog was so thick you could not see the tops of some icebergs when passing close by them, and when eventually we reached the entrance we found it closed up by the huge masses of ice. Fortunately we found the other entrance, and eventually at 7.45 came to moorings alongside a stage for fishing in a very secure harbour. After getting some food we had service in Captain Penney's large room, a most hearty gathering, and, compared with the miserable experiences outside, calculated to be especially welcome to us at any rate. Then we saw the sick folk of the place, and eventually retired to what we considered well-earned rest.

Next morning [3 August], after dispensing our medicines and getting an early breakfast, we started again on our journey, and at 9.30 a.m. ran into Square Island Harbour. Here, again, we saw several patients, mostly friends of last year. It was here we had a wedding on the *Albert*. Thence we made for Dead Island Harbour, but a thick fog again overtaking us, and the wind chopping round to the eastward, so as to make a nasty on-shore sea, we decided to run past and bring up in Venison Tickle. This we reached at 3 p.m.

Here we again found old friends, and among them unfortunately an epidemic of *la grippe*, also one case of right-sided paralysis, which we hope to send to Battle Hospital by the next opportunity. These have kept us busy till the present moment, and as I began by informing you, a strong N.E. gale is now howling round the *Princess May*, promising to detain us tomorrow also. Here I found the wife of the unfortunate man whose left arm was shot off last fall at the shoulder. He is still in St. John's Hospital. The agent here, Mr. Hawker, whose guest I am to be for the night, is endeavouring to get her and her little baby girl a free passage to Newfoundland. There is no possibility for a man crippled in this way to make a livelihood on the Labrador. Now I must close this letter and leave it here for the mail steamer to pick up when she calls.

Wilfred T. Grenfell

Thursday, August 3rd.   Went on shore to see a patient I had confined to bed; he slept in a bunkhouse with 4 others; the house was a log hut covered with earth sods and the bunks so narrow that for two to sleep in each the head of one man had to be next the feet of his mate; each bunk was 36 in. wide. We visited several houses but found nearly all the men out fishing; trap fishing has been a failure in this harbour this year and now the men have taken to longlining in deep water, which means that they do not return home till 11, 12 or even 1 in the night, and in this case the girls have little to do during the day but much in the early morning on the stages where work commences at daybreak.

Our hospital furniture, fire stoves &c. taken on shore & stowed in a storehouse; and commencement made in erecting the hospital; one cornerstone laid and a pile driven.

Sister visited p[atien]t this afternoon & sat reading for some time; he told her a weasel had been in & out of the room several times during the day.

Very few at our evening service, & most of these women. Several patients from Smoky Run & Bakeapple Bight.

Friday, August 4th. Day spent in visiting the stages & cottages of the people on shore – most of the men were away at the fish.

Saturday, August 5th. Another day spent visiting – when shall we get any really fine weather?

Sunday, August 6th. Mail came into Indian Harbr. (Paine's Cove) 4.45 – cold, bleak, raw morning. I rowed ashore, got a patient up and almost pulled his "mates" out to row him on board the steamer which would take him down to Battle hospital. Here was a man a week in a wretched bunkhouse receiving no help or sympathy from his skipper or mates though at one time he was near dying; his skipper did not speak to him for a week & the men would come in late & turn in without saying a word to him; his only visitor one day was a weasel.

The services were well attended – abt. 130 in morning & 156 in evening – the ship was quite full in the evening & sister's service for women was well attended.

At the evening service I went with skipper & a local pilot & a crew to Ice Tickle to enquire about wreckage seen & picked up off Belle Isle by two schooners. A large steamer making up Gulf of St. Lawrence went into Square Island on the Monday (July 31st) in the fog to enquire where Belle Isle was; on Wednesday night at 8 p.m.

two schooners coming down from New Foundland ran through very great quantities of wreckage abt. 25 miles s.e. of Belle Isle & picked up a lifebuoy, polarnaris [Palinurus?] stand & some timber – they saw pillows, hatch doors, kegs & numerous things & report that the wood was pounded up in short lengths & much splintered; in all probability, this was the remains of the steamer that went into Square Island; on the lifebuoy we could just make out "Straits of Gibraltar, Glasgow" & find she was a 1260-ton vessel carrying cargo & passengers; she probably struck [a] reef on n.w. of the island. Capt. sent all information to Lloyd's, London.

Monday, August 7th.   Saw several patients on shore. Two men & two women who live up the bay in winter but come out to the islands to fish in summer came in a jackboat & asked us to go & see some sick people; Sister & I left about noon with provisions, wraps, medicine chest, camera & gun &c.; it was 4 o'clock before we reached Pomeroy Island, where our first p[atien]t lived – a small log & turf house 13 × 13 – one room only – & there lived man, wife, a girl of 16 & 6 children (aet. 14, 11, 9, 7, 4, 2) all miserably clothed; we chatted, doctored, examined the seal lance consisting of "nolock" [*nuiq*] & "unock" [*unaaq*] used in spearing seal, and bought a muskrat skin; and after seeing an Esquimaux (Jefferies) & his wife, who looks as much a native as he does but whose father was an Englishman & mother a n.f. woman, so we were told – she had been deserted by parents on the coast & lived all her life among the Esquimaux in the bay – we went on to John Noel's house on the mainland opposite to Winter's Island, and there unpacked provisions & asked Mr. and Mrs. N. to join us at tea.

We went to see Mr. Oliver – an old Esquimaux who is very ill & lives with his Newfoundland wife & two undergrown sons of 17 & 7 in a miserable one-roomed hovel 12 × 12 × 6; they had caught no fish, having no gear – the boy had jigged all day & caught two fish only – but had had 3 quintals given them for mending a trap; at the time we were there the only food they had in the house was about 3 lbs. of broken hard bread (i.e. biscuit); their clothes were very old &

in rags, & they lay at night on a mattress with a dirty rug over them – no sheet & no blanket. Price of flour in Rigoulette is $10 a barrel (196 lbs.), tea 4/- a lb. & molasses 4/6 a gallon; last year they caught 9 quintals of fish & for this got 1 barrel of flour & 2 lbs. of tea for their winter's consumption besides a little powder & shot with which to shoot partridge.

After prayers at Noel's house we turned in; fortunately Mr. & Mrs. Noel did not offer the only bed in the house – it was a dreadful one – & fortunately too they had a large empty loft, on the floor of which we laid our rugs & slept fairly; before turning in we emptied our sack of clothing & settled to whom we would give the garments we had brought, but we were not left to ourselves, for between the planks which separated us from the loft of the house next door – it was a double house – we could almost see eyes peering to see what was being divided and occasionally heard "can you see?" in a sub-dued whisper.

Next morning (Tuesday, August 8th) I was up early shooting sanderlings, & knocked over a dozen before breakfast; they are said to be good eating & I hope Mr. N. enjoyed them. We took the Olivers some clothes – including a red petticoat & blue flannel shirt & then crossed a shoulder of a hill to see another family. There we found a boatload of people who had come from beyond Bluff Head & were on their way to get treatment at the "Albert" – 18 miles from their home; as one or two little operations were needed I could not help them then so they had to complete their journey; they rowed us round to Noel's house & then took us with our belongings over to Groves' at Pompey Island. Mr. Groves then rowed us across to Run by Guess (Mr. Maiden) & there we were put out by hearing Mr. Simms' bait boat, which was to have called for us at 3 p.m. by appointment, had made an early visit for bait & returned 3 hours before. Mr. Maiden had had a good spurt of fish & was very busy so we could not ask him to take us home and it looked as though we should have another night out. As fresh herring were being fried for us we were throwing the cast net for caplin & supplying Mr. Groves with bait, and then helped in emptying a cod bag containing 10 quintals into the trap boat, & again from the boat onto the stage. Mr. Maiden wanted us to stay the night, but seeing we were anxious to be back he offered to put us onto a part of Rodney Mundy Island from which we could walk home, so when his trap boat was going to haul the trap we got in & were taken to Edward's Harbour. Here Mr. Geo. Smith, the merchant, met us & gave us tea, & stowing our wraps &c. in his store we walked over the hills & reached the ship a little before 8 in the evening.

Wednesday, August 9th.   Visited in morning; in afternoon saw a few more patients & went over the hospital carefully; the building is getting on very rapidly as all the wood had been fitted in St. John's. Tea with Mr. Simms. Just as we were about to commence service a boat & six came to take me to Smokey Run – 3 or 4 miles – to see a patient who had been taken ill suddenly; a long, pleasant row in the evening light and a beautiful row back for the sea was full of phosphorescent animalcule[40] & the sky full of shooting stars.

Thursday, August 10th.   Rowed round to Smokey Run again & found pt. better; called on Mr. Jarrett – the agent – and walked home over the hills calling at one or two houses in Bakeapple Bight on the way. As we approached Indian Harbour were delighted to see the steam launch [*Princess May*] approaching the harbour, & by pushing on reached the shore & were taken on board by the dinghy; we had been very anxious about the launch & were relieved to find all well & that much good had been done at the harbours down the Straits and between Battle & this.

Friday, August 11th.   Breakfast with Mr. Simms – the agent. At 10.30 Grenfell, Sister [Williams], Capt., Dobbie & I start for the White Bear Islands in the steam launch; the morning was very fine & the sea calm but after we had gone half way the wind & sea getting up we feared we might not be able to return at night so turned round & visited Split Knife Harbour on Cut Throat Island; here we found several sick people, did our best, had dinner, & went on to Smokey Run again,

& then home. Tonight the wind is blowing a stiff breeze, & we are glad to be where we are.

Saturday, August 12th. The wind had moderated a little so Dr. G. & I went off to three harbours near to one another, viz. Horse Harbour, Emily Harbr. & Dark Tickle; he took the wheel & I the chart, & as the water was very shoal in parts we went slowly, I standing on the bows looking out for rocks. We met some very nice men at Horse Harbr. all of the name of Gosse & they seemed very glad to see us, having heard of our arrival in Indian Harbr. which they say is too out of the way of the people for the hospital – certainly one of these harbours would have been more central; we saw several sick people, including two bad cases of consumption, and then went on to Emily Harbr.; called on Mr. Apsie the agent & had to *ask* for lunch. The night before Mr. Burgess the revenue officer had been in Emily & Mr. A. had not fully recovered from his visit, finding it necessary to drink pints of water to keep his mouth cool; Mr. B. was a common fisherman till

Bully boats, stages, tilts, and store-houses at Horse Harbour.

he got voted into the House of Assembly, when he received his present lucrative post; he spends the summer cruising up & down the Labrador coast avoiding those harbours where he knows there are shebeens and manages to take plenty of spirits on board for his own consumption, which he has out duty free – i.e. smuggles – from England; he is a typical Newfoundland government official.

While there two men came to take me to Dark Tickle to see a girl & a boy – good men who do their best for their neighbours; I much enjoyed my tea with them & got back to the launch just as the water had risen high enough to permit us to get out of a narrow tickle & so save a long journey round the island. It was too rough for us to visit Brig Harbr. & as the wind had risen we thought it best to get away home as quickly as possible; coming across Smokey Run we found why it had received its name, the spray coming down the run to such an extent that the water seemed to be smoking. Very few birds were seen; but we saw several great glacier-carried rocks loose on the tops of the trap hills & many of the rocks bore traces of having been smoothed by ice.

When I got back I was called to see a woman who had been injured by the fall of the roof of one of the fish stages; the shores supporting the stage had given way, slipping off the smooth rocks & she fell with the floor, the log & bark roof falling in upon her, but fortunately one end of the roof fell on the pile of salting fish or she must have been near being killed; as it was she came off fairly well; our walk home from Paine's Cove in the dark was a curious one; Rogers led the way & Sister [Williams] & I followed going slowly as even when we were on the track we had to climb rocks & cross soft patches.

Sunday, August 13th. Dr. G. took morning service & the congregation of about 120 were very attentive; Capt. & some of the crew went off to Edwd's Harbr. & from there to Bakeapple Bight & Smokey Run holding services; the women seemed to like their afternoon service which Sister conducted. In the evening there were about 140, far more than I had expected as the wind was very strong; if the Labrador people do

Newfoundland fisherman's tilt,
Paine's Cove.

not respond well they will at least listen attentively to all one has to
say, but it is a bit discouraging sometimes not to see more evidence
of good done.

Monday, August 14th.   Last night heard mail steamer whistle at 11 o'clock, and this morning Capt. came into cabin with the mail – 12 English letters & 4
from Newfoundland for me. There was not much sleeping after
that, and I revelled in news for some hours before breakfast, long
jolly letters from home. After breakfast Sister & I went over to
Paine's Cove to see our patient & found her better & in coming
back went over the site which had been chosen originally for our

hospital. A more inconvenient & unsuitable spot would have been hard to find near here – on a raised beach 6 ft. above sea level protected on E. & W. but open to the N. & S. winds, which whistle through this gap in the long trap rock hills, and cut off from the rest of the main island, where the people live, at every tide; the distance of 500 yds. from any fresh water only adds to the other inconveniences; it was an interesting spot however for this level area is a raised beach and consists of pounded shells feet & feet deep; the people collect these broken fragments of shells & strew them on the earth floors of their hovels making a neat surface. Buried in the shells we found bones of a large sperm whale; from the way the bones were scattered & buried I should imagine the whale came ashore before the beach was raised, which was how many years ago? An old man here remembers these whalebones there 57 years ago, & says they have not altered in appearance since then.

We are very disappointed not to be able to get into the hospital this year, and it is not easy to settle how we can best spread our influence; at present we are concentrated strongly in Indian Harbour; Dr. G. will go north in the launch & I am anxious the "Albert" should move on too as the Capt. can do good missionary if not medical work, but Sister & I cannot stay here if we have no house to stay in. Today we have been over to Mark's Island near Smokey Run to see a large house built near a disused fish manure factory to see if we could not utilise it as a temporary hospital & centre for work this year; it is in a very central situation & would have done capitally if we had only heard of it two or three weeks ago, but now it will be of no use to us as it would need a fortnight's work to get it into order and that would leave us only about three weeks before we move south again.

We went on to Brig Harbour to see a patient with pneumonia we had been asked to visit & while there had tea with Mr. Strap who used to be Mr. Munn's [41] agent; he is an interesting man and has a great reputation as being "as good as a doctor"; however, he was glad to let us see a resident patient of his and took interest in watching us graft an ulcer on his leg. We heard there was a house & store empty at Dark Tickle, but it was too late to go there tonight as the time was gone & the fog coming up so we came straight home & did not arrive till 8.15.

Everyone speaks of the bad weather & bad fishery of this year; men who had 300 or 400 quintals of fish last year have only 100 now; they say they have had no summer at all this year and certainly we have had a most uncommon quantity of fog and cold winds with absence of sun.

Letter from Dr Grenfell to Frederick Treves, Chairman, MDSF Hospital Committee

ss *Princess May*, Rigoulette, Groswater Bay,
Labrador, August 15, 1893

Dear Mr. Treves:

Since my last letter and report to you we have made considerable progress, and, of course, had the usual difficulties. Everything at Battle goes well. Nurse Carwardine is excellent, and Bobardt has had his hands full. The last mail steamer took him up five patients, and we have three more going up – one, a girl of fourteen with a large psoas abscess. She had had it apparently three years. I let out a pint of pus at least. Another is a phthisical patient, and a third has a disease of the stomach. This patient is now in hospital on the *Albert* waiting for the next mail ...

I have visited a large number of harbours since I wrote last, and I joined the *Albert* at Indian Harbour last Thursday – that is, north of Groswater Bay – since when I have visited all neighbouring islands with Curwen. I am very sorry to say we cannot get this hospital into working order this year. The little mail steamer through bad weather was unable to land the material her first trip north, the result being that for about a month she carried it along this vile coast – I mean vile for navigation purposes. You know that not a light, foghorn, whistle, buoy, or other adventitious assistance is anywhere up the coast. When I found that in spite of all the exertions we could make we could not get into working order this year,

I made arrangements to have the hospital ready anyhow to use as a storehouse for the heavy goods during the winter.

All perishable articles I am sending to Battle Hospital, on which the burden of the work will now fall. Nurse Williams will return, therefore, to Battle by next mail. Plainly, there will be too much work for one nurse there when the house is full. Curwen will proceed with the *Albert*, using it as his hospital, while I shall continue roving in and out, and visiting scores of places otherwise inaccessible. The launch has more than repaid her outlay in utility already, I consider. Three vessels were lost from their anchors in neighbouring harbours during a recent gale; also two steamers were lost in the fog in the Straits of Belle Isle. One was called the *Straits of Gibraltar*. The Governor of Newfoundland's steamer picked up their crew, and we have some of their wreckage on the *Albert*. One man told me his schooner came sailing in the breezes through a scum formed of Dutch cheeses, candles, tubs of butter, &c.

Curwen has seen 335 patients, I have seen 263, and Bobardt, I suppose, about 200. Many are ordinary dyspepsia, caused by large and hurried meals of coarse indigestible food, and a monotonous diet of cod, bread, molasses, tea, and margarine. The exception is rather to have salt pork, or if they do have it it is used to cook the fish with, rather than to eat. Truly the affection is not necessarily fatal to life, but it tends to render life more miserable than necessary here, where comforts are few enough already. There is, too, as our lists show plainly, a substratum of really serious cases where untold agony and suspense, and even life itself, have already been demonstrably saved by the medical branch of this work.

So much travelling and being my own sailing master and pilot has left me scarcely a moment to spare for amusement, but one day, windbound during a gale, I steamed into a river mouth, and, with some raw meat as bait, which I had had given me that day, I landed several splendid trout. I have no respect for trout now, and none for what Mark Twain calls "trout liars." You can see the trout sometimes in scores feeding on offal round the stages, and with a stick and piece of string, a hook and some fish liver, you can get a meal in twenty minutes easily. They also take flies (in the river) as if they were determined to swallow rod and all. Shooting I have had none, except for killing half a dozen fat ducks on an island in the Straits. Anything in the way of fresh meat is a treat in this country.

Yours very sincerely,
Wilfred Grenfell

Tuesday, August 15th. Went off in launch at 7.30 to Emily [Harbour] to look at an empty house we had heard of to see if it would do for me for this summer; it was not available, being used as a store for flakes on which the fish is dried. Returned by 11 & after making various arrangements went off again up Hamilton Inlet with Sinclaire Simms as pilot in order to take Mr. Hollett the new Methodist minister to his station at Lester Point. It was a fine afternoon so we landed on Puffin Island to see the birds & investigate the mystery of their nests in the ground. We anchored at night at Ticoralak about 33 miles up the inlet; six of us slept on board, the crew in their cabin and the other four on the seats & floor of the cabin which was just large enough to hold us; the dog could not find room for himself on the floor so chose to lie down on my legs.

Wednesday, August 16th. Run on shore for half an hour for the pleasure of touching a tree; found four ripe bakeapples, the first found yet; started again before eight and on our way across to Lester Point saw & fired at several seals; the dog got very excited & wanted to go for them; he was very excited too at seeing a shoal of caplin & wanted to dive after them.

We landed & had a two-hour ramble in the woods after birds but saw nothing but a scattered jay or two; the mosquitoes were terrible and almost made one think the hunter's a miserable calling; found several interesting plants in the larch & spruce woods, including Linnaeus borealis and an orchis; the blue iris too was plentiful and the curlew or crowberries ripe.

Wilson's house, Rigolet. "The finest house in Labrador; no brick or stone is used in any house on the coast."

An hour's run brought us to Rigoulette, where we were welcomed by Mr. & Mrs. Wilson,[42] the local commissioned officer of the Hudson's Bay Co.; they are very nice English people and seemed really glad to see us, and together with their three little girls live in what is I suppose the best house in Labrador. Rigoulette is a beautiful place, well surrounded by good trees, and is very much warmer than any place on the coast outside; true last winter they registered 42°F. below zero but there was no wind & no moisture so that it did not seem cold at all; Mrs. W. & children were out for an 8 or 9 mile run on snowshoes every day last winter; the hottest month in the year is June although the bay is filled with ice then; last June they found the thermometer at 115°F. in their little cold conservatory on which the sun does not shine! We saw geranium, mignonette, fuchsia, pansy, and the blue meadow cranesbill or geranium so common in the English Lake District & other parts.

James Wilson, clerk-in-charge of the Hudson's Bay Co. district, and his family, Rigolet.

The day was bright & warm so we sat in a tent (!) till dinner was ready, and after the meal visited the storehouses & talked; we were shown a live porcupine that had been caught a few days previously in the woods; they are very common & are said to be good eating; the Esquimaux dogs sometimes make for them and receive what for in the shape of a mouthful of the sharp quills which are easily shed.

The company's flag with "pro pelle cutem" waved aloft in our honour and attracted people up the bay so that before we left we had seen a number of people who were ill. The most interesting person we saw was an old woman of 82 [Hannah Michelin] who keeps her husband of 78 who is beyond working; she is a half-breed Esquimaux & is a fine specimen, doing the work of two or three others; last winter she shot a great number of partridges walking 20 miles in a day and would herself dig a hole through 3 or 4 feet of ice to fish for trout with a hook & piece of meat for bait; she used to hunt & trap animals & drive the comatic or sledge but has had to give that up the last few winters.[43]

One lives here in a land of fish but at present I have not had time even to look for one; there are no trout within 8 miles of Indian Harbour but in parts of the inlet they are very numerous and will take anything, meat or red flannel or anything at all.

The evening was spent with the Wilsons but we slept on board.

Thursday, August 17th.

Mosquitoes dreadful in the early morning but when the wind sprang up they cleared away. Saw more patients & took photographs in the morning and after lunch we started back, tide with us but wind against; it was a fine, clear night till the last ½ hour when our old acquaintance, fog, came down again, but our pilot knew the way as well in fog as clear weather, steering by the sound of the breaking of the waves on the rocks – by the "rôte" of the shore as they say – and we made the harbour about midnight.

Mission Hospital Ship *Albert*,
Indian Harbour, Labrador, August 17

... Dr. Grenfell will have told you we found the hospital had not been begun; the wood had been landed two or three days previously only, the mail steamer having carried it up and down the coast twice, as she had not opportunity to discharge it on her first trip down the coast. A most unsuitable site had been chosen on an exposed raised beach, a mile from the harbour, from which it was cut off at high tides; but fortunately the agent who had chosen the spot had gradually come to think it unsuitable himself, and then selected a really good position 150 yards above his own house, on the only flat dry patch in the neighbourhood. We commenced building next day, and soon had the frame up; but it became quite evident that we should not get into the building this year. This was a very great disappointment to both the Sister and me, for we had been looking forward to some steady, methodical work among the people; it was the work we had come out to do, and the work we were hoping for. We have spent some time looking about for a house which we could turn into a temporary hospital, or even a house in which I, or Sister and I, could live and do our Mission and medical work; but although we have visited each harbour near, we have not found one that would be suitable. I believe the arrangements are that I go north in the *Albert* and that Sister goes to Battle to help Sister Carwardine. We expect the two carpenters who are at work on the Indian Harbour Hospital will have done their work by the fall, and that we shall be able to stow the stuff away in it during the winter, leaving all in charge of the old couple who take care of Mr. Simms' house and store, and that everything will be in order and ready for use at the commencement of next season. I have had several patients I should like to have taken into hospital; one man with ulcer of the stomach I sent down to the Battle Harbour Hospital, and another old fellow with cancer of the stomach I have at present on board, and shall send him south by the mail-boat. There is certainly room for a hospital on this part of the coast.

Our Sunday meetings have been crowded, morning and evening, for all comers, and in the afternoon Sister has always taken a service for women only. Weekday services are badly attended, as the men are out fishing far into the night, and often do not return at night at all, keeping out until they have a good boatload of fish. The people are very attentive, but do not respond at all well.

Last week Sister and I were taken to see some people eight miles from the harbour, and had to be out all night, being made as comfortable as possible. We went to one one-roomed log and turf cabin, 12 ft. square and 6 ft. high, in which lived an old Esquimaux who was dying of consumption, his wife, and two boys of seventeen and seven. They were all miserably clothed, and the boys undergrown. They had no fishing gear, except a trout net and [a] few jiggers, and the elder lad had spent the whole day jigging and caught two fish only! Last winter they received as their winter's diet one barrel (i.e., 196 lbs.) of flour and 2 lbs. of tea only, and had to fill up vacancies with partridges they shot. A barrel of flour in Rigoulette costs $10 which is only $3 70c. for cash in Nova Scotia.

Yours sincerely,
Eliot Curwen

Friday, August 18th.   When we got back last night we found a girl on board *very* ill with phthisis taken into hospital; quite pleasant to have a resident patient again but she was *very* ill & wanted to be sent home to N.F.

We weigh anchor and as the tide sets out of harbour "Princess May" tows us out; a great pity "P. May" is not strong enough to be really serviceable in towing "Albert"; she can only tow her in a dead calm – & then it will be into & not out of harbour of course – or when the tide is running strong with her. Really sorry to leave Indian Harbour and hospital with the hopes & plans unrealized.

A very light s. breeze so that we take all day in getting 30 miles; sat on deck part of day but in afternoon fog came in; pass thro' large quantities of seabirds sitting on water fishing for caplin; some seemed too fat & heavy to fly – Buffon's skuas I think – but for the fog I should have shot some for stuffing but Capt. thought stopping to pick them up would throw him out of his reckoning [of distance run].

At night put out to sea more as we could not see land & did not want to feel it, and as icebergs were in evidence.

WEBECK HARBOUR

Saturday, August 19th. Made Webeck Harbour, N. of Cape Harrison at 8 a.m., a lovely morning. Had not been in long before I was called to see a pt. ashore suffering from influenza. Fishing has been better here than up the coast; much of the fish has been "made," that is dried for shipping, and we saw for first time the fish laid out on the "bawn" [expanse of rocks] drying & women then piling it when dried.

In afternoon we could not get on shore because of wind.

"Princess May" came in after tea.

At 10 p.m. "Windsor Lake," the mail steamer, came in on her way south. Dr. G. thought best to send patient down to Battle hospital notwithstanding her serious condition, and not use "Albert" as hospital ship at all; Sister Williams went with her & will remain at Battle to help nurse there as, now that it is certain there can be no northern hospital this year, there will be no work for her except in Battle. I opposed sending patient s. because I considered her far too ill to be moved and because I think we ought to use ship as a hospital.

Sunday, August 20th. Another lovely day & mosquitoes plentiful. "No rose without a thorn." A crowd of patients, & when I had seen them all I found the ship well nigh deserted, & our boat gone on shore; at Webeck there is a chapel large enough to seat 100, built partly by the fishermen but aided largely by Hon. [James J.] Rogerson of St. John's;[44] here there is service every Sunday at 7, 11, 3 & 6.30 conducted by the men; we were asked to take the services today and our crew had taken the boat away with them so I had to stay on board.

Perfectly calm, peaceful Sunday morning; scarcely a ripple on the sea, a clear blue sky, warm sun, scarcely a sound to be heard; outside the harbour were several icebergs, and the mirage played great tricks with them, sometimes making them appear twice their natural size, sometimes showing them upside down in the sky, and sometimes showing bergs which were really out of sight beyond the horizon.

Services in afternoon & evening good & well attended; G. conducted them.

Saw several cases of night blindness; getting very interested in the subject.

Monday, August 21st. Morning spent on board printing photos & unpacking & stowing away drugs meant for Indian Harbr., but now needed on ship as so many of the ship's drugs have been taken on board the steam launch.

In afternoon went with boats to fetch fresh water; rambled over the hills; very uneven walking, ground covered with spruce & fir trees a yard high and with low-growing & creeping plants including Linnaeus borealis, bakeapple, curlewberry [crowberry], a curious Solomon's seal &c. The ground was made uneven by the great quantity of loose boulders lying about, great boulders many tons in weight & small, easily movable ones; some large ones were conspicuous on the tops of the hills and seemed to be lying tilted upon one edge, something like the Logan Stone on Dartmoor; like that one they have doubtlessly been dropped there by glaciers long ages ago.

Evening service very badly attended, all the men & women being so busy with the fish.

Letter of Dr Bobardt to the MDSF

Battle Harbour, Labrador, August 21

This fortnight I have nothing very fresh to chronicle in the way of news, except that the work is still heavy and we have to work hard

Hannah Michelin, 82, and her husband, 78, Rigolet. "He is too old and ill to work, so she supports him. Last winter on more than one occasion she unaided made a hole through 3 or 4 feet of ice and sat all day hooking trout."

Tuesday, August 22nd.

to keep up with it. The hospital is progressing. To-morrow we shall be rid of three or four patients; but, as the mail steamer arrives then, there will certainly be more to take their places. I am now living in the hospital myself, and so is the nurse. The patients come for admittance in a very filthy condition, and ere they can be admitted into the wards they have to be thoroughly scoured and washed. We could do with a gift of nightshirts and old change shirts, as the wardrobe of some of the patients is rather meagre.

I hold two prayer-meetings during the week at which I give an address on the "Life of Jesus Christ"; also two other evenings are devoted to singing practice, and last Sunday there were four meetings, with an additional prayer-meeting. It is rather a lot of work, especially as at most of them I sing, play the organ, read the lessons, and then preach too. But I love the work, and such meetings brighten the lives of these unfortunate people. I also have meetings at most of the houses I visit.

I have not yet had time to give you a special article, but no doubt you have quite a plethora of articles from the other doctors, who are both in the north doing their good work. Ere long I hope to give you a complete and more lengthy epistle.

Yours sincerely,
Albert Bobardt

I have a donation to the Mission of 56 cents (2s. 1d.) for hauling a tooth from a fisherman, the first local one. Nurse Carwardine gives most valuable assistance and works like a Trojan.

We are having a spell of really fine weather; flat calm in the morning but a little wind from the s. sprang up about 11.30 so we up anchor & proceed north; more water had to be fetched, and I had to go on shore to see a few patients, taking camera with me. Fish "making" – i.e. drying & preparing for shipping is going on very actively here, one vessel being nearly loaded. The chief family here bears the name of Legrow – this is the way the name is spelt – & their ancestors came from Jersey, England. Rest of morning spent printing photographs; had intended going fishing, for it's about

A trapboat returning with net full of cod.

time I caught a fish of some description, having been over 6 weeks on the Labrador.

Saw my 400th patient.

Clear of the harbour by dinnertime; once more we are among the icebergs; I have not seen so many or such fine ones since reaching Battle Harbour; 50 large ones easily counted; some are most curiously shaped, one like a sphinx, one like a pyramid with a tower by its side, another like a fine spire, but the most remarkable was more like the vaulted cloisters of Fountains Abbey than anything I have seen before – great arches supported on sturdy white pillars; nearly all the bergs showed signs of having been turned over in the process of disintegration, being terraced, each terrace being an old sealevel line; and throughout the afternoon we constantly heard the loud, sharp report or longer roar as smaller or larger pieces fell off a great berg into the sea; sometimes this report is like that of a gun, sometimes like a volley, & I remember taking the binocular and carefully looking for the man who had fired a gun, as I thought, as we were approaching Battle Islands. Some of the bergs had large & small masses of ice on their flat or sloping tops; they had evidently been separate once & become frozen into position, and their resemblance to the boulders so plentifully strewn about on the hills at Webeck & Cape Harrison was very striking.

The wind was very light so we had plenty of time to take in all we saw; the "Ragged Islands" are well named, but we were too far off to see whether they were geologically the same as the ragged & rugged hills about Indian Harbour & the "White Bears" [White Bear Islands].

Seabirds were plentiful & I was itching to possess some of their skins; however, every mile was important & putting off to pick up a shot bird would take time, so we did not shoot any till evening when we were becalmed; we shot a fulmar petrel & another bird I have not identified, big fat birds and good evidence of the abundance of caplin, the great bait used for hooking cod.

Evening spent developing photographs.

Fish pitchforked from trapboats onto stage.

Fish stage, Cape Harrison Harbour.

"Interior of tilt at Webeck Harbour, showing open fire, open chimney, cracks in walls, iron bake-pot, tea kettle, loaf of bread, &c. In this one room live 4 men, 1 boy and 1 girl, night and day."

HOPEDALE

Wednesday, August 23rd.

Last night we were in a dead calm surrounded by icebergs – not an overpleasant position; every now & then a loud report was to be heard as pieces of ice fell off; Capt's voice woke me at 6.30 so I went on deck and found him giving directions for altering the canvas so as to avoid a big berg; the wind was light but favourable; took several photographs and saw large pieces fall off a berg not far distant; we had not long passed one berg when it suddenly began to sway backwards & forwards without apparent reason; so much did it swing that a ledge running out some distance just under the water was raised more than 40 ft. to be submerged again as the great mass rolled back again; after thus swaying 3 or 4 times it gradually settled down in its old position.

During the day winds have been very light & fortunately, for navigation has been very difficult; there are numerous islands not

Chapel servants, Hopedale.

marked on the chart, & the islands charted are often not charted correctly & not named, and there seem to have been no soundings taken of the depth of water & presence of shoals. One or other of the crew has been stationed on the crosstrees all day on the lookout for shoals & reefs; it was not so cold up there although the presence of so much ice made one think it ought to be cold; thermom. in the shade was 72°F. and the air heavy & close as if a thunderstorm was impending.

Morning spent in reading & photography; afternoon ditto & skinning & stuffing.

At 7 p.m. after tacking 12 miles against a head (i.e. w.) wind we let go anchor in Hopedale, a large, perfectly safe harbour ("Best in

Labrador" Capt.), about ⅓ mile from the [Moravian] mission premises; the settlement is a very picturesque one with its very German-looking houses & church with red roofs; I did not go on shore, and by & by two of the missionaries set off to call on us – Herr Keastner [Kästner][45] & Herr Siemens [Simon];[46] they were both Germans but speak good English; they had been looking for our arrival & were very glad to see us. Several Esquimaux on islands we passed in the bay seemed glad to see us, & shouted their "auchenai" [aksunai] to us, to which we responded "achshuta" (i.e. "let us be strong").[47]

Thursday, August 24th. Hoisted sail & went out of harbour in order to come in again to a better anchorage; saw crowd of people looking very disappointed as we sailed out; on lowering mainsail Rogers got a nasty blow from a loose ring & gave us all a fright.

After dinner went on shore & was *most* warmly received; Herr Keastner the head of the station met me at the door & took me to his rooms where was Mrs. K.; he is a broad-headed, elderly man; she too is elderly, short, broad & Dutch-looking tho' really German; Mr. & Mrs. Siemens next came in, and then Mr. & Mrs. Hansen (Danes),[48] & last of all Mr. Fry, who has only just come out from Bristol in the "Harmony";[49] the two Danes & 3 of the Germans speak English well but Mrs. Siemens understands very little. They all live in one large house, each family having two private rooms only, with a common room for meals & a kitchen; and the harmony seems complete; all are very nice, but Mr. & Mrs. Hansen strike me most. One kitchen-maid is the only servant – besides the nursemaids – so the missny's wives do all the housework & take weeks in turns to take charge of the cooking.

The chapel is a large open room connected with the house by means of a passage; it would seat about 300 or 400 people; there is prayer from 9–9.30 every Sunday morning, sermon 10–10.30; service in English at 3 for the N.F. fishermen if there are any in the harbour, & litany in the evening in Esquimaux of course; and prayer several evenings during the week.

Mr. & Mrs. K. have three children with them, boys aged 6, 5 & 1½; Mrs. Siemens has a boy of 1½ & girl of ⅙ yr.; it is a rule of the Moravian Society that all children are to be sent home to Germany to be educated when they are 6; they remain at school till 14 or 16 and *never* return to their parents, going either into trade [with the Mission] or becoming ministers or mission[ar]ies in other parts of the world; Mr. & Mrs. K. have 4 daughters & a son in Europe whom they will never see again; the youngest daughter went home last year and there was no means of learning of her safe arrival till the end of July of this year, when the first mail arrived – 9½ months after the child had left; next year Gerhardt, their boy of 6, goes home; I think the thoughts of all of us were in Europe as we sang together tonight,

"Peace, perfect peace, with loved ones far away.
In Jesus' keeping we are safe, and they."

The Moravian missionaries never return home except it be for sickness; Mr. & Mrs. K. have been out 24 years & home once only during that time & that was 10 yrs. ago. This seems to me a most unwise arrangement, for they need the physical & spiritual refreshing that can only be obtained by a complete change & intercourse with other people; then again the want of more servants is very unwise for with so much domestic work the wives are quite unable to learn the awful Esquimaux language, & very few of the people can talk English. Expense seems to be the chief reason why no holiday is allowed; an unmarried man like Mr. Fry receives £9 a year & a married man £23 in addition to dinner, tea, a bedstead & a table which are provided; that is all.

After dinner I was shown the gardens and was as surprised as delighted with what I saw. Each missry. has his garden & grows vegetables chiefly but at one end has one or two beds of flowers in full bloom; the gardens so rich & in such order made me think I was in England again, for who expects to see Polemonium Richardsoni, poppy, nemophila, iris, mignonette, stock, agrostemma & pansy flourish in north Labrador? The large vegetable gardens were full of rhubarb just passing off, celery, cucumber, cauliflower, beet & carrot coming on, and lettuce, kohlrabi, cabbage, curly cabbage, spinach & parsley in good condition. We had great presents of rhubarb & lettuce, there being far more than the families cd. consume; at one time the N.F. fishermen used to rob the gardens but of late years – "since Salvation Army men came down" – the gardens have not been touched. After examining all the premises I was taken to see "the greatest work of all"; this was the view of the houses in which the people now live as seen from the grass-covered ruins of the old heathen Esquimaux huts of 150 yrs. ago; one hut had been examined by a party from Bodwin [Bowdoin] College;[50] it was paved with stones; I must borrow a spade & look about; outside each house was the koppenmodding or heap of shells, bones &c. &c., the refuse of meals.[51] From near these ruins runs a very fair path, made by the people last fall, through a spruce & larch wood behind the station, & on each side of the path very pretty flowers grew, including Linnaea borealis. It was a lovely day & the pleasure I got from my companions made the day a peculiarly happy one.

Tea was commenced & ended with a German chorale. Most of the people are away fishing, but are returning for the Sunday services. When I went on board I found a couple of dozen natives – men & women – on board singing and chatting in their curious tongue; before they left they assembled on deck in the moonlight & sang a chorale.

Friday, August 25th.

On board most of morning seeing patients & reading. Went on shore with Capt. to dinner at 12 o'clock. Long talk with Mr. Hansen after; heard noise outside, looked out & saw steam launch [*Princess May*] coming into harbour; before she arrived had time to see skin & fur winter dresses. Spent rest of day talking; Dr. G. proposes to go off to Nain tomorrow & to take Mr. Hansen with him; shall be sorry not to see more of latter.

Saturday, August 26th.

Awoken by Esquimaux singing chorales & M. & s. hymns[52] in honour of Capt's birthday; went on deck & found about 50 aboard; many had come in overnight hearing we were in Hopedale.

Moravian missionaries, Hopedale. Left to right: Frau Simon with Gertrude, Herr Simon, Mr Fry, Frau Kästner with Herbert and Gerhardt, Herr Kästner, Frau Hansen with Hans, and Herr Hansen.

Went ashore to take [photograph] group of missionaries; G. & Mr. H. started at 7.30. After breakfast came a distribution of cigars to crew; and then a salute of guns & decking the ship with bunting; the morning was fine & she looked very pretty with three rows of flags from topmasts to deck. By & by the E. boat returned; in the first was a Christmas tree covered with baubles to be presented to Capt. Ambrose, one of the most prominent of the people; this was followed by much singing & then came a shower of presents – mostly little feather & sealskin pouches & slippers.

Mr. Fry came off in a kyak (or kajak) – the sealskin canoe used by the Esq. when sealing; it consists of a light wood framework on which is stretched sealskin; so light is it that it can be easily carried by a man though very long; I got into it & paddled ashore to dinner, Capt. & Mr. F. following in "Mary Grenfell." The Esq. had a great day on board being invited to dinner, Dobbie feeding 74 of them; I

Labrador Odyssey

saw patients on shore & then photographed the band – a brass & stringed band trained to play really well by the missionaries – and the "leaders of the Church," fine old men and women; after much persuasion I got Josephine, Daniel's wife, to dress up in her real old Esq. dress, trousers and all, to be photographed; this old dress has quite gone out so far south as Hopedale, but is common in Hebron & Ramah & among the heathen.

Tea on shore. At 7 we all went to the chapel to a specially musical service; Mrs. Hansen played the organ, old Daniel the 'cello, & in addition there were 5 violins & Solomon with the pipe; they certainly played well & in good time; the choir consisted of 9 voices, mostly women; Lydia, the tallest woman in Hopedale, took the central position & sang with a clear good voice. There were 116 Esquim. present; the men sat on one side of the building & were dressed for the most part in white calico jackets with a red braid border the shape of the sealskin netsek [*natsiq*] or kursek [?] – something like a North Sea fisherman's jumper with hood attached; red shawls & red caps with blue strings made the women's side look gay.

At 9 o'clock on returning to the ship I found our friends crowding the deck again, waiting for the fireworks display; their faces were worth looking at as the rockets went up, for they were in great fear but at the same time were keenly delighted as the rockets burst & blue, green & red balls began to fall. Fireworks over, 2 of the native women brought their guitars out and sat down modestly in the crew's cabin and played & sang most prettily to a big crowd consisting of their own people, our crew, & men from several schooners in harbour: "Twinkle, twinkle, little star" & other hymns & German songs.

Sunday, August 27th. Another beautiful day. Service on board in morning attended by the few Esq. who could understand English, & men from schooners; after dinner I went ashore to take the usual afternoon meeting for schoonermen; in the middle of the service I saw something was wrong, for several natives & two missionaries left; a steam launch had arrived from West Turnavik (Capt. Wm. Bartlett),[53] a group of islands 30 miles to the south, to ask me to go at once to Ben's Cove, 5 miles from Turnavik, to investigate the cause of the death of two Esquimaux women who had been found dead in a native house & whose husbands had disappeared. Mr. Simon carried on the meeting, & Capt. & Mr. Fry accompanied me; we started at 3.30 but did not reach Capt. Bartlett's till 10 o'clock after a beautiful steam among the islands, at first by the light of the sun & sunset & then by the full moon. Tom Evans – a Liverpool man – who for 17 yrs. has lived at Turnavik taking care of everything in the winter, came in the launch to fetch me, & from him I learnt much that was interesting about the people, the dogs and wild beasts & birds and much too abt. Benjamin & Brown, whose wives were dead. On reaching Turnavik we learnt that there were 4 dead, the two wives, an old woman of 70 who was living with them as all her people had gone to the "World's Fair" on show,[54] and a girl of 12, a daughter of Brown's by his second wife; and that the two men had returned from the bay with a boatload of wood which they had gone to fetch to make coffins with.

Monday, August 28th.	Slept last night in Tom Evans's sleeping bag on table in Capt. B's room; our Capt. had sofa & Mr. Fry shakedown on floor. The bag is long enough to take a man of the ordinary length; it is made of the skins of 5 jar seals lined with reindeer's skin with fur on, and inside again with swan's skin flannel, and is what is taken to sleep in by the people who travel in the winter; it is warm & watertight, so that it is possible to sleep as comfortably in a bag in a snowdrift as in a bed at home.

Up at 5.30 & turned out to see the jacks [jackboats] going out of the harbour, which is one of the two prettiest – probably the prettiest – I have seen; was sorry I had left my camera on the "Albert."

We started early for Ben's Cove with 16 men and when there held a regular court; Capt. was elected coroner; it was a long, weary & difficult business but carried through as carefully as possible I think; a verdict of death from poisoning, probably from hemlock, was brought in, but we could not determine by whom it was administered. Hemlock grows plentifully about here & is very like what is known as "Alexander greens," which are eaten as a vegetable by some of the people.[55] Very great suspicion rests on Brown for there is very little doubt he killed his first wife & baby; & so badly did he treat his 2nd. wife that she died too; this his third wife came off best of the three while she lived, but looked at from an English point of view she must have led an awful life – Brown already talks of taking another wife; he is greatly feared by the few winter settlers here, and I should not be surprised to hear next year that he has been shot; his life seems to be a long story of crime upon crime, and I do not believe anyone of the jury thinks he did not kill these four women. We are sending all information & material for analytical examination to the authorities in St. John's.[56]

Returned to Turnavik at 6 o'clock; shot a sea pigeon on way home.

Report of Dr Grenfell to the MDSF, 18–28 August

Mission Launch *Princess May,*
Labrador, August 24, 1893

Dear Mr. Editor:

My last letter was written to you from Indian Harbour. In it I think I told you we found it impossible to finish the hospital for occupation this year. I also described, I think, my visit to the Hudson's Bay Company's station at Rigoulette. On Friday, 18th, I towed the *Albert* out of Indian Harbour, on her way to Cape Harrison, with Dr. Curwen, Nurse Williams, and a girl in a very dangerous condition in the hospital. That night the launch spent in Emily Harbour, and in the agent's house we had two minor operations. I find the administration of anaesthetics even now is occasionally necessary, without a second medical man to help.

Saturday, the 19th, I visited Brig Harbour, and found a patient whose leg we had grafted three days before doing very well. He had chopped his leg badly with an axe, and then had the wound neglected in the first instance. Holton Harbour we also called at, and gave away a lot of literature and saw patients. This is a very large centre of people, and all very anxious for the "Gospel ship" to call. It is not an easy harbour to make, however, and we got a photograph of one large schooner still standing on the rocks, her last resting place. We shall, however, endeavour to call on our way down.

The next part of the coast is unsurveyed, and so we were glad of a strong southerly wind to show us the rocks by the breaking water. About 6 p.m. we steamed into an unmarked cove, where we saw some masts. It is called by some King's Bay, and is a harbour large enough to hold the British Fleet. We visited the few vessels anchored here, and then called at Sloop Cove, only waiting to tell them the *Albert* would be in the next harbour for three days. East Turnavik was our port next day. Here we found the planter in trouble. The schooner in which he had brought down his people, ninety-six in all, had been wrecked in the bay, and was now lying as a hulk dismantled at the side of his harbour. The puzzle to him at the time was how in the fall he should get his "crowd," as they are called, back again.

This night we heard from a returning boat that the *Albert* had passed north, and was probably in Hopedale, so at daylight next morning we left for Windsor's Harbour. Here also two wrecks had occurred; one, a Danish brigantine, called the *Erling*, had struck in getting out of the harbour, and had been abandoned and sold, and the unlucky captain had returned by mail steamer to St. John's. The other was a fishing schooner, which had run ashore in fog, in a strong breeze. The planter received us most cordially, and we met here again many friends of last year. The bulk of his men were, however, further north in four schooners looking for fish. His schooner, the *Thresher*, we met going out, bound for Exeter with fish. She is a much smaller vessel than the *Albert*, but carried 2,000 cwt. or quintals of fish. We left at night for Double Island.

We found one poor fellow very ill in Long Tickle, and I arranged for him to be sent to the *Albert*. The look of gratitude in the eyes of his wife for a tin of soup and a bottle of bovril was worth much, any kind of the commonly used foods for invalids being unobtainable up here. I fear the poor fellow will lose one hand, or at least a good part of it. We had this morning towed for seven miles a "bait skiff," manned by five men, and going a row of twenty-four miles to obtain lance fish [sand eel] for baiting the lines: twelve miles each way is a long row in a heavy boat well laden, and they were right glad of the pull.

Our next port of call was the Ironbound Islands. Here we found another well-named group, with steep perpendicular sides; they lie well out in the Atlantic, and the unprotected cleft on which the fishermen were anchored boded ill if an onshore wind should set in and find them unprepared. The planter who usually fished there had gone much further north this year, as he so often had his stages for the fish swept away. After seeing patients and distributing literature, we went on to Cape Ailik, and thence to West Turnavik. In endeavouring to pass between an island and the Cape we went aground, but fortunately by a little manoeuvring got off again without any damage. We had a very warm reception in Turnavik, but as fish was very scarce near here, most of the boats were away fishing. They are all open boats, yet they will go away for three days to a week at a time. The men take some salt for the fish, which they split, and they will bring back from 14 to 20 cwt. At nights they sleep rolled up in the sails.

After leaving Windsor's Harbour at 6 p.m. we determined to spend the night in Double Island, a summer settlement of Eskimos, most of whom were known to us. Our first difficulty was to find where it was, for though among countless islands of bare rocks, those we sought were not marked in the chart, and the way was unknown to us. Meanwhile the wind rose steadily till we had a strong head breeze, and the water was flying over the launch in showers of spray. We were forced to go along dead slow in order to give ourselves a chance to get off again if we struck a reef, a not unlikely occurrence, as they lay in every direction. The strong wind, however, proved a good friend, though it soaked us through, for the rising sea breaking over the shoals warned us of otherwise hidden dangers. Just as the sun set, we made out a building through the glasses, and cautiously threading our way along, we came up as near as we dared and blew our whistle. We were answered from the shore, and soon a small Eskimo boat came paddling swiftly towards us.

They had hardly come aboard when another boat followed it, and the latter paddled ahead of us as a pilot, till we were advised to let go our anchor. It was soon apparent that our anchor wouldn't hold us in the wind, so the Eskimo carried a long hawser ashore and made it fast round a rock. Where it caught the edges we lashed our empty coal sacks on, to prevent the rope chafing through. Then hauling our anchor and sheering over we dropped it again, and were soon riding safely to the two fastenings. Getting into one of our guides' boats, I was rowed up the narrow strip of water between the two islands under which we were sheltering, and as we got nearer the scene became most interesting. Behind the islands was the lurid glow of the setting sun, against which the island stood out as a black foreground, while the tiny turf-covered huts, built by the Eskimo for the summer, began to be visible. Hurrying in every direction were the little Eskimo men, women, and children, getting the fish, which had been out on the rocks all day drying, into small stacks before nightfall. These figures hurrying and jumping from rock to rock looked like silhouettes against the sky, the whole being completed by the picturesque dress, the many fine dogs, and the kajaks or skin boats.

Soon a crowd was down to greet me, and I shook hands and said "Auchenai" with every man, squaw, and picaninny that could get near for the crowd. They really are very nice, kindly people. Clear hazel skin, dark brown eyes, and jet black hair make the children exceedingly pretty, but the straight-set eyes and flat faces spoil the effect to the European eyes as they become adult. The two men being aboard the *Princess May*, and being absolutely alone, for some time I could make little progress, but eventually found two who could talk some little English. All remembered us from last year, and one of the first remarks was, "Eskimo plenty tanks [thanks] come here," then much smiling and nodding. They had seen the *Albert* passing north two days previously, and were drying up their still green [salted but undried] fish in order to be free to hurry after her.

Hearing one was sick I went off to the hut to see him, followed by all the crowd. The small low hut, made of poles and covered with turfs and rinds of firs, was absolutely devoid of furniture, while the windows were made of the gut of the square flipper seal, dressed fine, and neatly sewn together. The sides of the room were laid off with an edge for the bedding, very much as the pictures in Dr. Nansen's "First Crossing of Greenland"[57] shows, each family having its allotted place. All slept on the floor on skins and blankets. A flat box was brought out and put into the middle of the room for me to sit on, and a cleverly made lamp supplied with cod oil was lit up. The stove was made of sheets of flat iron, and the chimney was the round side of old meat tins.

Then the patients came and knelt or squatted on the ground in front of me, as their affliction called for, while the whole of the rest of the house was filled by the merry-faced crowd (who were all welcome), and who stood round trying to show their joy at seeing us by attempts at conversation, laughing heartily whenever I tried to repeat their Eskimo. It was now dark, and time to get back. The little launch with her bright light was rolling in the breeze at her anchor, and in spite of her small size was a palace to the humble abodes of these contented people.

At sunrise a stray Newfoundland boat passing south descried us, and brought me a patient, while two boats full of Eskimo passed for Hopedale. Before leaving for Hopedale with an Eskimo guide I was called to remove a frostbitten toe, unhealed since the winter. The patient was a girl of about seventeen.

Under the guidance of an Eskimo we reached Hopedale safely, and last night was spent in the company of the Moravian missionaries ashore. If I am to get further north it is imperative I should leave at once, while there is still hope of some "civil" weather, and so, in company with Mr. Hansen, of the Moravian Mission, we rounded Cape Harris, a wild headland of high perpendicular cliffs – like Achill in western Ireland – and found the *Albert* at anchor in the harbour. Sunday [27 August] broke a flat calm and a hot sun, and it was quite evident that the ship would not hold the people at the services. We decided, therefore, to hold morning and evening service ashore, while the crew should take charge of the afternoon gathering. A large wood building had been erected for "keeping prayers" by the people themselves, and this was filled three times over. It was a day not to be forgotten soon, though the work was not light, for we had many patients between services.

On Monday [28 August] the *Princess May* left to visit all the stations to an island called Turnavik, where we were to meet the *Albert* again. The harbours visited included three in the "Ragged Islands," aptly so called from their very ragged high peaks. Here were many craft anchored, and moored fore and aft in each case, for the clefts affording shelter were so narrow there was no room for even the smallest to swing. That night we spent in Roger's Harbour, in some island called Adlavik. The icebergs were very thick all round here, and one enormous fellow we saw capsize with a roar like thunder. The fragments of broken ice came bobbing up a good quarter of a mile from the main piece. In the morning we visited Long Tickle, formerly a larger summer settlement than now. It may appear remarkable that much of the snow in clefts and shaded places is not yet melted, nor will it probably melt at all this year. I think this is unusual, for the fall is not very great, apparently, and June, July, and August usually disperse it all.

The *Princess May* will leave to-morrow before breakfast. As the mail steamer does not go further north than Hopedale, except once more, later in this fall, we shall be beyond reach of the mail, and so I must close my account thus early this time. Dr Curwen will probably write you also.

Wilfred T. Grenfell

Spreading fish, West Turnavik. At right, Capt. William Bartlett.

Moravian mission station, Hopedale.

Moravian mission station, Hopedale.

Inuit winter houses, Hopedale.

Tuesday, August 29th.	Another good night in sleeping bag; morning very wet so kept in; mail steamer not arrived today so cannot return to Hopedale yet. After dinner Mr. Fry & I went out fishing with Mr. Eli & caught 30 or 40 fish in a couple of hours. Back to tea at 7 & chat later on in evening. About 10.30 see a vessel with a light three miles off – she can be nothing but the steamer, for none of the schooners carry lights at night; pack up & in a little time we are bundled aboard & reading letters, then writing.
Wednesday, August 30th.	Up early to finish letters; went into Windsor's Harbour at 6 a.m. Hopedale at 10; slept on couch fearing the bunks for they have a very bad reputation. Arrived on board & found one of our crew had fallen from halfway up the mizzenmast while scraping it and was badly hurt. Brought with us a man from Long Tickle who had been very badly treated by the Dr. on the mail boat;[58] he will have to lose all one finger but I hope we shall save the hand.
	Tidings just come in that Nathaniel, an Esquimaux who was aboard here on Saturday, was drowned last night at Double Island while fishing.
	Mail boat gone on to Fanny's Harbour & will be back in a few hours.
Thursday, August 31st.	No sooner had we reached the Albert yesterday than a smart N. breeze sprang up, & when I had finished my writing it was too rough to go ashore. Today the wind has not abated – a hard gale blowing – so that I have been confined on board, skinning birds, & clearing up, & printing photographs. The mail steamer which should have returned last evening did not arrive till 4 p.m., having been weatherbound further down; we put our mail on "Mary Grenfell" & manned the boat with four oars but the wind was so strong she drifted to leeward & would have gone across the harbour onto the rocks had not one of the men caught hold of the dinghy, which was riding astern.
	A long trapboat came aboard later on & we bribed the men with a lb. of tobacco to take our mail for us. The mailboat dropped an

Inuit family, Okak.

Inuit with deerskin tent, Okak.

anchor, but the chain broke, so she had to put a rope ashore & hold onto the rocks.

Friday, September 1st.   Wind moderating; glass still very low. At 11 Messrs. Simon & Fry came on board & released me, taking me ashore to dinner in afternoon. I saw several Esquimaux patients, Mr. Keastner acting as interpreter; one house I visited was very interesting, being built very much in the style of the old Esq. houses, there being no walls, the roof sloping up from the ground & the small square window in the roof being filled not with glass but with the scraped gut of the "square flipper" seal; the window being already broken I was allowed to help myself to a little of the membrane.

Lydia's house was very large & clean; she was busy at her needlework; sews *very* well & has a good sewing machine; she showed me how to dress sealskins; was sorry to find she was suffering from consumption – a disease *very* common among the Esquimaux; she is the tallest Esq. I have seen.

Tea on shore. Many fishermen on board in evening; there are 48 schooners in harbour going s., many with scarcely any fish; one crew of 10 & 2 girls had only 30 quintals!

Saturday, September 2nd.   Find it very hard to even write diary, friends ashore being so very kind & grudging us any time we spend aboard. Mr. K. says, "I seem to have known you for years already"; it must be a treat to have some visitors, for their life is a very lonely one. They give us the whole of their time and I wish the weather was better that we might be out more.

Today was fine however; kept busy on board till 11; ashore to dinner at 12. Examined meteorological tables (Mr. Simon's); highest temp. in last 4 yrs. was 98°F. in shade in 1889; coldest last winter 26°F. below zero, i.e. 58° of frost; warm weather lasts so short a time that average for year is 28°F.; the day has been warm, but tonight thermom. is 36°F.

Visited graveyard & saw graves of many missionaries & their children, including 2 of Mrs. K. & 2 of Mrs. H.; the oldest was that of Swen Anderson, born in 1746 & died in 1816 – stone was freestone & in very good preservation; the oldest slate stone was 1855 & well preserved; but an old (abt. 1820) Purbeck marblestone was illegible; the inscription on the wooden "stones" over Esq. graves were painted in black paint; the wood had been much worn where not painted, but so great was the preserving action of the paint that in many cases the inscription stood ⅛ in. above the rest of the wood.

Saw several very old heathen Esq. graves; the bodies (man & wife) were laid on the bare rock & stones had been piled up over & around them; in one case the bones (skulls missing) were plainly seen & reached through the stones; the people very much dread the bones being touched.

From the heathen graves we walked to the remains of the houses of the heathen times, and scraped about in the "koppenmöddings," as they would be called in Denmark, or heaps of shells & bones, the remains of the meals of the days of long ago; the shells were mostly mussel shells & there were thousands of them; bones belonged to various animals. I found part of a whale's scapula & vertebra, several pieces of seal's skull & scapula, deer's lower jaw & various bones belonging to animals I could not identify right off. I was greatly rejoiced at finding the horn socket of the iron tip to a seal harpoon and a piece of the runner of a komatik or sledge made out of the rib of a whale. Mr. Keastner was much amused at my eagerness & Mr. Fry gave me much help.[59]

Run of patients at night; many with bad teeth which were duly removed.

Letter from Dr Bobardt to the MDSF

Mission Hospital, Battle Harbour, Labrador,
September 1893

These lines will again give you the information that we are all well here, and everything progresses well.

For the wants of the people the hospital is not large enough – that is, if one admitted all who wanted to come into the hospital and be treated as in-patients, but many of them are really not ill enough for this. Our capacity is eight; that is all we have bedsteads, beds, and bedding for. I have had about 400 out-patients, the majority suffering from rather bad ailments, and needing attendance.

There has been one death in the hospital, a young girl, aged twenty, suffering from scurvy. She came here from the north, in the mail boat, and was almost dead when she was brought here. Poor girl! She had been cook on one of the fishing smacks, and was in a most pitiable condition on her arrival here. I have never seen a more filthy and miserable case in my experience; there was never any hope. It seems a great pity that such a system of employing young girls on board these smacks should exist. Their environment is by no means always of the purest, and they have a very hard time of it, struggling for the few dollars they earn and an existence.

The hospital, as I said, is now full, and always is filled when the mail boats arrive. They have always brought a full complement of patients. Already some, sooner than return without treatment, have stayed out at some of the settlers' houses, so as to be under medical treatment. There is not the slightest doubt but that the work done and to be done is absolutely necessary, and one can feel satisfied sometimes in hearing how grateful the people are to have their bodily wants attended to. And then one has many opportunities of preaching God's Word to them. How the settlers got on before I know not. I suppose they had to get well or perish.

I have been holding many services.

Albert Bobardt

Sunday, September 3rd.   Cold, wet, raw. Service on board in morning; abt. 40 present. In afternoon I took service in the chapel ("Hidden treasure") & had a congreg. of about 140. The dogs seem to have a great aversion to the services, for the bell may ring for anything else & they will be quiet, but when it is for service the "Hopedale band" is many & deep tongued. Missionary's house turned into hospital outpatient department, patients being dark-skinned, black-haired Esquimaux needing Mr. K's assistance as interpreter. The men & women have very long, straight, jet-black hair which is worn very long & a man must be very old if it is to turn at all grey; Mr. K. has never known an Esq. with hair of a lighter colour.

In evening chapel again, full of schoonermen & women, Capt. conducting.

Received present of a beautiful bunch of flowers from the garden; the stocks, mignonette & pansies could not be beaten in Hampstead, and the nemophila is the finest I have seen anywhere. We are kept well supplied with greens & lettuce.

Monday, September 4th.   Patients on board till 11; foggy so schooners cannot get away although the wind is fair.

Operated on a native, Mr. & Mrs. K. assisting valuably. Shall be very sorry to leave Hopedale; in fact I am almost a member of the

Employees of the Moravian mission, Hopedale. Left to right: Sybilla (Frau Hansen's nurse), Benigna (Frau Simon's nurse), Bertha Anderson (kitchen girl), Benigna (blubber yard), unnamed woman (blubber yard), unnamed woman (Frau Kästner's nurse), Lydia (needlewoman), and Salome (washerwoman).

household, having dinner & tea and many cigars with them every day. After dinner showed Mr. & Mrs. Simon my photographs; too wet to do anything out of doors; saw more native patients in their own houses. At 5 Capt. & I gave a tea party on board; they all came, and we got on pretty well; the two little boys of 6 & 4 were much taken up with the two kittens and much preferred plain biscuit, which they knew, to figs & French plums, which were new to them.

In the evening we gave a magic lantern lecture on views of the Holy Land in the chapel; there were 110 men & 40 women; Capt. worked the lantern while I explained in English to the fishermen, Mr. Keastner interpreting to the Esquimaux.

This morning I bought a very fine seal harpoon from Nathan; he had used it for 5 years, and I was interested to see that the walrus ivory socket for the iron point was of exactly the same size & shape as the socket I had found in the refuse heap of a house, which had

Brass band, Hopedale.

been represented merely by a depression (square) in the ground for more than 100 years & dating from the old heathen time – the missionaries have worked here 120 years. Later in the day Mr. K. gave me a very old lamp used in the heathen time; it is a large, heavy soapstone open dish & burnt three wicks.

Tuesday, September 5th.   A quiet morning spent on board & seeing patients on shore. After dinner went over the storehouses with Mr. Simon & bought two sealskins – a ranger & a whitecoat. In evening there were many schooners in bay so we had a meeting on shore, abt. 60 attending.

Wednesday, September 6th.   Dull wet day. Saw dogs being fed & regretted want of sunlight for a photograph; they are fed on blubber & caplin every other day & know well when to expect & how to appreciate the meal; they fight over the food, the weakest going to the wall; this time the weakest was "Silver," the leader, who has a swollen face & lame leg, the result of recent fights with his neighbours.

Labrador Odyssey

I took a spade & dug over the remains of the old heathen houses; found a few pieces of bone from a komatik but nothing of any value.

Mr. Keastner & I went in Josiah's house to ask about the moss commonly burnt in the open soapstone lamps; J. when he understood our meaning brought out a very old lamp similar to the one Mr. K. gave me on Monday (called kollik [*qulliq*]); he said it was very old & had never seen it used (he is 58); he made me a present of it & said he did not want payment, but was delighted later in the day with a present from me of powder & shot.

Dr. G. & Mr. Hansen returned in steam launch about 5.30 after 12 days absence; they had been to Zoar, Nain & Okak and had had a good time; was relieved to see them as we had had no news of them from any schooner passing by here from the North; they had been on the rocks 4 times.

In the evening Daniel & Clementina came in from Double Island; C. had Benjamin's baby, & they report that the night before Asa Benj. the boy of 12 was taken ill suddenly with the very symptoms shown by the 4 women before they died – weakness, coldness & loss of sensation in extremities & throat & breathing symptoms – and that Benj. was much cast down about it; Ben. & Tom Brown had left Ben's Cove & gone to Double Island to fish; they told us everyone believed Tom Brown had killed the women.

Thursday, September 7th. Up at 4.30 & Mr. Hansen, G., Capt., & I start in steam launch for Double Island 20 miles away; after going half an hour it was thought necessary to put back as it was very rough outside and the piston of the engine was needing repairs badly – "She can only run half an hour more," said the engineer. Greatly regret having to give up going to ferret this case out, but there was no other way of getting to the island so we had to give it up; some new light had been thrown on the matter by the suspected cause of the death of two Esq. three yrs. ago (Joel's brother & his wife), and I was *most* anxious to obtain the flour & molasses for analysis.

No special incidents; heaps of kindness shown to all of us, but this is an everyday occurrence; much enjoyed long talk with Mr.

Benjamin and son (left) and Tom Brown.

Hansen. In evening visited about a dozen schooners in the harbour in Joel's kayak – or flat-bottomed canoe made of sealskin stretched over a light wooden frame. By the bye Joel many years ago murdered his infant child in Newfoundland; this he has confessed to the missionaries.

In the evening we had 104 men & 30 women to the service in the chapel.

Friday, September 8th. Gerhardt Keastner's birthday; he is 6 yrs. old & next birthday will be spent on "Harmony" on his way to Europe.

Morning spent on board; shore to dinner; took photos of the Esq. dogs feeding; they are fed every other day on seal's blubber & caplin in order to keep them from pillaging the gardens; they are hungry animals & eat anything that comes in their way, usually visiting any empty fishing boat that is by the rocks for what they can get; one day they found the chapel door open & demolished the hymn books that had been handled by greasy hands & had well thumbed pages. They eat the food given them as though they never expected to be fed again, fighting for every scrap most vigorously and it is necessary to stand over them with a long walrus hide whip to prevent the dogs belonging to the Esquimaux joining in the meal.

This afternoon was celebrated by tea in the gardens – true German fashion, a band being the only element missing.

There being fewer schooners in the bay we did not have more than 50 men at the service.

Saturday, September 9th.   Morning on board reading & seeing patients; had arranged to go for a long walk in afternoon but this was prevented by rain; wind strong from N. Long talk with Mr. Hansen in evening.

Sunday, September 10th.   A fine day but a good deal of wind in morning; the painter of the missionaries' dory broke & the little boat drifted from the ship onto the rocks; fortunately not much damage done. "Princess May" dragged anchor & would have been on the rocks had she not been fastened to us by a rope.

Visited schooners to tell them of the services; there were 74 in the harbour, all going south with their fish. Some were good-sized vessels – that is up to 96 tons – but some very, very small & totally unfitted for so long a voyage; 74 is the largest number I have seen in the harbour at one time.

From 50–60 in the morning meeting; in the afternoon the chapel seemed quite full, there being 246 present; while we are here the missionaries refuse to take any service for the fishermen, asking us to relieve them; the people seemed to enjoy the service though some were very sleepy & all unresponsive apparently; I cannot make the N.F. fishermen out; they are unlike any other class of men I have seen; as often as not I have to ask for "thank you" from a patient, & they will receive books, woollens & even coals &c. without showing any gratitude; should I hail any of them in a boat with "Good Morning" or "What Cheer, Old Skipper?" I have learned to expect stares and not words or signs in reply.

There were about 350 at the evening meeting and it was with utmost difficulty that we could find seats for them even on the floor; G. spoke to them on the subject of sleep at a [prayer] meeting &c. as the urging of the devil.

Patients till 11 p.m.

Report of Dr Grenfell to the MDSF, 26 August to 11 September

Princess May, Hopedale, September 5, 1893
Dear Mr. Editor:

As I was leaving the region visited by the mail steamer, I was obliged to post my last letter to you early. We left early on Saturday, August 26, for Zoar, which is the second station of the Moravian missionaries, and is sixty-five miles north of this. I was accompanied by one of the Moravians, an old friend of last year, the Rev. P.N. Hansen, a Dane and an earnest Christian evangelist, able to speak German, Eskimo and English – invaluable accomplishments to us – in order to interpret for the natives who should come to visit us.

The charts north of Hopedale are very imperfect, and so except for the general direction, we discarded their use entirely, especially as we found the large number of islands made it quite impossible to recognize individual ones, and so the outline even and names (of those that rejoice in names at all) became useless. We borrowed instead a long wood ladder from the Mission station and lashed it upright against our mast. From the top of this we could see shoals that were whitish long before we were in any danger, but black shoals were more troublesome – that is, those covered with the long larix weed [*Rhodomela cobfervoides*]. On our way we met a solitary boat, a settler going up his bay, and he was indeed glad to meet us and receive a bundle of reading. We were quite free this day from icebergs, the outer islands keeping them out, and the tall trees on the side of some of the passages in the bright sunlight made me think of Switzerland.

At night, about nine, we dropped anchor in Zoar, and our steam whistle brought out the solitary missionary, the Rev. G. Schultze.[60] Most warmly he welcomed us, and we were his guests over the Sunday. Five years ago here an Eskimo had fired at the missionaries and endeavoured to break into the store, and so the Society had thought wise in this place to close the store, the result being many of the Eskimo have left for a Hudson Bay station some twenty-five miles away, where they have stores at hand. Zoar will, therefore, soon be abandoned as a station, though, but for the mosquitoes and sandflies, we agreed it was the most picturesquely situated and best protected of all. Sunday was, therefore, a very quiet day, and my two men on the launch, the missionary, his wife, Mr. Hansen, and one Eskimo, formed our whole congregation. We were really glad of the rest.

Monday morning, August 28, we were early at work loading the *Princess May* with wood, for we were now beyond the regions of coal. A queer picture she looked when we had finished, smothered all over with chopped wood, and not room to move from one end to the other. We left five sacks of coal here for our return journey. All day long we steamed north, but went by mistake five miles up a bay in a large island called Kikkertavak, so that we lost some time. Mr. Hansen had once been to Nain by komatik and dogs, but the country then was deep in snow, and all the water also frozen and snow-covered, so that he was unable to identify the usual land-marks. At sundown we sighted high cliffs in our passage, which we thought preceded the entrance to Nain Harbour. It was now rapidly becoming dark, while we continued to steam on and on, hoping every minute to sight the Nain Mission-house lights. At length the man in the boat sang out that the water began to be shallow, and before we had time to stop her we touched a soft muddy bottom.

We were soon, however, off again, and, retracing our way a short distance, dropped our anchor in two fathoms of water. In the night the peculiar position of the launch roused me, and I got up to find Mr. Hansen had rolled on to the floor. Climbing on deck, I found we were high and dry, and the *Princess May* was also lying down at rest. The returning tide floated us in the morning, while we gathered more wood from the bank. At 8.30 we sighted a tent, and made out a boat also at anchor. Here we steamed, and soon a kajak came off to us. Then we went ashore and found it to be a tent made of reindeer skins. Two Eskimo women, dressed (as they all do) like the men, with skin trousers and mocassins, emerged and warmly welcomed Mr. Hansen, whom they knew at once. We found we were close to Nain, and as a young Eskimo named Cephas was just about to start thither with a boat-load of salmon trout, we offered to tow him in return for piloting us. This we did only too well, for we towed his "dory" or flat-bottomed boat right under water, and had to delay while we re-collected the trout that were loose.

We received an exceedingly warm welcome in Nain from the Rev. A. Martin,[61] superintendent of the whole Moravian Mission on this coast, and from his colleagues, Mr. Kahle[62] and Mr. Waldman.[63] We also met at this station Miss [Mary Hannah] Ridgeway, a young Manchester lady who had come out a fortnight before in the *Harmony* to be the bride of the Rev. Mr. Townley.[64] Mr. Townley was away in Ramah, and would be unable to get down until the return journey of the *Harmony*. Here we had a few Eskimo patients, and spent an exceedingly happy day.

On Wednesday [30 August] the fine weather tempted us to pursue our journey, especially as the Eskimo were chiefly out at their fishing stations, and would have time to learn we were coming down, and so to gather at Nain by then, if they wished to see us. Our charts extended no further, and I only had the loan of an amateur chart made for the *Harmony*, which proved to be more valueless than my last; so we arranged with out friend Cephas, who was an old Okkak man, to take us down, which he did very creditably. He, to the end of his life, will probably be a great man, having had charge of one of the few steamers that have ever been to that station.

The distance travelled this day was 95 miles, a good record, as we had only wood to burn and a strong head wind the latter part of the day. The coast becomes simply magnificent as you get north. Cape Mugford rises over 3,000 ft. almost sheer from the sea, while the "Kiglapeit" Mountains and the "Kaumajet" also rise to even greater heights, more or less abruptly along their whole extent. We passed many Newfoundland fishing schooners during the day, anchored in coves and bights, all the way down; while north of us still would be at least 800 schooners, carrying from five to fifteen men each, and one or two women. These were mostly beyond Cape Heyford, between that and Cape Chidley. Being late now in the year, and the weather being already boisterous, while at eight it froze and during the day we had some snow, I thought it advisable to go no further north this year in a vessel only 8 ft. wide, and not a good sea boat. Thus, beyond going north to visit two Eskimo stations next day, returning the same evening to Okkak, we now reached the turning-place of our cruise this year.

It was nine o'clock exactly on Wednesday night, Aug. 30, when we dropped anchor in Okkak, while we vigorously blew our steam whistle to salute the station. Soon we saw moving lights on the shore, and launching our little boat we made for the nearest. These we found to be a number of Eskimo, who, in return to our salutations, escorted us up to the Mission-house. The missionaries had just begun to guess something had happened, and we might have fallen from the moon, so great was the surprise of receiving visitors in this out-of-the-way place. Mr. Jannasch,[65] the head of the house, told us that, except for Lieutenant Peary's steamer which had called to buy dogs, he did not know of any steamer having ever been to Okkak. Mr. Hansen was, of course, well known to them, and a warmer welcome than these self-sacrificing servants of God gave us I never want to experience. We have all felt that our intercourse and conversations with these Moravian brothers and sisters have been a privilege such as it is seldom our lot to obtain. The parting always was a task, even though we only were with them two or three days at longest, especially when we remembered our own homes and loved ones in England that we hoped to see at Christmas, while these self-sacrificing people are here for life, separated from country, home, and friends, in this bleak and frost-bound land, cut off from almost every privilege of civilisation. Will our readers remember in their prayers the difficult work and special difficulties of these brave servants of Christ.

The two days we were at Okkak we had plenty of work. Sufferers from all kinds of complaints were brought from many neighbouring stations – some who had lost limbs from impossibility of skilled help – two men blind, whose sight might still have been theirs, and others who showed only too clearly how great a boon the visit of a medical man even occasionally would be to this large population. There are 350 Eskimos in Okkak, and constantly fishing schooners are visiting the harbour on their voyages north and south. It is not usual, Mr. Editor, to harrow our readers with details of surgical and medical cases, but to enforce the point I wish to insist on I will record here the details of one case only at Okkak. A young man of twenty-five, named Abraham, in the fulness of health and strength came for advice with the following history. Two months before he had broken his right arm at the shoulder, and had had done for it only the rough treatment his brother Eskimos could render. The arm ever since had been very painful, and was now fixed at an angle of about 45 degrees from the body, so that, besides the pain, the poor fellow could not work, at that season of the year on which almost a whole year's diet depends. On examination we could find no evidence of broken bone, but what appeared to be a deep abscess, and a *very* extensive one. This eventually proved to be the case, and before an hour was over the pain had gone, the limb was movable, and the man's life was almost out of danger. The gratitude in the poor fellow's eyes was ample reward, and he asked Mr. Hansen to say, "Money he had none to pay with, but he would ask his Saviour to make a reward for him." I can only echo the prayer, and trust that God may enable the MDSF to extend a work the privilege of having a part in which would alone make life worth living for.

We left Okkak at eight o'clock at night, and, taking watch and watch, steamed all night back to Nain. We had to pass through a great deal of ice, which, unknown to us, a strong easterly wind had brought on the shore, and at times between cliffs and icebergs, it was not easy to get along; but there was not a breath of wind, and the moon did not fail us, so we saved a day, and by breakfast-time were once more in Nain.

It being Saturday (September 2), we determined to stay over Sunday, our men meanwhile cleaning up the *Princess May*, and reloading her with wood. We found a number of Eskimo had collected here for us, and also one or two English settlers were here. We were entertained in the Mission-house, and on Sunday had a nice English meeting in the afternoon. Numbers of patients again attended till nearly eleven at night, Mr. Hansen kindly interpreting for me. Early morning (September 4) we made preparations for starting, having obtained photographs, as usual, of the station, our hosts, and many Eskimo friends. We had obtained a guide, who wished to go part of the way to his fishing station at a place called Tak Tok; but rain, wind, and fog made him decide not to risk his boat, which we were to tow, so eventually we left alone. The first thirty miles we made easily enough by the help of a rough sketch of a special chart made by the *Harmony*'s captain, and by our own chart, made as we came up. But then coming into open water, the sea lop [choppy wave] and the dense fog determined us to seek shelter for the night, and we ran up into an uncharted bay.

Mr. Hansen and myself landed, in spite of the rain, to stretch our legs, and were much surprised to find when we reached the rocks that they consisted of Labradorite, a kind of stone which shines with resplendent blue sheen when seen in certain lights. The small cabin of the *Princess May* was very welcome when we returned, and our sleep was unbroken on the lockers which serve for beds, as we rocked to our anchor. The fore deck had, we found, become leaky, and, as accommodation was always very poor, there being only just room for the two men to lie down, our steward and mate and boat-swain and able-bodied seaman, combined in the person of Llewel-lyn Owen, one of the *Albert*'s men, henceforth took up his quarters on our cabin floor, where we spread a couple of sealskins and dogskin pillow for him. We left the bay at 4 p.m., as soon as the daylight enabled us to pick our way out, and again in thick fog we steamed to Zoar for breakfast. Mr. Schultze gladly welcomed us, especially as his last child, a little girl of seven years, had left him by the *Harmony* three weeks before for Germany, and was ill at the time, and he expected us to bring news of her. We had seen her at Okkak, waiting to leave the coast, and were indeed glad to be able to report well. We felt very much for Mrs. Schultze; all her children, eight in number, are in Europe for education, and she is now quite alone. She told us she would be glad to have the care of a child to cheer the house again, and laughingly suggested that Mr. Hansen should lend one from Hopedale.

After lunch we left again for the south, expecting to anchor at night in Davis Inlet, a station of the Hudson's Bay Fur Trading Com-pany. Alas! no such fortune was to be ours, for at 6 p.m., though in good light, we had the misfortune to run on a narrow reef with a falling tide, and found it impossible, in spite of all our exertions, to get off again. We at once proceeded to take precautions to prevent her from chafing. Our wood ladder was lowered over the starboard side, and the vessel listed over on the port side. Then the ladder was run underneath on the starboard side, and made to rest on flat rocks. Between the ladder and the bilge we then lashed a very large block of wood, and then made the vessel lean over on the top of it, putting all the weight now on the starboard side to keep her resting on it, and so lashed all together. Having taken all other precautions we thought necessary, we turned in to sleep two hours at a time till we should float again, which we did safe and sound at 2.15 a.m.

At 3.30 a.m. we dropped anchor in Davis Inlet; at breakfast time we went ashore to call on the Hudson's Bay Company's agent, but found he and all hands were away up the bays collecting trout. The quanti-ties of sea trout to be caught may be guessed by the not unusual catch of one man this year. He took ninety barrels of two hundredweight each for the season, that is in all 20,160 lbs. of trout – a quantity that will make the ears of any trout fisherman tingle who is accustomed to fish English rivers. Of course I need not say they were netted.

This night we reached Hopedale, passing Fanny's Harbour, near Cape Harrison and Malta Harbour, which Dr. Curwen had undertaken to visit from the *Albert* by sailing boat. We passed forty to fifty schooners, all bound south, looking like small North Sea fleets at times. We counted twenty-seven in one batch. We steamed close alongside as many as possible, and threw them a bundle of reading aboard as we passed. As we neared Hopedale again our spirits rose, though, as I had arranged for the *Albert* to leave for the south on the previous Friday, we did not expect to find her in harbour.

Some Eskimos sighted the launch as she came down the run and as we rounded the harbour point we found the Mission flags up, the *Albert* all decorated, while guns were fired, and boats came off to meet us as if we were Royalty itself. These people are a most loyal people. All such days as the Queen's birthday are kept religiously, and the missionaries told us that unwarlike as they are, they had actually repeatedly asked if they could help when England was going to war in Egypt, and had actually endeavoured to drill – an effort not encouraged, however.

They are more convinced than ever that Her Majesty the Queen will await our arrival at Yarmouth, and both Dr. Curwen and myself are charged with repeated messages of gratitude to Her Majesty for the Hospital Gospel Ship. A more demonstratively grateful people I have never met. It may be interesting to learn that no holiday or fête of any kind is kept without it ends in service in the chapel – the people would not consider it a holiday otherwise – and the teaching most appropriate for the particular occasion that can be derived from God's Word is then given. Thus the Queen's birthday serves to introduce the subject of how God would have His servants act towards those in authority over us, and so on …

Yours very faithfully,
Wilfred Grenfell

Monday, September 11th. G. has settled to go south in launch; we are to wait a few days longer because so many schooners going south call in at Hopedale.

Having had no exercise off board for several weeks & feeling doughy as a result I got Mr. Simon & Mr. Fry to come off in a boat with two of our men; we hoped for enough wind to take us about 3 miles to "Black Head" – a very bold trap rock head – but were disappointed & had to row; neither Mr. S. nor Mr. F. had been to a certain large pond or small lake – N.F.ders call all sheets of fresh water "ponds" – about a sq. mile in extent, so it took us a long time to find it in the broken country; at 2.30 we had given up hopes of finding it, so made a fire & had dinner.

We found the water at 4.30 & fished for an hour but got not even a rise; the bottom was all sand & stone & there being no mud or vegetable growth on the bottom I doubt if there is a single fish in the pond. At 6 o'clock as it was beginning to get dusk we heard a loud calling and saw a large goose in the middle of the pond; it was certainly not shy as it made a great noise, probably calling for its mate, but its mate was more wary & kept out of sight and so did not receive a shower of shot about it; unfortunately Mr. S's gun scatters the shot very much & so the bird could only have received one or two pellets; he dived & came up nearer the other side and continued to call in a laughing manner; I went round & lay in wait and at one time he seemed to be coming within range, but he turned back and kept well away, and after keeping me lying down in wet moss for half an hour he gave a "ha ha" as I got up to walk away.

It was nearly dark when we got to our boat & it took us 1½ hrs. to row home.

Tuesday, September 12th. Morning fine; wrote letters & printed photographs. Dinner ashore & then another chat with Mr. Hansen. Mr. H. went over & corrected with me the notes I took of the address I asked Zacharias to give [on our behalf] at the end of the Sunday afternoon service: Z. is the man Mr. H. takes as guide & interpreter on his komatik journeys in the winter; he is one of the "chapel servants" and is the brightest Christian in Hopedale, not subject to the fits of depression which all the other Esquimaux, even Daniel, suffer from. The interpretation runs, "My dear friends, we have not all the same language but we have the same love to the Saviour; so it is always: if we are one with Him, we are joined to one language & one love in Him. Love each other because Jesus Christ brought love to us; therefore if we are joined in love to Jesus like we are here together in this house we shall be brought to Him and stand before His throne as one Assembly. This love is prepared before Jesus Christ descended from heaven; therefore we shall all bring praise & thanks to Him who has first loved us; it is our duty to do that every day."

"The people of the world cannot join in our coming together and cannot love one another as we can, but only the people of God can rejoice when they come together. We must always develop it in our daily life, that we are Sons of God. None of us know when we shall be called from this world; therefore we ought to be prepared to enter Eternity."

"We are here that we shall have food for our souls – not for the body – as our bodies must have daily food, so our souls must be fed day by day. We shall love one another in the name of Jesus that His love may reign in us; because we are baptized in one baptism we are really one in Him and shall be with Him forever."

"Perhaps tomorrow we shall have to depart from some of the friends we love, but we shall not be separated from them when we have come to our Eternal home. Therefore in the name of the Lord we wish to bid you good-bye."

In the evening we had some music in Mr. Hansen's room, and after that a service in the chapel; the sharp ears detected the whistle of the mailboat during the meeting and at the close we met the Capt. of "Windsor Lake," who had come ashore; our Capt. went about getting coal from "W.L." for our launch, and I returned on board to see patients, finish my letters and wait patiently till Capt. returns with our letters.

Good night all.

Wednesday, September 13th.	Morning spent on board. Afternoon spent visiting Esq. patients.
	Good meeting in evening; was asked to visit a girl on a schooner in the harbour; saw her 11.30; very ill.
Thursday, September 14th.	She came on board 4.30 a.m. & at 7 Dobbie called me saying, "There's a female patient on board and her schooner's left!"; divided hospital into two with curtains and stowed her safely – pleurisy with effusion.

Dinner 11.00; at 12 Mr. & Mrs. K., Mr. & Mrs. S., Mr. H., Mr. Fry, Capt., I & two Esquimaux (Ambrose & Joshua) got into the "Mary of Hopedale" and went for a "sail"; there being no wind we had to bend to the oar and rowed & rowed & rowed to Illuvertalik, aksenai-ing all the Esq. we passed on the road & shooting a couple of "sea pigeons." On landing on the island Mrs. K. set about preparing tea, the Esq. fetching wood and water while we walked to some old heathen Esq. graves at the end of the island; we found nine but none of them were perfect, having been visited by a destroyer who had removed all the bones before I had a chance; in the old time the body was laid on a bare stone – should the man's wife or the woman's husband "break the heart" the two bodies were laid side by side – and built over with large stones loosely put together so that in a perfect grave like one here at Hopedale the bones are very visible from outside.[66] Hearing there were two more graves at the other end of the island Ambrose guided Mr. H., Mr. F. & me but these we found completely broken up; Ambrose pointed out a cave in which he had slept with his parents when out fishing ten years ago. We saw a shallow hole in a bank made by a fox for shelter, but no birds were visible except a flock of ducks about 800 yards out to sea, & these proved an excellent target for the rifle for a *short* time. Were very glad of tea after the walk. Too little wind to sail home, so another long pull. Reached harbour 7.30 – ten or eleven schooners in, so service at 8.

Friday, September 15th.	Another still summer day – yesterday & today two of the warmest days we have had, $\tau = 78°$. Last night was very warm & contrasted

with that of 9th when т. was 30°ϝ. on shore & 35° on board. Dr. G. wants us to be at Turnavik Islands for Sunday, but today it is too calm to leave. The afternoon was spent in dentistry; in the morning Mr. Simon [a trained metal worker] made a tool in the blacksmith's shop to my pattern and after dinner I used it in stopping one of Mr. H.'s teeth. Walked along the Jubilee Walk – the walk built last fall to commemorate the 150th year of Moravian Mission work – with Mr. & Mrs. H. and much enjoyed the small trees & wild flowers and views across Avertok to the islands outside; the flowers in the garden do not cease to surprise me; I took a bunch of stocks, mignonette & pansies on board and all on ship agree that we have never seen pansies finer in size or quality.

No schooners in tonight so evening spent in playing & singing, concluding with "Ein feste burg."

Saturday, September 16th.   s.ε. wind very light & sometimes dropping altogether; Capt. decided not to sail as he did not wish to spend Sunday at sea in a calm; the wisdom of this was seen later in the day and felt too by those who had a share in rowing the "Mary Grenfell" home from Black Head. After dinner Mr. K., Mr. H., Mr. F., Capt. & I went with Ambrosius & Joshua – two Esquimaux – in one boat to visit some old graves at Black Head – a high trap-rock ending to an otherwise fairly low schist island.

We landed & walked a mile over very rough ground and on the way disturbed a flock of geese but could not get within range. We found 5 or 6 graves, but only one of these was nearly perfect, some of the stones of the others having fallen in; the graves, like the others seen, consisted of loose stones built round the body, which had been placed on the bare rock; I found parts of 3 skulls, but none perfect, and various other bones, but they had all been well "weathered." In one grave, evidently that of a woman, I found a number of teeth of a polar bear perforated in one fang for stringing together, probably for a necklace, and several pieces of thin copper, shaped with several perforations, which were used probably as ornaments, being sewn to the sillapak [*silapaaq*];[67] with these were two small, triangular plates of stone, perforated near the most acute angle & used probably in the necklace; a small disc of ?lead, a ?lead needle of a large size, a bone handle for [a] knife with the remains of an *iron* rivet, the bone button for [the] walrus hide sling which connects the dogs' traces with the komatik, and the broken remains of a soapstone lamp similar to the one Mr. Keastner had given me, but smaller; in this grave the only bone seen was a piece of a rib. In another grave I found a large piece of a whale's bone which had been hollowed out. The graves with most bones contained no other objects of interest.

Ambrose told me they were very, very old; no doubt they are more than 150 yrs. old, but how much older it is not possible to say without knowing more of the early trading opportunities of the people; there is plenty of copper in Labrador, & near Hopedale too, but I believe there is no evidence to show that it was ever worked by the people; nor is there any reason to believe that the iron rivet in the knifehandle was a native product. I was very interested to hear Ambrose say when I showed him the knife handle that perhaps it was the handle of a stone knife, for it showed he was familiar with the fact that 100 or 200 yrs. ago knives were made of stone; Mr. Keastner tells me that when he was in the North 24 yrs. ago he saw many knives & daggers of stone beautifully shaped.

Near the graves were two large circles marked out with stones; these are the sites of two tents – reindeerskin tents – which were much used in summer in times gone by; they are still largely used in the North of Labrador & Dr. G. saw them at Okkak, but now at Hopedale there are only a few tents & they are of calico.

While at Black Head the wind changed suddenly to E. & blew very hard for a short time, and when we got back we found two schooners had collided in the harbour, but no damage had been done.

After tea I attended Esquimaux service in the chapel and tried to follow in the singing; Ambrose, our Esq. companion of the afternoon, played the organ really well; service concluded with "Eine feste Burg." Mr. K. & I groped our way arm in arm to a patient's house & then I went on board.

Sunday, September 17th.   An interesting but trying day, for saying "good-bye" is never pleasant. I went on shore to the 10 o'clock Esq. service as Ambrose had told me his baby was going to be baptized. This baby was born on Friday week, and on the following day I asked for an introduction; the baby was then very little darker than a European baby of the same age but had a characteristically flat face, and I was very interested to see five or six days later that it was much darker in tint. I noticed this same change in the baby of Sarah – widow of Nathaniel, who was drowned three weeks ago – which was born the same day as little Seth Ambrose.

The babies were well wrapped up in clothes, arms and all, not tied to a board as in Norway but fixed so that they could move as little as if they had been; outside all was a large white handkerchief which was knotted over the child's chest. Each baby was then placed on a pillow & covered with a muslin veil and then carried to the table at the appointed time, Seth Ambrose by Josephine and little Lydia by Benigna, two old women who were dressed for the occasion in their sillapâks. Mr. Simon baptized them, and after the service the children were taken to Mr. S.'s room to be untied – for I found it was customary for the missionary to lend the baptismal clothing and after the ceremony to give the parents a few clothes for the child. Mr. S. tells me clothes are lent for the baptism to ensure uniformity of appearance & decency, for some people are very poor & have no clothes for the children; he tells me he remembers one child being brought for baptism when it was a week old with nothing on but a big pocket handkerchief – this was at Hebron a few years ago; and at the same time the wife of a man who had murdered two of his children before & was the terror of the neighbourhood used to come to chapel with her child sitting in her amaut[68] – or the hood of the netsek or sillapâk – absolutely naked, & this even in mid-winter.

Mr. Hansen took the 11 o'clock service for schoonermen. At dinner we had new potatoes & carrots – the first taken from the garden this year.

At the afternoon service there were about 120 people, mostly schoonermen; Ambrose played the organ again; I told him I would give out the number of a hymn, then he was to play the tune and after that I would read a verse; but whenever I gave out a number he would play the tune on the opposite page of the book, coming back to the right tune when we began to sing, and this he did he told me because he thought I should like the variety!

Saw patients on board from 4 – 5.50 and then went on shore to tea, passing on the way several boatloads of Esq. who were off to the ship, Ambrose magnificent in a scarlet military uniform among them.

Capt. took evening service; there could have been very few men left on the 20 schooners in the harbour for the chapel was nearly full; *all* our crew was present, the ship being left in sole charge of my patient, who is himself a skipper, and he had instructions to let no one on board till we returned.

The Esquimaux had asked to give us a farewell meeting because they knew we were to leave tomorrow, so when the English service was over the bell was rung and all the people came; it was a very pretty sight, the women in their pinks & blues on one side of the chapel and the men with their straight black hair in their white sillapâks trimmed with red on the other; Mr. Keastner presided, and after the singing of "Safe in the arms of Jesus" in Esquimaux he read an address which seemed to be about Labrador, *Albert*, Capt. & "âniasiorte" [*aaniasiurti*] (or doctor) as far as I could make out; Daniel then got up & spoke, Mr. Hansen interpreting somewhat as follows: "Therefore before the living God we are thanking & praising because both our spirits and bodies are being cared for; but not only that, for our bodies also have experienced love from you. I personally know, for I have been in many places, that if the Gospel had not been brought we should have been enemies to God. I have experienced being hated by men because of faith in God. Now I know quite plain there is none in heaven like the Lamb of God; He alone is able to change the hearts. We should not have shown love to the fishermen coming down here if it was not for the love of Jesus. Therefore we are thankful you have come and want to say good-bye to you and to all believers. May He in His great love help that we may be among the redeemed."

Titus spoke in much the same strain, but it was harder to take down what he said; he exhorted all to mutual love, and spoke of God's reading the heart while man sees the outside only: "Therefore tell the believers in England that it is because of the long forbearance of Jesus Christ, which is the same as it was before, that we are still alive; therefore we are thanking and happy. I will close in this way."

Captain next addressed the Esq. thro Mr. Hansen, and then one of the people prayed; then we sang No. 11, "Free from the law, Oh blessed condition," we in English but they from memory in their own language, and after that I said a few words, Mr. K. offered prayer and we closed with "Abide with me."

I went to the door to shake hands with Daniel & Titus, and again received their blessing; and then everyone would shake hands and each wish Godspeed, or at least so I thought, for of course we could not understand one another; and when the men had gone the women came and this was much more trying, for they wept out their "nakutlarpotet" [*nakutlapotit*: thanks] and other messages.

Immediately after this service we went to the missionaries' house for another farewell meeting, or "love feast"; Mr. H. presided and took prayers, and the solemn little service ended with vain attempts to give expression to the feelings of thanks felt. It was late before we got on board, & 11.45 before the last patient had left.

TURNAVIK

Monday, September 18th.

A day of great contrasts; beginning in fog, fair wind and the company of friends and ending in fair weather, headwind and disaster and nearly loss of our dear little vessel. Capt. was very opposed to visiting Turnavik (West) in the "Albert" for the harbour entrance is so very small and thought it was enough if the steam launch called there; the launch did call on her way N. and we did not as we were far out to sea and we should have lost much time; besides the capt. of the ship, thinking it an unsuitable harbour for his ship, was justified in not putting in as the responsibility if any accident should occur would rest on him entirely & not on the Superintendent [Dr Grenfell].

Dr. G. left Hopedale & wished us to proceed to Turnavik on Thursday after receiving coals from "Windsor Lake"; Thursday & Friday we were becalmed, & Sat. was a headwind, so we did not leave till this morning. We left Hopedale with much regret, not only because we were leaving friends behind, but because we were leaving the best harbour for working among the schooners as they passed South – one Sunday 600 attended the meetings & in 3 weeks I had 250 patients. After leaving it was still a question with the Capt. whether he would go to Turnavik or go out to sea clear of the islands & rocks and sail straight to Holton; *no* good purpose could be achieved by going to Turnavik – the steam launch had been there going N. & going S. too, and Capt. & I had been there 2 days – and the dangers in sailing to it through the runs great and the difficulty in making the narrow harbour much greater. Capt. is in a very uncomfortable position as Dr. G., who is Superintendent of the Mission and has Capt. Trezise's appointment in his hands, gives orders as to where the "Albert" shall call but takes no share in any of the responsibility should a mishap occur in the attempt to carry out an injudicious or unsafe order.

A large number of the Esquimaux came off to bid us farewell again, and Capt. & I went ashore to bid good-bye once more; we received two beautiful bunches of flowers – that from Mr. Hansen consisted of stocks & mignonette. As we weighed anchor we were surrounded by boats of Esquimaux cheering and our gun rockets were answered by a discharge of guns and lowering of flags. The missionaries are really sorry we have gone; they are expecting the trading ship "Gleaner" and when she leaves they will see no one from the outside world till July of next year!

We had a pleasant run south but as there was but little wind made but slow progress; 20 schooners left Hopedale ¾ hr. before us but we passed them all & late in the afternoon they turned back to Windsor's Harbr. We had a long beat against a headwind from Windsor's Harbr. to West Turnavik & it was almost dark before we fired a gun rocket as a signal that we wanted a pilot. Capt. [William J.] Bartlett himself came off with a crew, & after shaking hands I went below to finish a letter, but came up again 10 minutes later in a hurry when I heard much running about on deck to find that we were lying broadside to the wind across the mouth of a cove, the bowsprit almost touching the steep rocks on the w. & the stern – well as soon as I got on deck it began to bump, bump, bump on a low ridge of smooth rocks to the E.

I at once saw what had happened; Capt. B. in his pleasure at seeing us again and in overconfidence had mistaken the blind tickle for the harbour mouth in the dark, and when he had found out his mistake had dropped both anchors to bring her up and prevent her running her bows between the rocks & getting jammed; this had the result of getting her broadside onto the rocks, and as a strong wind was blowing straight in, the position of the dear old boat seemed hopeless. It was not long before we had 50 or 60 willing men on board, but it took from 7 to 10 o'clock to get her clear off – three hours of hard pulling on ropes & cables attached to anchors we took out in boats, but even we should not have got her free unless the wind had dropped markedly & almost suddenly; the wind freshened again late in the night, and all next day it blew so hard that no boat was able to leave the harbour.

After getting clear she was taken in tow by six great trapboats which took her into the harbour & helped in the mooring. The bumping on the rocks was bad enough on deck, but down below it seemed ten times worse; my patient, who was in bed & ill with pleurisy, was not unnaturally greatly alarmed at the banging & quivering of the ship as she rose & fell heavily, and it was hard to imagine how a ship could stand this knocking about without springing a leak.

We got clear off, I am thankful to say, but it has been a bad thing for Capt. B., who is a downright good fellow, for his enemies will say he did what many men do on this coast, namely tried to wreck the ship to buy her cheap – only this summer [Capt John] Hennessy at E. Turnavik has bought two vessels – one a schooner of his own he *put* on the rocks, called her a wreck, put her up for auction, sold her for $30 to *himself*, *sailed* her to his harbour & made a fish stage of the wornout thing and now applies for the $1600 insurance! The other boat was one that touched on the rocks; he had it put up for auction, sold it as a total wreck for $100 (including her cargo of salt) to himself, got her off later in the day, put a crew in and sent her down the shore fishing!

Letter of Dr Bobardt to the MDSF

> Mission Hospital, Battle Harbour, Labrador,
> September 18, 1893

Since my last letter I have been kept busy. Since July 13 there have been 390 out-patients, and since July 20 there have been 27 in-patients, some suffering from severe forms of disease, others bad enough, but getting well after a few weeks' rest. One man had a very bad hand, which had been bad since the commencement of the summer, so it kept him from his duties. I amputated the middle finger of his left hand; he is now almost well; he has been in the hospital for five weeks. Another man, aged thirty, has been in the hospital since July 20, having been brought from a fishing village up the Straits of Belle Isle in the launch *Princess May.* He is very ill with phthisis, and I doubt whether he will ever get well again; still, he has been skilfully nursed by Nurse Carwardine, and I am certain but for such he would have been deceased long ago.

The use of the hospital has been conclusively proved when one considers the number of patients treated; all, of course, were not suffering from severe diseases, still there have been numerous poisoned inflamed fingers; quite a number of sore throats, which might have scared the neighbours very much, as the inhabitants very much dread diphtheria, for in Newfoundland it has wrought such great ravages in families.

In the summer one has not the best opportunity of judging the condition of this people, and one can only speak from hearsay as to the condition and state during the winter. The people seem to lack clothes very much. One man, a father of a family, had for his best a pair of trousers patched at the knees and in the seat, and these had been given him by his father. They originally belonged to a brother who was lost during the winter, having perished out in the snow. The grateful way in which he spoke of his father's gift was very touching.

Albert Bobardt

Tuesday, September 19th. A big run of patients; blowing hard & raining, so attended to patients on vessel & on shore all day.

Wednesday, September 20th. s. wind again so cannot proceed south. Instead went to see a patient at Island Harbour 12 miles from here in Ch. McNeal's boat (jack). Started at 11 a.m. but had to beat against a light wind round the point & did not land till 6.30.

Old Mrs. McNeal, aged 85, very ill & feeble; found 9 other jack-boats in the little harbour – there after the herring – so had a good meeting in evening. Ch. McNeal is a great hunter in winter & told me many deer stories; his aunt, Mrs. Lyall, is the great curiosity hunter of the coast and a good talker, so we got on well & learnt much about the few settlers on the coast.

Thursday, September 21st. While the jack was being ladened with barrels of herring & trout I went up the brook with McNeal's hopeful [son] of 7 yrs. & tried to find a few trout; it is not pleasing to hear that big trout were so thick at the beginning of *last* month that they could be caught with the hand, and that at the end of *next* month they will be thick again, when you know there are none there now.

In the afternoon the wind was contrary & it began to rain so there was no getting back and the time was spent talking & seeing the fine dogs & buying a good fox skin – cross between black & red.

Friday, September 22nd. Started in very light wind at 9 a m ; wind soon got stronger & from s.e.; that is, it blew straight from Turnavik; by 1 o'clock we had

Fish bawn, Emily Harbour. "After lying in salt 3 or more weeks the fish is washed and spread in the sun; it is spread for two days, gathered into piles each evening, then left in piles two days, and finally spread on the bawn for two more days."

made 3 miles good only and as it looked blacker & the lop was rising we thought it safer to run back to Island Harbr. again.

At 4.30 I went with Ch. McNeal to look for partridge, having first got into some of his sealskin boots; it was very wet underfoot & we walked through & along the edge of the woods for 1½ hr. without seeing any game at all; coming back another way we put up 5 or 6 plump-looking birds in the wood & shot one each, but the others got away & it was too thick for us to trace them; later on we shot a muskrat in the brook and then passing by a part where wood is usually cut in the winter I was shown the "clock" or sundial, a tall stick left standing in a clearing and a smaller stick as a guide to the hours.

In the evening after prayers Mrs. Lyall skinned the muskrat.

Labrador Odyssey

Broomfield family, Long Bight. "This family lives in a one-roomed log hut, the only furniture in which are a stove, a plank bunk, a box and two barrels. All are very scantily clothed, the children being practically naked, and often in the winter they all have to keep indoors. In October, they had already begun their winter's diet – 4 barrels of flour, 1½ lbs. tea and molasses – that was to last till July."

Saturday, September 23rd.

Started at 7 a.m. with a good wind; at 10.30 when abt. 3 miles away from Turnavik were met by Capt. Bartlett's steam launch with Capt. Trezise, Tom Evans & Bob Bartlett[69] on board; they had come to fetch me to take me to "the Cape" to see some old Esquimaux graves – two, one a single one of an old woman, the other contained skeletons of man & woman lying side by side; found remains of huts, & tischikoot [*tasikqut*][70] & a wooden bowl for washing skins in the single grave, & a button (copper) in the double one, outside which were the remains of the man's kyak.

Reached home abt. 4 p.m. & saw patients straight away till 11 p.m.

Sunday, September 24th.

Took service in a store in morning; as many people came as could find room among the barrels of flour & molasses; meeting again in afternoon & evening & the rest of the day *very* busy seeing patients.

Princess May in Hamilton Inlet.

Report of Dr Grenfell to the MDSF, to 24 September

Princess May, Emily Harbour (windbound, with
heavy westerly gale), September 23

Dear Mr. Editor:

My last letter was dispatched to you from the Western Turnavik
island after returning from visiting settlers in Kipakok Bay. I was so
impressed with the needs of these people that I determined to miss
no opportunity of visiting them, and as I could get wood enough in
the bays, not to run away with our stock of coal, I left early next
morning for Chensovik, Aillik, and Makkovik Bays. I have since
visited nearly all the settlers as far as Hamilton Inlet, have collected

statistics as to their numbers, ages, means of living, educational and moral condition, and have also visited since then Long Island, Manak Island, Aillik, Cape Harrison, Tinker's Harbour, Holton, Emily, Horse Harbour, and Dark Tickle, so you will understand our work has been constant. We have learnt much that has opened our eyes, and which, when reported to our committee in St. John's, will, I think, without doubt, lead to some remedial measures being undertaken by the Newfoundland Government. Altogether, as far as I can find, between Nain and here are some 300 souls, of English descent, who live all their lives on this barren coast. They live by trading codfish with the Newfoundland visitors in the summer, or by the fur they catch in the winter months, which is traded with the Hudson's Bay Company or the Moravians. Life is desperately hard for many reasons for them, more especially since the Mountaineer Indians and Eskimo have greatly reduced the fur animals, and the settlers are too poor to compete with the Newfoundlanders in catching cod – the latter being, as a rule, better equipped and fitted out. Beyond this the prices are very high. Sugar varies from 9d. to 1s. per pound. Kerosene oil goes as high as 60 cents a gallon, while flour is 6 to 8 dols. always per barrel of 196 lbs.; and I have had some old receipts sent me showing it at 14 dollars a barrel. Other things are in proper proportion; but the worst of all, perhaps, are clothes, which are absolutely unobtainable at reasonable prices or in good qualities. The old clothes gathered by the M.D.S.F. are priceless here, while many settlers in this climate have not even seen wool as good as is used in our ordinary North Sea helmets, mits, and mufflers.

Here, then, come in some of the worst features of settlers' lives. I will take one family as an instance to explain my meaning. Richard Broomfield, his wife, and seven children (all young) live on a promontory in Adlavik Bay. His nearest neighbour is his brother, about ten miles away up another bay. In October all Newfoundlanders leave, and with them all chance of obtaining fresh supplies of food till the following end of July or early August. – i.e., seven to eight months at least. Mr. Broomfield's house is a single-roomed wood or log house, with a central worse-for-wear iron stove, leading by an iron pipe through a hole in the ceiling; the furniture is one bed built out from the side, one box, and a couple of old barrels. In a small store adjacent he has the winter stock of food – four barrels of flour (to be commenced next week), a little molasses, a few dried cod, 1½ lbs. of tea, and a small stock of powder and shot – too small by far. Besides this he has a couple of old salmon nets, a few hooks, and two old single-barrel shotguns – one for his boy (now useless, as the ruffle is broken out), the other his own. I may say marvellous work is done with these old weapons. With a single ball this man will kill a seal only showing its head from the water better than many would do with a Winchester rifle. Clothes I can scarcely go into details about here. Suffice it to say that in winter, in the awful cold of 20 and 30 deg. below zero, they are driven to go out and hunt for their daily food; and for sheer want of warm clothing, even the father of the family cannot at times go out. The two eldest boys were dead; "They took sick," was all the mother could tell me. Of course, there was no one to help. The next eldest was a girl. I proposed that the family should come to the doorway to be photographed, that my statements might be capable of ocular substantiation. Till now, the children had all crouched down in one corner, except the two eldest boys; when they moved I discovered the reason. The mother just said, "They are ashamed, sir, because they have no clothes." She told me, "Times has been so bad, we have had no new clothing for three years." This year, from July 20 to about August 20, this whole family lived on the game they shot each day, or the trout they caught through holes hammered in the ice. Those who had the privilege of sending old clothes by the *Albert* this year may well rejoice, indeed, to know that this family will be well clothed this winter, and also helped to get more for themselves by the visit of the *Princess May*.

When a man is as far down as we found this poor man, he is incapacitated as it were from doing his best. All hope in life seems knocked out of him, and he goes from worse to worse. I look forward to seeing a new home altogether here next summer. His two little lads, just big enough to pull a single scull each, their father rowing two behind them, came off to say good-bye, and their happy little faces, especially when they saw we were taking their gun to be mended, will long live in our memories. One of the little lads had a commencing curvature of the spine, from improper feeding.

A gale came on next day, and we ran the *Princess May* into a river, as we wanted to plug one of our boiler tubes, which, alas! had given out. Opposite us on the bank was the remains of a former settler's house. The man's name was Olliver. Some three years ago he had fallen into the same condition as our friend Mr. Broomfield. He had five children. When his food had been some time exhausted, he went off, taking his last possessions, and old Jack plane and a trout net, with him. Having no dogs and komatik, he had to travel afoot over the ice and snow, and came to the house of the best-off settler about, Mr. Tosten Andersen, a Norwegian and a splendid man. He asked for food. Mr. Andersen showed his barrels of flour and said, "To part with any more than I have already done, means we must all starve together." This is about thirty to forty miles from where he lived. Olliver then trudged on twelve miles to a Mr. James Thomas, whose reply was just the same; two days later he reached Mr. Broomfield's house on his way back to his own. Here the reply was just the same. No more was known till three days later, when Richard Broomfield was summoned to the Ollivers' house. On the middle of the floor, his shirt off, and shot through the head, his own gun beside him, lay Mr. Olliver; in a heap in one corner lay the three youngest children, scarcely dead from blows from an axe which lay beside them. Mr. Broomfield's story is simple and intelligible.

It appears on reaching home Olliver sent his wife and eldest daughter out to look for food, and his eldest boy with his gun to look for game. It is supposed he determined to spare those who might provide a living for themselves. He then destroyed the three helpless infants himself. Virginius of old [who according to Roman legend sacrificed his daughter] acted much the same way.

Mr. Tosten Andersen, at whose house I spent the best part of a night, says, "If we could get goods at reasonable prices, we could make a living well enough, and want no help. But now there is no selfish good in making more than you need, for you are obliged to be charity officer for the whole country round." When he came to Labrador American fishermen brought down the necessaries of life cheap. Now, everything is highly taxed and dear, "and yet we reap no advantage from the Government. No provision is made for the starving. Little or no law is administered on the coast. Education is absolutely ignored, and our spiritual welfare is relegated to one visit from a Moravian missionary in his dog sledge during the winter, or our annual visit to the Moravian station at Easter." These brave Moravians travel far over the ice, often at great risk, to visit these our scattered English brethren. They also shall not lose their reward.

Lest I should be misunderstood, I should say this question agitates the minds of the Newfoundland fish-planters in the neighbourhood as much as anyone's, for they find it unremunerative to fit out these settlers with good nets, &c., and yet are too good-hearted to be able to let them go unprovided for. I know not a few barrels of flour and supplies stand nominally as debts, but actually are gifts year after year to their struggling fellow-fishermen near their temporary summer stations.

For Sunday we steamed to one of the largest Newfoundland stations, called Long Tickle. It was dark before we dropped anchor, but we went ashore, and gave notice of Sunday services. On both sides of that large natural harbour small shelters have been built by the fishermen for services, and they hold prayers in each, two or three times each Sunday. We had a good gathering in the morning on the western side, and during the afternoon visited on the eastern side. Here was the wife of an in-patient on the *Albert*, a poor fellow who had had to undergo an operation, depriving him of a part of his hand. She was glad indeed to get news of his welfare. But the feature of the day was the evening service. When we reached the little building we found it full to suffocation, and a crowd outside as well. So, as the day was warm, we decided to have service on the hillside. Accordingly we all journeyed up the rugged hill, and, finding a natural arena, settled down and had service. Irresistibly we were reminded of the [anti-episcopal] Scotch Covenanters meeting on their hillsides. The picturesque dress of the fishermen, the wild grandeur of the scenery, the number of small fishing vessels lazily swinging to their anchors in the spacious harbour below, made it a scene not easily to be forgotten. The singing sounded well in the evening stillness, and the meeting did not disband till the sun had sunk behind the horizon and the stars were shining out brightly overhead.

At Planak Island we found a poor fellow very ill – the doctor in the mail steamer had asked us to call and see him. This is a strange little island, and is supposed to have received its name from some bygone warrior Indian of a similar name. High on the hills is the grave, certainly, of an ancient warrior. Like all the Eskimo graves, it is open, the body being simply laid on the bare rock, and a tomb of loose stones being built over it. Inside you see the whitened bones all still in place, the skull face upwards, as if watching and waiting for a resurrection morning. Beside him lay the remains of his kajak, his spear, sword, dagger, knife, harpoon and gun; while in a small cache beside was his file, skin dressing tools, bracelet &c. All these graves are placed in prominent positions, where even the bones can look down on the old harp-seals as they swim past, or watch the flights of wild fowl, who of yore paid toll so often to the warrior's skill.

In one old grave, long since partly demolished by the hand of Time, and the fall of rocks broken off in the winter frosts, I picked up among the bones two rough cut wooden dolls, much battered truly, but meant, we thought, to represent the dead man's patron gods. Yet the Eskimo have no word of their own for God, for sin, or even for love.

On Tuesday [19 September] we tried to get round Cape Harrison, but a heavy sea drove us back – and glad enough we were to get back, though while seas were true we did better than a larger boat. So large were the swells we could count twenty as we ascended the side of one of them. Here we were again among old friends, and had a few patients. Next day we managed to creep round the cape, and after visiting Tinker's Harbour, brought up for the night in Holton Harbour. The fog and rain had been very dense, with an increasing wind, yet we had many visitors, and anxious inquiries as to whether the *Albert* would visit Holton. They promised her a royal welcome, and were intending to keep a good look-out for her, and tow her in with ropes if she did not come otherwise. A very large number of settlers are here, and also at a place half a mile away; but the harbours are not good at this period of the year. Here again we had several patients, and in addition to those working from the shore, fleets of schooners coming from the far north daily visit the harbour for shelter or other purposes, as they fly south'ard before the approach of winter.

Think what a population this is – 3,200 schooners from New-foundland alone! Nova Scotian schooners with crews from twelve to eighteen, and many brigs, barquentines, and steamers waiting to take cargoes of cod to various parts of the world. One steamer with 10,000 quintals left Battle Harbour last Saturday.

On Saturday [23 September] we anchored in Emily Harbour, and had patients from two neighbouring harbours. Sunday we also spent here, and held services. There is only one store [merchant premises] here for services, and as there are a great many people of various denominations, the usual method was adopted, and we had Church of England service in the morning, Methodist in the afternoon, and Salvation Army in the evening. I wrote you also that in the Straits the Roman Catholics consecrated the same building according to their own rites, and used it whenever a priest came along.

We have to rejoice that the [MDSF] bazaar at Yarmouth [England] went off so well, of which I saw an account in to-day's mail. We must, Sir, have an "Eskimo" stall next year, for we have had several curiosities given by them or the settlers to us, made of skins, or feathers, or bone; while the skin dresses and many curiosities might well form an interesting show.

Yours ever sincerely,
Wilfred Grenfell

Labrador Odyssey

Monday, September 25th. Fine day with a smart north wind; it took 5 hours hard work to get anchors up and haul the vessel out of the harbour, so that it was 11 o'clock before we up sail & started; in the first 4 hrs. we made 9, 10½, 11, & 10 knots an hour and during some of the puffs reached about 13; we made Webeck Harbour about 4.30 & thus made the 63 miles in a very short time.

Patients thick again & kept me busy till 10.30 p.m.

Tuesday, September 26th. When we reached the harbour (Webeck) yesterday we found we had missed the mail steamer – she must have been in one of the small harbours as we passed along – and so lost the chance of "answering" the letters she was bringing for us, and too lost the opportunity of sending our letters down to Hopedale; this is the first time we have missed the mail, and hope it will be the last.

Today has been a very quiet day below decks, for the wind has been blowing too strong for visitors or visits and being southerly the greater part of the day we were not able to sail; tonight it is N.W. and if this continues we shall up anchor and be off as early as possible tomorrow morning. I have much enjoyed a quiet day reading and writing.

Wednesday, September 27th. Wind blowing hard from the west, but so hard we cannot heave up our anchors although the wind is fair; the wind is so strong that if we were out we could not get into Holton Harbr.

After dinner we shall probably start as the wind is moderating and we are *very* anxious to be getting south now. I only hope we may not lose the mail steamer again.

HOLTON

Wednesday, September 27th. After dinner weighed anchor & started in company with "Girl of Devon," a three masted schooner collecting fish for Munn & bound for Plymouth. The night closed in very early & by 6.30 we had a fine dark sky with the setting sun lighting up rain falling on Cape Harrison with a curious crimson-vermilion colour on one side of the vessel, & on the other an almost full moon breaking through the clouds.

By the bye we hear of reports of a volcanic eruption at Cape Harrison in N.F. papers & "Westminster Gazette";[71] the first news the Cape Harrison fishermen had of it was from their terrified wives at home, and it seems that this quite foundationless report was taken home by someone (?a sick fisherman & a gullible one) on the mailboat. The cape is a fine mass of basaltic rock rising 1026 ft.; all the rocks in Labrador are volcanic – granite, trap rock, schist & basalt – but there is no evidence of volcanic action at a date subsequent to the time when glaciers overflowed the country.

It was 9.15 before we were off Holton and as Capt. did not know the harbour & saw in the chart there were many rocks, I went in with the mate & a crew in "Mary Grenfell" after we had fired a gun rocket. We had a long row of about 4 miles and at 10.20 met the "Princess May" coming out; Grenfell towed us back and learning he really wished us to come into the harbour we lay off all night to come in at daylight.

Thursday, September 28th. Up early & as no pilot came out we fired another rocket at 7.30; this brought "Princess May" & a fisherman out and in an hour's time we were anchored. Morning spent in mooring her – the harbours are so narrow & so full of schooners that it is necessary to moor a vessel like ours with two anchors on the bows & cables astern to prevent her swinging with the tide & wind into other craft; Dr. G. took in new stock of food, drugs, clothes, coal &c and after dinner left for Emily & other harbours & will hope to meet us at Gready [Harbour] on Saturday.

Early in the afternoon the "Windsor Lake" arrived so I went on board for our mail; while on board I learnt that the Superintendent of Police, who is a J.P., and two constables had gone N. in her to arrest Tom Brown, the husband of one of the 4 women found dead, and that having found him they were taking him to St. John's. It may or it may not be right for Tom Brown to be arrested, but it is pitiable to think that in order to take him and having insufficient evidence to take him on the charge of wife murder they have arrested him on the charge of a doubtful crime that he committed 12 years ago, convicted him and sentenced him to 4 months imprisonment; if the same treatment was meted to all it would be a small percentage that the arm of the law would not reach. My belief is that these men were sent down to arrest him on any or no charge in order to take him out of the way for a time; the end aimed at may be all right but the means adopted is unjust.

The afternoon was spent in reading a delightfully long lot of letters – from Mother, Etta, Isabel, Ellen, Bessie, Edward & Cecil, and several others.

We had a full service on board at 7 p.m. & after that I had plenty of custom at the dispensary while Capt. was busy at the book locker.

This morning my patient having recovered she joined her father's schooner, which was lying in the harbour "making" fish (i.e. sun drying the salted fish); she went without saying "good-bye" or "thank you" to anyone on board, but this was due I think to ignorance on her part; unfortunately she is not the only Newfoundlander ignorant in this way. She had only been to school one year, when she was 7 yrs. old, and then had to walk 8 miles daily as there was no school then in Bay Roberts; she made some slight progress with her writing lessons while on board but was not very persevering.

INDIAN TICKLE

Friday, September 29th.   Called at 7 a.m. to see some patients who had come in 3 or 4 miles to see me; as we began to weigh anchor more & more patients came off so that I was busy till 9, delaying the departure of the ship. Holton is a big harbour & I was sorry we were unable to stay longer; we must be getting south though.

A moderate breeze took us along between Teapot & Coffee Pot Islands, then by White Cockade, down Cutthroat Tickle between Cutthroat Island & Entry Island; all the rocks & hills were very bare

Charles Flowers's tilt, Indian Harbour. Grenfell is seated at left, and at right is Flowers, the "winter man" or custodian for Simms, Job's agent.

– perhaps the barest I have seen on the coast – and on the tops of the hills were great glacier-borne stones; we passed by the entrances to Smokey Run & Indian Harbour and continued by the Ducks, crossing the mouth of Hamilton Inlet between George Island & Tumble Down Dick; the wind moderated very much & then dropped entirely, so that at tea time we were outside N. Stag Island, and at midnight rolling about in the slight swell & unmanageable a little south of S. Stags.

We did not land at Indian Harbr., as we wanted to get on & Dr. G. was going to call in the steam launch; we hear the hospital is finished & locked up, the carpenters having gone home. I should like to have seen it and seen some of the people again, but it is just as well we did not land, for we have had a good deal of unpleasant correspondence with the agent [Simms], who has thwarted us in

Labrador Odyssey

Indian Harbour Hospital.

our work considerably, and now that matters are quieter again it would be a pity to open the subject again, which would be inevitable if we were to meet, and it will have to be gone into with Mr. Job in St. John's.

I got into our boat, though, off the harbour mouth as I saw a Great Northern Diver – a large & handsome bird – but he wasn't to be caught by my chaff [i.e., deceived], diving whenever we got two gunshots off or more.

The morning spent printing photos, looking about & trying to read; the afternoon ditto & developing plates; by 7.30 I had 23 developed (using hydroquinone for them); washing is by far the worst part. In evening cleaned up & skinned birds.

Saturday, September 30th. We passed Gready Harbour in the morning and having a fair though light wind continued past the "Devil's Lookout" – a high, bluff island – and the Gannet Islands and arrived at Indian Tickle in the afternoon. The Gannet Islands is a famous breeding place for birds, and we saw some hundreds of ducks close inshore; as the wind looked like dropping Capt. would not stop and let us try & shoot a bird or two, and his wisdom was evident afterwards as we were no sooner anchored than the wind ceased entirely.

Called on Capt. Windsor – the agent here – a very old man & staunch Methodist; he had just built a chapel, and the Methodist body wanting to buy it they had asked Mr. Hollett, the missry. at Rigoulette, to come down, inspect, advise &c.; was very sorry to see Mr. H. for it means we shall not have opportunity for taking service tomorrow as he will have the chapel.

Very busy with patients in evening.

Sunday, October 1st. A lovely & calm, even warm day. Mr. H. took service in chapel in morning; in afternoon Capt. W. lent me a boat & crew & went with our mate to Salmon Point, where 3 families of settlers live; all were out except Willm. Parr – a fourth brother – who lives at Fox Bight and Jim Parr's children, 3 girls & 3 boys; two of these children had no boots or stockings and none of them had more than one layer of clothes on and none to fall back on in the winter. They all got into our boat & came across to Fox Bight to Will's house, where we had a congregation of 20. Back by 6 p.m. to find a number of people on deck, so we at once decided to hold service again and by service time had the ship crowded.

Tuesday, October 3rd. Yesterday (Monday) was calm & sunny so at 8.30 Capt. & I start in the "Mary Grenfell" with "Sails" & Jack Bishop (an extra man we took at Turnavik) for Rocky Bay, taking kettle & the needful with us; called at Salmon Point & took Jim Parr in; first game we saw were 5 curlew on the point, but we were not able to bag one; throughout the day we saw a great quantity of game but got very little, for the birds are very wild; we saw 4 or 5 Great Northern Divers – or "Loos" – but cd. not get within 150 yds. of one; it is a very shy bird & ranks next to the seal for the length of time it can keep under water, so Jim says; by Eagle Islands we came across between 100 & 200 ducks, but they all took to wing before we got within range; landing on Narrow or Juniper Island at 1 p.m. we walked 1½ miles through low spruce & juniper trees while the boat went on to light the fire; I came across two coveys of white partridges; they got up out of range & were hard to follow, being very quick & seeming to know where I should have most difficulty; this partridge differs from the spruce partridge in many respects; in winter it is quite white & resembles the ptarmigan; just now it is changing from the darker summer plumage, the wings only being white; I saw about a dozen birds in all but only shot one; neither Capt. nor Jim got any; a small flock of golden plover flew by as I was examining a large rent in the knee of my knickerbockers caused by being caught by a stiff branch.

Didn't Jim enjoy his dinner! never before had he had any tinned meat, and no cheese for 20 years or more; he has hard work to live, having no wife & 7 children; last year he started the winter with only 2 barrels of flour but was able to buy two more during the winter at Cartwright with some fur he shot.

After dinner I put an explosive bullet within six inches of the head of a seal at about 200 yds.; he didn't like the whiz & disappeared with a great splash. Sailed across the bay and landed to walk ½ mile through woods to where Jim's winter house is; all along the narrow & soft path were the recent footprints of a large company of deer; they led from the edge of the water right past the wooden "tilt" and then went on through the woods to the hills; there must have been a large company, for the footprints were very numerous, some large & some small; Jim said they were not 24 hours old. It was dark when we got in the boat again to row across to Narrow Island; we landed and built a tilt for the night by firelight by rigging up our two sails to wind'ard using the gaff, boathook & oars for spars; the night was very still & we thought warm, so after tea we sat about and got Jim to tell us of some of his hunting experiences, and how he sleeps in the snow when out after the deer; we wrapped ourselves up in our big coats & tried to get some sleep for an hour, but it was all in vain, for Jack would begin to bawl like a goose & wake us up in a hurry.

Moon – a small quarter – rose at 9.45, so at 10.5 Jim & I pocketed a biscuit or two & went to look for geese; after an hour's hard walking, now over stones, now on the tops of a dense, low growth of spruce & juniper and now over very soft but dry & springy moss which would give about 3 inches to the foot, or jumping from one clump of grass to another over boggy ground, we reached a large pond & heard two Great Northern Divers bawling, making a noise like a very liquid laugh; no goose was heard there, but lower down we heard some "quonking," and in another half hour had reached the lower & smaller pond, where we heard two or three.

It was settled that I should remain where we were while Jim crept round & got a shot if he could, driving them my way so that I should have a shot as they flew over my head. I lay down under a bush at 11.30 & was interested hearing Jim "tolling" for the geese (i.e. imitating the note) and leading them to where he could get a good shot; unfortunately it was too dark to see well, so he spent his time & waited till they got near; after waiting 1¾ hrs. I saw the flash of his gun and then began a great noise as a large number of frightened birds rose and flew quacking in my direction; unfortunately they were too high & the night was too dark for me to get a shot. I walked round the pond & found Jim putting on his clothes, for he had had to wade some way out to pick up the two birds he had killed – this was at 1.15 a.m. We walked to the upper pond to which they had gone, but they had left again before we reached it, so we stood for some time, tolling for a bird that flew backwds. & forwards, but though it passed close above us we could not see it.

We got back to our camp at 3.40 thoroughly tired; it was the hardest walking I had ever had, and coming at the end of a long day my legs were very tired; how Jim ever got back with those two birds slung over his shoulder on his gun I do not know; one weighed 11½ lbs. & the other was less, but they made me stagger as I tried to carry them; he of course is accustomed to this kind of work & tells me he has often carried six home on his shoulder.

Called at 5.15 as the sun was thinking of getting up & at 5.30 we started back to the same pond to see if there was not yet another bird killed but not found overnight; in the first long pond we saw 10 "Great Northern Divers" but could not get a shot, & near the second pond we came across the feathers of two white partridges, all that was left of a meal a fox had recently eaten.

We walked through the woods till after 8 but did not see a bird; I met Jim & walked along the shore towards the place we expected to find our boat and was greatly surprised to see him stop and hear him utter several deep, uncanny growls; he had seen a seal rise not far off and by imitating the growl of a seal was trying to draw it within gunshot; young seals are easily "tolled up" in this way, but this one was old & had a wiser head.

Sailing back we saw very few birds, so when we reached the ship about 2 p.m. we had only 2 geese, 2 partridges, 2 sea pigeons & one golden plover.

In evening we had service on board as usual.

Wednesday, October 4th. In morning Wm. Parr called to take me to see his wife, who was ill at Fox Bight; my hands being dirty I asked for some water & was directed to the washing tub, half full of far from clean water, but as it was all the water in the house it had to do; as I finished washing, Mrs. Circum's girl of 13 came in, so I asked for a towel to wipe my hands on and she immediately took off her white neck scarf & gave me that; she did not know what a towel was & only knew I wanted to dry my hands & gave me what she dried her hands with.

I found this girl was standing in *all* the clothes she had, with the exception of a print dress she kept for Sundays, and her all consisted of a well mended stuff dress, a piece of calico under the body, a pair of stockings & a pair of boots.

I got back to dinner of roast goose & found it good; and then we had the clothes out and looked up some good warm clothing for all the Parrs & Circums & if they are not warmer this winter than last it will be no fault of ours; they were really grateful.

I saw patients from 2.15 till 6 – one long string; some were Esquimaux who had come from Red Point, and it was quite pleasant hearing one old man talking in his mother tongue; he had been up from Hopedale 20 years or more but being very deaf he had scarcely learnt English.

Dr. G. arrived in the "Princess May" & in the evening we had a magic lantern lecture in the chapel.

Thursday, October 5th. Jim Parr slept aboard last night & came to my cabin at 6 a.m. to ask me to fulfil my promise to look at his eyes before he left for his home; his expression when I jumped out of my berth in something else than my dayclothes was first class.

The day has been a great change from the last few days, cold, foggy & strong s. wind; however, Dr. G. went off in the steam launch; he is a great anxiety to us. I did not leave board all day except to visit a man with heart disease in a schooner near; there are several schooners lying round us unable to proceed south, the wind being s. & the sea too high.

Friday, October 6th. Rain all day & strong winds, at first s. & late in evening N. Again it was too rough for me to go ashore; for this I am sorry as I want to see more of Capt. Windsor, who is a nice old man.

Many of the patients I saw down the shore are in the schooners near us, going home, so in the morning several came to see me; Mr. Percy of Smokey Run asked me to go on board the schooner which was taking him south to see his wife, who was too ill to come & see me. I had heard something of the want of comfort & misery endured during the passage to Labrador & back on board the schooners, but had formed no idea of the terrible hardships & discomforts that have to be put up with. Instead of being led to the companion I was taken to the main hatchway, which was partly open, allowing the rain to fall on barrels beneath; there was no ladder, so I had to let myself down; two lamps, one on each side of the ship, showed where the people were, and being directed which way to go I had to crawl to my patient; she was lying on a feather bed which had been spread over her husband's cod trap & her own domestic goods and was so near the deckhead that she was unable to sit up in bed; I had to lie on my side, raised on an elbow, to talk to her.

This schooner had been down the shore fishing and had 400 quintals of fish in this hold; planks & bark were laid over the fish and a tarpaulin and then the space above this was divided among the crews that were taking passage home in her; into this space they had to put all their belongings – traps, crockery, window frames, barrels of clothing, molasses, food, &c., &c., and on the top spread their bed; it was a curious sight as I lay talking to my patient & looking about; all sorts of things were lying about and the rain was coming in & wetting much; across the other side there appeared to be an untidy heap of clothes but by & by it moved & I saw it was two girls in bed trying to hold up a quilt; there were no screens in the hold, and in it 2½ crews – men & women – are huddled together. They told me this was a very good boat for going home in as there were so few crews & therefore more room, and they must be right, for in some schooners there are 12 or 14 crews of from 4 men & a girl to 8 men & 2 girls in a crew. Mr. Smith of Edwds. Harbr. tells me of one schooner of 56 tons and 92 people on board. When there are a number of people on board it means there is scarcely standing room on deck, so that the women remain down below during the whole passage, which may last from 4 to 18 or 19 days.

From visiting that schooner I went to another to ask Mr. Smith, the agent of Edward's Harbour near Indian Harbr., to come to dinner, and from there to see my patient with heart disease; this vessel is Irish & Roman Catholic throughout and consequently dirty, but the Skipper was pleasant & clean enough; just as I was getting into my boat a man asked me to see his baby, which had "thrush,"[72] so I had another opportunity of seeing how these poor people travel to & from their summer's work. It was really terrible to be down there – in this case the main hatch was on & covered with a tarpaulin and the atmosphere below consequently none of the freshest – and impressed me more than ever perhaps with the fact that women ought not to come to Labrador fishing.[73]

There was no need to "let myself down," for the hold was too full for that to be necessary; the difficulty lay in reaching the baby's mother when I had sighted her, as I had to go along on my side in a manner not unlike the sidestroke in swimming, with the deckhead immediately above me and barrels of clothes, pots & pans, nets, &c. below and about me; the mother, who was in bed, & unable to sit up, as the least raising of the head would have brought it in contact with the deck above, passed her 12-day-old infant along sideways to me.

Getting out of this hole could not be accomplished in a dignified manner as legs *had* to go first, and in order to let me pass, a girl had to squeeze herself into the groove between two puncheons of molasses; in this place lived six women & three men, the rest of the male members of the crews being stowed away forward. I am not surprised the owners & skippers try to keep us from visiting these places where the people are stowed; the skippers take as many crews as they can get into their schooners because of the freightage money; the people have to provide their own food and wait their turn to cook at the galley, which is on deck, in even the worst of weathers, and for the accommodation provided for his crew the skipper pays 25 cents (or 1s. 0½d.) for every quintal of fish he catches, so that if he catches 100 quintals of fish he pays £5.4.2.

Mr. Smith of Edwds. Harbr. & Mr. John Spracklin of Indian Harbr. helped us to eat one of the geese we shot in the early part of the week, and so enjoyed their company & cigars; they stayed to tea and spent the evening, not going till after supper; I was glad they came & stayed as we became better acquainted than we could during the busy days we spent in Indian Harbr. and they are men of influence.

At our evening service our hold was nearly full with people from the schooners.

Saturday, October 7th.   October truly: strong, cold N. wind and foggy; not a tempting day to go to sea, & though we are very anxious to be going, as it is high time we had left the coast, Capt. determines to stop, for the fog may become thicker any moment and there is too much wind to make entering the Labrador harbours safe.

Wind too strong all day for me to go on shore in our boat. Mr. Jarret's "Maida" – a square-rigged schooner of 116 tons that went on rocks in Smokey Run last year; she was immediately put up for sale by auction as a total wreck, bought by Mr. J. for $60, got off rocks & towed to his stage within six hours and is now worth £400 a year to him, as he takes his crews down & up from N.F. to Labrador in her & charges each crew 20¢ for every quintal of fish they catch – the "Maida" came in and anchored close by us to take in two more crews. I went on board with a sack of woollen caps & some bundles of literature for distribution; there were 12 crews on board – 66 men & 24 women; the skipper of each crew had a bunk in the after cabin, but all the other men & the women were stowed in the two holds; each crew had a given space allotted to it – six feet from before backwds., half the width of the ship in width, & from the top of the fish to the deckhead in height – and in this space had to stow everything they had, as well as themselves; the smallness of the room given to each crew leads to certain results in every schooner; one is that the women are not allowed on deck, and another is that in an overcrowded vessel like this one, not half the men are able to get below deck to lie down at night. The Capt. told me there was not standing room on deck for all the people, and said that if he was caught in a severe storm and had to batten down the hatches many of the people would be suffocated.

It is terrible to think of the people having to travel in this way, although when I went down into the hold the people were all at tea, sitting up in groups, and from the noise & laughter one would think one was at a happy picnic party. Women certainly ought not to be allowed to travel in this way; in England they would not be allowed; and for the men the government ought to charter the sealing steamers to take them down & up in spring & fall; the colony lives by the codfish caught, but the colony in no wise recognizes that the codfish catchers are human.[74]

DOMINO

Sunday, October 8th.   Strong wind gone, only light northerly breeze; the presence of the Methodist minister in Indian Tickle, and the many reasons pressing us to go south as quickly as possible, determined us to set sail and if possible reach Batteau Harbr. for evening service. We sailed out directly after breakfast but the wind being very light & then dying away we drifted slowly with the current & tide & did not reach Domino till 5.30, when it was beginning to get dark – a journey accomplished at the rate of a mile an hour! At one place the tide was setting us onto a rocky island, so we had to put out our boat and tow the ship away past it.

A large number of people came on board, but when the first bell for service rang about half left; at the service I chose hymns I thought everyone would know, but not a man outside our crew made any attempt to sing; only one man prayed when several were asked to; it was the most fast asleep congregation I have seen on the coast, and it had an effect on me which was both chilling & very warming.[75]

Monday, October 9th. We have spent the day outside this dangerous harbour (Domino) in an exposed situation and a dead calm. Being quite exposed from the N. we have lain with sails set, holding on by a kedge anchor only, ready to be off with the very first wind. In order to cause no delay should the wind rise I have not been ashore except to shake hands with Skipper Isaac Bartlett, with whom I stayed when I visited the harbour before; rowing up the harbour I saw several crews taking their goods to the schooners waiting for them, rolling barrels & carrying nets, pots & pans &c. into their boats; several crews had already left as was evidenced by the empty window frames & the wide open doors of their houses or tilts. The window frames are always taken home lest they should be stolen, & the doors left open that the warm spring air may have greater facility of getting to & thawing the snow which always finds its way into & fills their miserable hovels in the winter.

This afternoon I got into the boat & in about ½ hour shot 20 "tickerelsies" – a gull something like a kittiwake which is as good eating as partridge. The mailboat came in but we had the disappointment of finding that Dr. B. had detained our mail at Battle Harbr. without any instructions from us, a proceeding that has annoyed us greatly.

A day like this cannot but force upon us the fact that with a steamer we should do ten times the amount of work we can do with the "Albert"; here is a fine day absolutely lost on account of want of power to move on; moving along the coast with a heavy vessel is dangerous work at the best of times, & especially now when the weather is far from dependable; during the whole season we have visited only 11 or 12 harbrs. with the ship out of the 150 or so on the coast; the steam launch has of course visited many more but the "Princess May" is not the "Albert" & has not the facilities for doing good that the ship has, and I have had from 30 to 100 patients in every harbr. I have visited within two days of the launch. Among the advantages of steam over sail are:

1. Get about in all winds & weathers.
2. Time now utilized in tacking agst. contrary winds & waiting for favourable ones after the want of a harbr. have been supplied could be made use of in forwarding the work of Mission.
3. More rapid progress from port to port.
4. Navigation far more sure & reliable.
5. Much assistance cd. be given to schooners by towing in calm & strong breeze.
6. All sick cd. be conveyed to hospitals under good treatment & at less expense.
7. Each hosp. cd. be visited 3 or 4 times a season.
8. The disappointment & annoyance strongly evinced by persons in harbr. where "Albert" has not called on account of undue risks in case of bad weather would be avoided as a steamer would be more manageable.
9. *Far* more people would be reached, & those visited once only would receive three or four visits.

Tuesday, October 10th.   This is now the 7th day practically lost for want of better means of progression – from Wed. to Sat. of last week on account of contrary winds, Sunday from want of wind, so that we took 8½ hrs. in sailing 9 miles & so got in to Domino for one service only, and yesterday & today from calm.

The harbr. being a very unsafe one during N. winds – the prevailing wind at this time of the year – Capt. asked me not to leave the ship for more than ½ hour at a time as the wind might get up very quickly & he would have to put out to sea clear of the islands before the wind got too high. Consequently I did not leave the ship all day & found plenty to do attending to people who came off to see me, some for medicine & some, poor halfbreeds from Spotted Islands, to see if we had any clothes we could give them. Wm. Dyson brought me his summer's ac[coun]t, showing what exorbitant prices he had been charged for his food by a certain Mrs. Kelly, who keeps a store & liquor shop at Black Tickle; he cannot read himself & so can't keep an ac[coun]t of what he buys, and is obliged to pay all this wretched woman charges him on trust, ignorant of the fact that he is charged $2.50 for "sundries," and often has to pay 20 or 30¢ more for a given quantity of an article one day than another; his bill came to $36 for the year & being allowed $30 for his fish he is left in debt to the extent of $6.

His brother John Dyson caught 21 quintals of fish and has spent it all buying the following: 2 shirts for self, one for boy of 20, two for girls of 13 & 6, pair of boots for wife ($2) & pr. seaboots for boy ($4.50), 10 gallons of molasses at 3/6 a gallon and one barrel of second quality flour for 7½$ (=31/3 for 192 lbs.); this flour & molasses form his winter food supply; he has no seal nets, and his chances of shooting birds are not great.

Capt. was out shooting birds near the ship in the morning and was startled at the sudden appearance of a great "square flipper" seal with long whiskers close beside the boat with a flat fish in his mouth; Capt. killed it but it sank beneath the sea and was lost; the skin is a valuable one for making the bottoms of kamiks [*kamik*] or sealskin boots, and I was sorry to lose the chance of a seal chop, which I have been hankering after all the time I have been on the coast.

At 5 p.m. the wind began to blow, & being anxious to get south, & most anxious not to be caught in Domino by a northerly gale, a quarter of an hour saw our sails set & anchor weighed and farewell rocket ascending. As we sailed E. to clear Roundhill Island the wind blew stronger & stronger and when I turned in at 10 p.m. we were sailing gaily in a stiff breeze at 7 or 8 knots an hour with our topsails struck.

FOX HARBOUR

Wednesday, October 11th. At 3.30 a.m. I was awoken by a noise as of things rolling about & banging together so jumped up to place my spectacles in a safe place & remove my empty cocoa cup from the table to the floor and adjust one or two other things; I had not turned in long before I was out again to go on deck to see what was up, as we were rolling heavily and Capt. was giving orders; I found we were lying up to the wind & in the trough of the swell as the "five finger" or iron ring at the end of the standing main gaff had broken and that consequently the peak of the sail was all adrift and the vangs [guys] no longer steadying the gaff, which was swaying backwds. & forwards as the vessel rolled.

I saw I should be no good and as it was cold & wet on deck I was soon asleep again but woke up several times to be conscious we were still rolling. In the darkness it was a difficult matter to put to rights; the mainsail had to be lowered, & from 3.30 till 8.30 we were lying to with mizzen, fore & jib sails when at about 8.30 land was sighted; through the driving rain we found we were 2 miles s. of Battle Harbr. and that we should have to beat to wind'ard. Oh! how the ship danced, & how she threw us all about! no one dreamed of breakfast till 11.30, when we were in smoother water. Capt. wd. not attempt to make Battle Harbr. as the ship would not get any shelter till she was in the mouth of the harbr., and then if there were many vessels there she would not be able to avoid running into some of them as she would of necessity have a lot of way on. So we made for Fox Harbr., 6 miles to the N. of Battle, where we have much more shelter, while this gale lasts and where we shall be able to continue our work, *when we can land,* among the very poor people I visited one day in July from Battle Harbr.

At present then we are at Fox Harbr., unable to land because of the sea, and unable to rejoin our friends & get our mails, which are 6 miles away only.

I have a patient on board with an abscess deep in his palm, needing poultices every 3 hours; I took him on board because it would be impossible for him to attend to it on a schooner in which he would not have room to lie down below decks; I wish it were possible to take more people to N.F. in the ship.

Thursday, October 12th.

After breakfast Geo. & John Holley came off; the wind had moderated but a high sea was running outside and breaking heavily on the rocks about Battle Harbr., so we decide to remain where we are, and as no small boat could go across we are letterless for another day. Capt. & I go ashore & spend morning investigating needs of the people again; some are very, very poor; Mrs. Thoms & her six children without a change of clothes! Mrs. Sampson told me she had not had any new clothes for six years; they are as badly off for food as for clothes; e.g. Mrs. Thoms started last winter with two barrels of inferior flour, 1 cwt. of hard bread (biscuit), 8 gallons of molasses & 4 lbs. tea; during the winter she was able to get 3 more barrels of flour with two otters her boy shot & the little she could earn making sealskin boots.

The merchants seem determined not to allow the people to make money, in fact to get as much out of the people as they can; they take their salmon, cod, herring & fur at a price they name & give in return what provision they like, always arranging prices so that there is nothing on the credit side; it makes little or no difference to the settler if he makes a good fishery during a season; for example, Mangrove does not expect any more provisions for the winter this year than he got last (viz., two barrels flour, ½ cwt. bread, 7 gallons molasses & 3 lbs. tea) although he has taken more salmon (he has 9 quintals at $5 a quintal (£1.0.10)). Mangrove said, "God knows when I had any money last; afore I was married I had a scattered shilling," & that was many years ago, as he is 64 now & a widower; he has not had an account from the merchant for 16 yrs. Geo. Holley has not had an acct. since 1884, so that he does not know if he is in debt or not; he has a cod trap & with his 3 brothers has no doubt he has made $700 this year, but he does not for a moment believe he has anything on the credit side and fears to ask. In one way it would do him no good to receive an acct. yearly as none of them can read; we looked at some old accts. of his and could see how very carelessly they were kept; to give but one example, the 1883 acct. closed with a deficit of $17, but there was no reference to this debt in the acct. of 1884, which commenced as if there was nothing either for or against him and closed with the two sides balancing to a penny.

After dinner we returned with six large bundles of clothes and some hard bread; it was a real pleasure to see the women opening the bundles and finding good flannel and cloth clothes; I am afraid the men must have felt out of it, for besides a few flannel shirts we had no men's clothes left; however as a rule the men are better dressed than the women.

Most of the people from the harbour came to service on board in evening, the second time only that there had been "prayers" in the harbr. this year.

As the night was dark & clear we fired a gun rocket and then burnt several flares which could be seen from Battle Harbr., so by now I expect it is known we are not far off.

Friday, October 13th. Another day spent within sight of Battle Harbr., "So near & yet so far." Wind s. veering to N.W. towards evening. The day has been overcast & rainy; but it was neither the wind nor the rain that kept us back. The sea outside is tremendous and breaks on the rocks, throwing up the spray to a great height [on the] Battle Harbr. side of the bay; outside this harbr. the sea was *breaking* though there is 6 fathom of water, the height of the waves from crest to trough being according to Capt. 24 feet (4 fathom). The s. end of Battle Harbr. – the water lying between Gt. Caribou & Battle Islands – is nearly closed so there is a great "undertow" in a N. gale – the waves & surface water being driven s., not being able to get out at the other end coming back below the surface; this undertow

Brown family, Fox Harbour: "Family consists of Mr. B., his 2nd wife, 1st wife's brother and two daughters, and his own two boys by 1st wife. House consists of one room and porch: it is a log hut banked up with 2 or 3 feet of earth outside. The clothes worn were a present from Mr. Hall on the occasion of Mr. B's wedding two days before photo was taken."

Interior of Brown house, Fox Harbour, 13 × 12 × 8 feet: "Central iron stove held together by chain. Behind it is seen Mr. and Mrs. B's bed; to the right is shelf on which brother-in-law and his boys sleep; the girls sleep under this shelf on the floor."

makes mooring very difficult work and often leads to vessels being dragged away out of harbour, to be blown back again when the moorings have gone & broken on the rocks. The undertow in Battle Harbr. must be very great for there is nothing but it to account for the swell that has set into this (Fox) harbr. which faces it, though at a distance of 6½ miles, the swell coming in in a direction opposite to the direction of the waves & swell outside. This morning we up anchor & come further down harbr. into quieter water and so get less rolling.

During the morning I went the other side of harbr. to see Brown, who lives in the worst house I have seen in Labrador; I took my camera, hoping for a picture that I knew would startle the folk at home, & I wanted a view of the two boys of 7 & 8, as when I had seen them in July it had been a wonder to me how their tattered garments kept on their bodies, for "cover" them they made no pretence to. Great was my astonishment then to see the house swept and clean, a few alterations made in the one room, the holes in the roof where the dogs had fallen through mended, and the two boys washed and in well mended clothes! The explanation was to be found, I soon saw, in a new inmate of this one-roomed house (13 feet by 12), for Brown the widower last Monday week had been to another harbr. to find a Newfoundland woman he had met & had a conversation with in the early summer, and now that her summer's engagements were over he brought her home & married her at Battle on the following day. Her first ten days' work had certainly altered the appearance of Brown's house & children. In this one room, built of logs well banked up with earth outside, live Brown & his wife, his first wife's brother & her two daughters (aet. 12 & 14) by a previous husband, and his two boys of 7 & 8.

During the summer there was another wedding at Fox Harbr.; Widow Thoms, who owns half a schooner and half a house & fish stage, married Mr. Wakeham, a gentleman absolutely devoid of property, yet he had the cheek to tell her in church at Battle Harbr., "with all my worldly goods I thee endow"! They are neither of them very young; she is nearly blind, and he very attentive. The

"Fish bawn, Battle Harbour: the fish are being piled for the evening. In a few days this fish was put on the brig *Blanche Currie* (Capt. John Jones) and taken to Leghorn, Italy."

"father giver" is an old man who "gave her away" on her first wedding and was heard to remark that next time he would keep her himself. Their three "bride's girls" were three old married bodies.

BATTLE HARBOUR

Saturday, October 14th.

A lovely day – bright sunshine & light wind with clear sky taking the place of violent cold wind and rain. The night had been cold, & some water spilt on the deck had been frozen – practically the first new ice I have seen. At 8.30 our anchor was weighed, & we were waving adieus to the people who congregated on a hill and waved their handkerchiefs. As we left Fox Harbr. there came the realization that my work on the Labrador was finished, as at the only

"Fish on flakes at Battle Harbour. Settlers' houses and church in distance; this church has been built about 46 years but has had no minister for more than half the time."

other harbour to be called at (Battle) the medical and mission work is in Dr. Bobardt's hands, and this feeling gave a gloomy colour to the rest of what would otherwise have been a very pleasant & invigorating day. I was particularly pleased to have two patients before I left Fox Harbr. as they brought the number of patients I have seen up to 1001.

Our friends at Battle – Dr., nurses & Mr. Hall – we found well, and the hospital pleased me greatly; it has those characteristics of warmth, cleanliness and brightness that a hospital should have, and much good work seems to have been done in it; Dr. B. has seen 505 patients – a larger number than I had expected.

Dr. B. rowed out to the harbour mouth to meet us, bringing our mail; I received letters, most welcome letters, from Mother, Mary, Ellen, Etta, Margaret & Annie, but no newspapers ("speakers," B.M.J. or L.M.S. "Chronicle");[76] I greatly fear newspapers disappear on the mailboat, for Mr. Job has sent me a bundle of papers *every* mail but only one bundle has reached me, a fact for which I can get no explanation from the mail master.

How good of all at home to make & send more flannel clothes! I hope they will arrive before we leave the coast – a mail is due on

18th. – but even if too late for this year's distribution they will be of great use next. What we are bound to say about the condition in which we find the people is sure to lead us into trouble with those who have interest in keeping matters much as they stand, and already much exception is taken to a remark or two in one of the letters published in Sept. "Toilers."[77]

While at dinner report came in that a flag was hoisted half mast on an island a mile away only; as a heavy sea was still running, a large, well-manned boat was sent to enquire the trouble and later in the day brought back news that a woman had been taken ill suddenly & died in little over an hour; the heavy sea & temporary absence of all men from the island had rendered sending for Dr. Bobardt out of the question.

A schooner came in during afternoon & reported Dr. Grenfell at Snug Harbr., 40 miles to the north, waiting for the sea to quiet; he had made several ineffectual attempts to get on his way south.

Sunday, October 15th.

Another great change in the weather; during the night a hard wind from the south sprang up, and by breakfast time the wind was blowing so strongly down the harbour & the lop [choppy wave] getting up that going on shore appeared doubtful. We were already well moored, having two heavy anchors & one kedge anchor down, and two steel wire ropes ashore, but so great is the undertow, doubtful the holding, and changeable & unreliable the weather that Capt. put a great 9-inch hawser ashore astern.

Four hands put me ashore to service, but they had to return to the vessel in case of eventualities. I waited a few minutes before going into the church to take in the view as the waves were breaking with great force on the many islands off the harbr. and the spray was being thrown very high by waves which were breaking over some sunken rocks not far off; it was a wild, cold, dreary scene, and as it began to drizzle I felt glad I was on shore & not out on the sea. The October gales have fairly settled on the coast, and the rocks have a savage & relentless appearance.

Dr. B. has had a difficult work in Battle, & both this morning & this evening he was straight & pointed, and the people must be hardened indeed if what he said did not strike home to some.

Afternoon spent talking to Mr. Hall. At tea we had eggs! They reminded me of the fowls I had paid £2.0.0 for and from which I had had such expectations which I had hoped to realize at Indian Harbour; when I found we could not live ashore this year, & finding the sea voyage interfered with their laying eggs, I lent them to some people in Batteau Harbour who were going to look after them, keeping the eggs but preserving the birds alive so that I could pick them up as fresh food, or game, on our journey south; as however we were unable to call at that harbr. on our way south I am speculating as to what has become of them, and whether they will prove a total loss or pay anything on the pound.

Wind continued high so I concluded ship's boat could not come for me even if I whistled (the usual signal) for it; I was sitting in hospital, arranging with Sister to stay the night, when Capt. & three of the crew arrived; they had come ashore to see if I was going off to the ship tonight; so off I went.

Monday, October 16th. Fine sunny day, less wind. No sign of Grenfell. Morning spent taking clothes, Indian Harbr. furniture, drugs &c. ashore and stowing them in one of Mr. Hall's warehouses.

Ducks at dinner at Mr. H's – rather fishy. At two put on my sealskin boots and trudge over the hills to Indian Cove, the other side of Great Caribou Island; followed a clearly marked track till it disappeared and then made across hill & vale; I found later that I had started well, but kept on when I ought to have turned off another track; the track I kept on was just as well defined as the one I ought to have taken but it has not been used for 15 yrs. It was the track to Bradley's house, which 15 yrs. ago was taken up bodily and run on rollers over the snow, up hill & down vale to its present site half a mile away, and is great evidence of the durability of the rocks and of the little weathering they undergo.

Inuit patients aboard the *Albert*.

One patient very ill with rh[eumatic] fever. My little lad who I saw with diphtheria in July scored off me by getting well, I am glad to say.

Dishonesty is certainly the best policy on the Labrador if money making is the end & object of life. On Saturday schooner "Annie Brown," 20 tons, went on rock in Assizes Harbr. under suspicious circumstances; she had made a bad voyage down shore, taking 50 quintals only; in this harbr. lives only one man (Joy, Conelly's agent) who keeps a store to supply sch. as they shelter in the harbr. for the night, and Geary, who is "making," i.e. drying his fish there. Indian Cove is only a mile away, and two men from there, passing just after the sch. struck, learned that she was to be sold but not till later; they went home & were back within two hours to find she had been sold already – sold without the 24 hrs. notice law requires, & sold when there was only one bidder, for Joy had acted [as] auctioneer and Geary, the only other man there, had bought her & paid $11 only. The 50 quintals of fish were sold separately for $8 – at present the value of fish is abt. $3 a quintal. It is not hard to see through this – the sch. made a very bad voyage & the skipper & crew knew they would make nothing out of it, not receiving a winter's diet even, so they wrecked their craft, selling it for nothing, but not till they had arranged with the buyer to share the profits of the transaction.

Service in a cottage in evening at Battle – full to overflowing, and the heat!

Tuesday, October 17th.

A beautiful & still, sunny day; two days ago we thought the coast "savage" and now today are almost minded to go and look for primroses! Much of the day spent in going onto the hill with the glass, looking for the steam launch. In afternoon the woman who had died on Saturday at Big Island was buried; a procession of six boats kept in line by a rope brought the corpse, and after the service in the church conducted by the little schoolmaster it was taken to the picturesque graveyard – a small, level plot between three rugged, rocky hills and the sea – a peaceful spot on a day like this.

The "Princess May" turned up in afternoon, much to our relief, and in evening we went to crowded cottage meeting at Trap Cove.

Wednesday, October 18th. Snow! Cold & raw; so unlike yesterday; snow did not lie, but from the flagstaff, Belle Isle – 15 miles away – was seen to be covered. After dinner photographed wards &c., visited the fish carrier "Blanche Currie," which is taking a large cargo of fish for the Mediterranean. What a tremendous quantity of fish is eaten! This one – a small vessel – is taking 240 tons of dried fish, & she is one of a great many.

I have put on 8 lbs. since I left Battle in July: 11.5 [stone] then, 11.13 now, and am thus the weight I scaled at Queenstown.

s.s. "Windsor Lake" came in, bringing letters from Hopedale; many lying reports has she spread along the coast about us; every man on board save one is a Roman Catholic & all hate us.

Dr. G. gave magic lantern in evening in a store & during it Rev. Waghorne,[78] the archfalsifier, turned up; he is to come on board tomorrow morning and will have to explain the reasons why he deliberately tries to estrange people against us, saying we are liars; but we have him on the hip, and if he is worldly wise he will have some "pressing engagement" & not come, for we have only to tell him his bishop's & the Cathedral curate's written opinion of him.

Thursday, October 19th. Rev. Waghorne spent an hour on board this morning, and a more pitiable object I have not seen for a very long time; he is interesting as a pathological specimen but a deplorable specimen of a man. His two charges against us is that Dr. G. has been bold enough to state in public that there is much poverty among the settlers on the coast, and that "they live & die without the knowledge of God"; this last is taken as a charge agst. the Established Church, and has not the "beloved Church" been working on & off for 38 yrs. in three centres along the coast? We point out that there has been no clergyman on the coast for 18 months, that the last man at Battle was not all that he should have been, that another late clergyman on the coast is now in gaol, and that a harbour 10 miles from here – taking it as an

Battle Harbour Hospital: dispensary
and consulting room.

Battle Harbour Hospital:
female ward.

Battle Harbour Hospital:
male ward.

Battle Harbour Hospital:
Dr Bobardt's room.

Medical staff and crew of the *Albert*, probably taken at Battle Harbour before their departure. From centre left: Capt. Trezise; Eliot Curwen (in fur hat); Sister Williams. Front row: Alfred Bobardt, Wilfred Grenfell, Lorenzo Rumbolt, Sister Carwardine. Standing at right is probably George Hall, Baine Grieve's agent.

example – has not been visited by a minister of any kind for 7 yrs. These facts bore out our statement that the spiritual needs of the settlers have been "neglected." "Not at all, not at all; these are only isolated instances you mention, and on them you have no right to say the people are neglected; it makes us mad to hear it," &c., &c., &c.

It is sad to think of this man – the only minister of the Established Church – wandering about in Labrador botanizing & spreading misrepresentations & untruths; where he is known he is harmless, where not known poisonous. The Bp. of N.F. strongly recommends us to have nothing to do with him on the coast, and the

Cathedral curate writes of him as an "egregious ass." Before he left he denied making several statements which we have in his writing, and when we told him politely he was a falsifier & that we did not believe what he said he heaped coals of fire on our heads by asking if we had any tobacco we could give him!

The day was cold & bright. Thermom. about 32° all day. Day spent in photographing rooms in hospital; leaving Indian Harbr. hosp. stores &c. carefully labelled & stowed in hosp. here, and in roaming over the island, telescope in hand. In evening Dr. G. gave another magic lantern lecture on astronomy and various other subjects; it lasted 2½ hrs., and so new is a representation of this kind that some of the people were sorry when it was over.

Report from Dr Grenfell to the MDSF, *25 September – 20 October*

ss *Princess May,* Snug Harbour, October 11, 1893
Windbound, NE gale

Dear Mr. Editor:

My last letter was, I believe, sent to you from Emily Harbour, where I was awaiting the arrival of the *Albert.* As she did not arrive, and we on the *Princess May* were short of many necessaries, we steamed back to Holton Harbour to look for her. Here we lay two days, and on the evening of the 27th, about ten o'clock, after service ashore, we saw her rockets out at sea. An hour was sufficient to get up steam, and soon we went out to offer her a tug in. A breeze off the land was, however, rising, and the captain decided not to venture near the land in the dark, so the *Princess May* returned to her anchors. Holton is a very barren place, but a very large number of fishermen are there all the summer, and a cordial welcome awaited the Mission ship.

Early next morning we took out a pilot and brought in the *Albert.* After restocking the *Princess May* we left for the south and spent that night in Emily, giving a magic-lantern lecture on "Bible Scenes" to as many as could gather. This place is the largest centre of fishing on Labrador, and is the district where medical needs will be supplied by the hospital at Indian Harbour. Two large steamers were loading with fish for the Mediterranean markets, and also three or four barquentines and schooners were at anchor, loading with fish for foreign markets. So bad is the weather at this time of the year on this coast that no chance must be missed of getting the fish aboard when once it has been dried, so that long after dark the men will be working away by torchlight, numbers of boats hanging on alongside the steamers like they do "boarding fish" in the North Sea, except here it is carried on in natural harbours.

Next morning [29 September] found the *Princess May* at Smokey Run. Here the Newfoundlanders were all ready to start for home. The fish had all been dispatched, and the people were leaving together in a brigantine before the approach of winter. The same evening we reached Indian Harbour, and at once proceeded to visit the hospital. The building was completed with the exception of the chimneys, and the whole building had been erected in six weeks. I enclose a plan of the hospital inside, and hope to send you a photograph of the finished building by an early mail. We determined to christen the building that night, so we published a "lantern lecture" and laid out the large room with every available economy of space. An hour before the time for the meeting, I went up to try the lantern, and was surprised to find the building full – so much so, that I feared my watch must have lost an hour, which, however, proved not to be the case. The hymns were thrown on the sheet in the usual manner, and a really hearty gathering was the first one in the new hospital. The keys and care of the effects brought from England are in the hands of Mr. Simms, the agent of Messrs. Job Brothers, to whom Indian Harbour practically belongs. Mr. Simms has superintended the erection of the building. During the winter a Labrador settler has promised to keep an eye on the building, as he does on the houses and stores in the harbour.[79] His name is Mr. [Charles] Flowers. He had just come back from a few days' hunting in the bay, with a fine black bear skin as one of his trophies. It is by the help of fur, "fish," and salmon that these "liv'eres" eke out their precarious existence.

Labrador Odyssey

On Saturday [30 September] we crossed Hamilton Inlet, and passing many islands put into Pack's Harbour for Sunday. Here we found again the Newfoundlander[s] preparing for home, while many Labrador men had come in to get their winter supplies. The planter, Mr. Lawrence, kindly emptied a store for us, and on Saturday evening we again had a lantern exhibition, as a good preparation for Sunday and a good means of announcing the services. Many of my slides are from famous pictures of the life of Our Lord, such as Doré's, Da Vinci's, &c., and being well reproduced make excellent subjects, when introduced among the scenes from Palestine of the places in which the events actually occurred. Sunday as usual we held three services, and the store was well filled indeed each time. Pack's Harbour must contain about a hundred fishermen, when the liv'eres who get supplies thence are counted in. It makes a lovely harbour, though it is really a narrow strait between two islands.

Next morning a volunteer pilot took us to Cartwright, across the shoals in the mouth of Sandwich Bay. Here we found a girl whom we had sent to Battle Harbour hospital just returned. Everyone was loud in their praise of the hospital, and the girl, who had been suffering with an internal abscess, told us she would like to have stayed there for good. Cartwright, like Pack's Harbour, was fairly full, for the company's dealers and settlers from further in the country were just getting supplies, and preparing to seek their winter homes in the woods. That night, therefore, we stayed there, and had a meeting in the school-house, leaving at daylight next morning. On our way to Gready Island, where we expected to meet the *Albert*, we landed by request on an island called Huntingdon, to see some settlers. These families are, perhaps, the most independent on the coast, and, with sturdy sons to help them, seem to make quite a comfortable living. A terrible accident, however, overtook three of them last winter.

One day in March John Davies, his two sons, and his mother-in-law went out over a hill to get a first view of the sea, as a break in the floe ice had occurred. While skirting the hill William Davies' nose commenced to bleed, and he stayed a little way behind the others. While he stayed a noise above was heard, and a huge avalanche of frozen snow came crashing down the hill. All ran for their lives, but the three front men were buried alive. William, however, had time to mark where his father fell, and when the avalanche had passed rushed to endeavour to find him. The father was four feet below the surface, and could be neither seen nor heard by his son. With the energy of despair, the son worked away, tearing up the frozen mass with hands and feet. Judge of his joy on shortly coming right down on his father's head. The man was face down, and unable to move, but was mercifully preserved from suffocation, as his head was over a bank. It became then only a matter of time to free him entirely. The father told me: "I first thought of scraping my way out, but found the weight on me so great that as I lay, my arms outstretched, I could not even close my hands. I heard my son walk up to where I was; I heard him stop over my head and commence to scrape away the snow with his feet; but, though I kept shouting to him, he never heard a sound from me. The other poor fellows we could not find, so we returned for shovels. At last we found them. They had caught across trees, which had also been swept away by the avalanche, and had probably been killed in the first rush."

Mr. McCrea, the agent at Gready Island, extended his usual hospitality to us that evening, and we found it a rest to have an evening off, for all hands were engaged loading a Bristol ship with fish, and so we could not get a meeting. The *Finlaggan*, of Campbelltown, had already departed.

Next day we reached Indian Tickle, and here found the *Albert* at anchor. She had missed both Gready and Emily Harbours. Here we had a grand meeting in the evening, in a new wood building which the people have erected for services, and which the Methodists are hoping to be able to use as a centre for a Labrador summer missionary next year. It was crowded to overflowing with people, some of whom had come across the water in their boats.

October 5, it blew hard and rained, but being able to get the shelter of some islands we steamed to Red Point, and thence on to

Domino, the fog and rain being very thick before we let go our anchors. Here we soon had patients aboard. The rain fell in torrents all night, and we found the roof of our cabin had sprung leaks, so that we were unable to keep our rugs dry till morning. Fortunately we had sea boots which were waterproof.

Friday, the 6th, we reached Batteau. This is a very large station, but all small planters. It is a dismal, dreary place, as, indeed, most of these islands with fishing stations on them are. Here a strong northerly gale came on, and kept us over Sunday. On Saturday afternoon, still in heavy rain, alternating with mist, we managed a walk over the island. In the bay we found the skeleton of a young whale. The skull I could not lift, but two of the huge vertebrae I carried off. At night we had a cottage meeting, and Sunday being fine, we managed three good gatherings in different cottages, or rather huts. The plan for the huts here is to build the whole of poles close together like a shed, and then partition parts off. The planter [owner] has one end, the women the middle, and the crew the other end. This is a better arrangement as far as ventilation goes than the series of small mud huts and close small bunkhouses as adjuncts. In these small huts large stoves are used which form much carbon dioxide gas, and make the air very often close and very unhealthy.

From Batteau we crossed the bay and reached Punchbowl Run. A heavy swell was still running and a tremendous surf breaking over all the shallows. Here we got inside islands and steamed along to Seal Island. About fourteen families of Labrador folk dwell on these islands, numbering in all some seventy souls. Here we found two poor folks very ill indeed – one poor woman especially, on whom it was necessary to perform an operation, but whom a long period of suffering had most terribly weakened.

One of our great difficulties in medical work has been always the impossibility of procuring proper food for our patients. Seldom can they get goats' milk, and hardly ever tinned milk. Beef tea, and so on, are unknown on the coast; and fresh vegetables, eggs, or any kind of fresh meat, except very unpalatable seabirds, are very rare and hard to obtain. We have once, or even twice, ourselves had a piece of reindeer given us, and I shot one porcupine on the shore one day, which ate most excellently. Beyond that, except for some wild geese, we have only tin meat to use for them, and naturally not enough of that for all. The special foods I got, prepared after Dr. Nansen's method by the Bovril Company, have been invaluable. Chocolate in sticks, and dry biscuits, with from 10 to 25 per cent. of the albumenoids of meat in, have done wonders for some of our patients. They are not known out here, and would be of inestimable value to the Moravian missionaries in their long winter journeys over the ice, and also, I should say, to the Hudson's Bay people, &c., who cannot carry much in their komatiks when driving ...

On Sunday, October 15, we held three crowded meetings on Square Island. There are nine Labrador families here, and, as is customary, several schooners had come in for Sunday. Most of the residents are earnest Christian people, and some old friends being aboard some of the schooners from the north, we had what I may almost call "family" meetings; for the sense of brotherhood bred of the *knowledge* of a common Father and inheritance is more than merely congregational in a lonely land like this. The same spirit is often felt in North Sea meetings, nor have I ever felt it so strong elsewhere, so that in spite of the heavy gale and sea outside, we have never had a more happy Sunday. Monday morning we crept along under the land, the strong wind having veered offshore, and hammered down the sea a little. We visited Ship Harbour and brought up for the night in France's Harbour, where Mr. Penney prepared a large store for us, and at night we had a crowded meeting.

We had visited during the afternoon also a place called France's Bight and George's Cove, where dwell fifty-three Labrador folk. They told me it was seven years since a clergyman had visited the place. Time was too short to allow me (even were I qualified to do so) to christen the number of children desirous of the rite, and my certificate to marry, promised in St. John's, not having arrived, I could not marry an anxious couple. I was able, however, to make use of some of the warm clothing still remaining.

On Tuesday we reached Battle Harbour, where we found the *Albert* and all hands belonging [to] the hospital awaiting our arrival. Here we stayed till Friday morning, the 20th, when we left to cross the Straits of Belle Isle; the *Albert* was to follow later in the day. These three days were not idle ones, for we had crowded evening gatherings, and settled up the hospital affairs for the winter. Dr. Bobardt was to leave as late as he could, and catch the *Albert* in St. John's, while Nurse Williams joined the *Albert*, and Nurse Carwardine was to come up by the last steamer. The hospital will be closed all the winter, and the key entrusted to Mr W. Baine Grieve's winter agent, who will open it, and light fires there, before the people arrive next spring. The windows will be boarded up to prevent the ice and snow from breaking them in. The addendum has been built on since I sent you a photograph of the building, and it greatly adds to the accommodation, but there is yet much to be done to get the building into perfect order. We have found it will be quite necessary to double board the floors; nothing else seems to keep out the wind here. I have sent the [MDSF] Hospital Committee a plan of each hospital, which may be interesting to our readers. Sister Carwardine was very glad to hear of the oilcloth and carpet which are coming; such accessories will be invaluable, but are much too expensive luxuries to provide, when so many more useful things are still needed …

W.T. Grenfell

TRANSIT TO ST JOHN'S

Friday, October 20th.

Dr. G. left in "Princess May" at 6.30 but whether he was going down [the] Straits of Belle Isle or across to the "French Shore" I do not think he knew himself. He left instructions that we are to proceed to St. Anthony, if we don't find him there to some other place, & if not there we shall find him at a third harbour. Sufficiently vague.

Morning bright & light s. wind; but glass falling & wind rising. Sister Williams is to go s. in "Albert", Dr. B. & Sister C. following week later in mail boat. Many good-byes & much expenditure of gunpowder & dynamite. Steam launch "Pundit" tows us out; we then hoist sails, flutter our wings, discharge final salutes and bid farewell to Labrador.

Wind rose & blew big guns; the sun was warm, and the old lady danced gleefully, poking her nose into wave after wave and covering her deck; the tide was setting up the straits & the wind was blowing down from the w.; consequently, the sea was a very broken one. Never has she danced so much in the N. Sea.

I was able to realize the difference between the misery of being below decks in the rain, as when we were going into Fox Harbr., and the exhilaration of being above decks & in the sun today. The first 19 miles we did in 2 hrs., 5 mins.; this brought us to the E. end of Belle Isle, near enough to see the three houses built & kept provisioned by the Canadian govt. for the use of shipwrecked mariners. While under [the] lee of the island we took in two reefs. Two positions & two positions only were possible: either the vertical one on deck, or the horizontal one below, and as the evening got colder the one position was exchanged for the other. Sister turned in early & was soon very miserable; and everyone from Capt. down to Lorenzo Rumbolt, aged 10 – a protégé of Dr. B's[80] – felt at one time or another that the land was preferable to the sea. When we started I thought we were well off with 4 stewards on board, our own & his assistant, Battle Harbr. steward & the young Lorenzo; I was surprised at not being asked to have any dinner – the thought of it was bad enough; the sight of it would have been dreadful – but soon found our steward was in bed with a bad attack of asthma & the other three horizontal for another reason. At 4 I lay down & read "Timothy's Quest"[81] and at 7 went on deck to find the wind had dropped suddenly and that we were rolling helplessly in the swell within sight of Cape Bauld, the most northerly cape of N. Fdland.

The swell was heavy and our rolling consequently very great, so great indeed that the strain on our sails & spars was so severe that our main boom – a great red pine spar 14 in. in diam. – snapped in the middle and left us for some time without a mainsail. What made matters worse still was the fact that in the stress of wind the mainsail had split & was now very ragged, with 13 holes in it. The mainsail had to be lowered, the sheet of the sail secured and tackles and a sliding wire rigged up, and the canvas hoisted again. Capt. decides to run for St. John's & not attempt to meet Dr. G. on the "French Shore" as it would not be possible to beat the ship against the headwind into one of the harbours now that the boom was gone & the canvas split. Oddly enough, on the same day of the same month last year, within 10 miles of the same place, the very same accident occurred, the boom being broken, but that time from weight of wind.

Saturday, October 21st.	Spent *all* day on deck – rough but bright & sunny. Not a sail seen, no beast or fishes, only tickeralsies & bull birds [dovekies].
Sunday, October 22nd.	Not so rough by any means; wind from N. & fresh so we make 9½ knots – or abt. 11 land miles – an hour. Why does one get so abominably sleepy the first few days of being in the open sea? Three bull birds flew on deck this morning; they are like very small guillemots and are very bad flyers.

We find that our boat, "Mary Grenfell," had been lifted by a sea on Friday and dropped onto a bucket, so that one of the planks has been stove in – but the pretty chapter of accidents was not complete till 10 p.m.; I had just turned in, but when the steward came to say there was something worth seeing on deck I soon turned out in light attire to find a hole in our mainsail the size of the mizzen; only ¼ hr. before I had dotted up the rents that had been blown in the old canvas during the gale of the two previous days – 13 in number – and had I thought the thirteen were soon to become one I should have waited on deck to watch the process. However, here we were with the main boom gone, & the mainsail represented in outline only, a condition of affairs which wd. bring the ship into the category of "unmanageable "

Monday, October 23rd. She proved "unmanageable" too during the night, for the wind dropped & left us rolling, rolling backwds. & forwards – or rather sideways all night. This did not disturb my sleep, however, & when I awoke at 6.45 it was to hear Capt. order a hand to hoist a flag. I was soon on deck to find we were off St. John's – but about 4 miles off, in something approaching a calm. After a time a tug came out and took us by the nose, and I was quite glad to see the foresail we had rigged in place of a main stowed away before it could be seen from shore.

Right in the Narrows of the harbr. we passed the remains of a Norwegian bark which met its fate on the rocks 8 days ago – two lives lost; what a pounding it had had on the rocks!

Trousers & black coat – ugh! Necessary I suppose. Away to the post office to find most of last mail sent to Battle, but letters from Mother & Etta & papers detained; too pleased at this irregularity to be cross about it. Mail expected in today, and one off home this afternoon. Only 10 or 11 days from home now.

Capt. Trezise to the MDSF

St. John's, Newfoundland, October 26, 1893 … I am in hope of hearing some news of Dr. Grenfell by the mail which arrives to-night from the north, as I think he may have succeeded in crossing the straits before the gale sprang up; otherwise he may have put back, if possible. Consequently we shall not leave here for a few days if such is the case.

Knowing the *Albert* would have to be docked here, and with a view of expediting matters, immediately I arrived here I made arrangements for docking, as vessels are sometimes delayed two or three weeks to wait their turn, and I was enabled to dock on the evening of the 24th inst. The vessel was dry yesterday, and as soon as Lloyd's surveyor had examined the keel, which was badly frac-

Labrador Odyssey

tured in the after length, I wired you. We estimate the present repairs will cost £150.

Joseph F. Trezise

Report of Dr Grenfell to the MDSF, 20–26 October

… Leaving Battle Harbour at daylight on October 20, we made Henley Harbour by midday, a strong head wind rising all the time and making any attempt to cross the straits impossible. In Henley we found a good many people, including four Labrador resident families. The harbour is a very remarkable one. It is made by three islands, two of which are capped by perpendicular basalt cliffs, flat on top. They present a very imposing appearance, while the approach to Chateau Harbour, which we visited next day, is almost grander still. The latter is in a landlocked bay, several miles long, very narrow, however, and steep high hills on each side. The entrance also is through a narrow defile, and the whole presents the appearance of an enromous grave dug out and the bottom filled with water. At Henley we had a good gathering in the evening to see the magic lantern, and also on Saturday for prayers. We found here Mr. Pitcher, the schoolmaster and lay reader from Battle Harbour, with whom we combined for our Sunday services. Monday, again, was too rough to leave, so we steamed up Pitt's Arm and went to Antelope Harbour, both of which are inside the Henley Islands. In the former there are only the winter houses of the residents, though a couple of schooners were now in for shelter.

At daylight on Tuesday [24 October] we attempted the straits; and, though a head wind rose steadily as we neared Newfoundland, we had not much water over the launch. The distance across is twenty-eight miles, and is made worse by the strength and uncertainty of the up and down tides. The *Princess May* took four hours and a quarter to cross – an excellent piece of work, considering the head wind and sea. The *Albert* had, we expected, already crossed, and was awaiting us with coals and supplies for the return voyage (which we dare not carry across ourselves), so we determined to press on along the French Shore. The sea and wind rose rapidly after we left Cape Bauld, and before we reached Fortune (the first harbour we could make) had become serious. The wind being on shore made the little vessel roll heavily, and in rounding the point to take the harbour, so nearly threw her over that it tossed the compass out of the box and rolled it overboard! This was an irreparable loss, as it was the only "spirit" compass we had, and was borrowed from the *Albert*. A card compass is scarcely any use in so rolling a vessel as the *Princess May*. Thus was our joy at having crossed the straits turned to sorrow, and from that time to this (Thursday) we have been clinging to two anchors with the south wind freshened to a whole gale. We found in Fortune many old friends of last year, especially Mr. Az. Alcock, a merchant trader on this part of the coast. We found the ss *Ingraham*, of St. John's, had left the morning we arrived. She was badly damaged, having had some of her planks knocked off in the straits by the sea, and had come in here to be beached to prevent her sinking.

W.T. Grenfell

Friday, November 3rd.

Today is 3.xi.93, & the last time I wrote was the day we reached St. John's, viz. 23.x.93 – a serious falling off!

All last week was spent calling on friends & printing photographs. Mr. Job met me shortly after landing & told me he was expecting me to stay with him [on the South Side], so on the Tuesday he sent his launch to the ship for my things.

The Governor was warm, & disappointed I had made other arrangements & cd. not stay at Government House as he had rooms ready for all three of us. Nothing could be done by way of arrangements for [a public] meeting till G. arrives & there is no good thinking of holding a meeting till after the general election on Monday next, Nov. 6. The days went quickly, I seemed busy, yet there appeared little to show for my energy at the end of each day.

On Saturday Mr. Job, Mr. Edgar Bowring[82] & I started on a 40-mile drive down to the South Shore with guns, tent, provisions, &c;

the country was very fine – wooded in parts, often bare & bleak, and the coastline was rugged but in parts the wood came down to the water's edge – unfortunately however the fog was so thick that we could see very little except the rough road & the trees immediately surrounding us.

We stayed at Mr. [Michael] Cashin's[83] at Cape Broyle – he is the governmt. candidate for the Ferryland district – & while there received a visit from Geo. Shea[84] his opposition colleague.

Early Monday – which was a fair though dull day with a cold N.E. wind blowing – we started off. We had much baggage so needed two men in addition to our two guides to carry the stuff. They started off before us, a queer-looking party with packs on their shoulders & cups, frying pans, kettle, bags &c hanging from their shoulders & round their waists. During the morning we moved 5 or 6 miles into the country over very rough ground to a tilt near Gull Pond – a somewhat dilapidated log hut which had not been seen for two years. After a hasty lunch of tea & sardines we went off to look for birds leaving two men to repair the tilt & set the tent; birds were plentiful on the rough barren ridges & hilltops but very wild, getting up 50 yards or more in front of the dogs & flying a mile or more before settling again, so while we had plenty of walking and had plenty of opportunity of seeing the dogs "standing on birds" the end of the day saw us with 21 birds only. The ridges & hilltops were strewn with loose stones & rocks & on the very tops of the highest nobs were great masses of ice-carried rocks often settled on an edge.

Monday night it began to rain, & the rain did not cease till we were home on Wed. night; all Tuesday it came down in torrents so we kept in the tilt till the water came down through as freely as it did outside, & then leaving the tent to be fetched another day we packed up & made tracks home, arriving at Cape Broyle about 3.30 without a dry stitch on.

The presence of a Dr. in one of the outports is so unusual that the people thought they would improve the occasion by visiting him, so that on Tuesday night & at each harbour or cove we passed through on our way back on Wednesday I was kept very busy & our progress forward was much delayed.

On reaching the ship Wed. evening [8 November] I found there was no news of Grenfell & that great anxiety was felt for his safety, seeing it was 12 days since he left Battle Harbr. The Governor had wired to every station round the island making enquiries, the mailboat "Virginia Lake" received instructions to call at every harbr. & cove to look for him & even to go across [the] straits & search on the s. Labrador coast, & a sealing steamer "Leopard" had been taken off electioneering duties & sent in search; worst of all I found a report of his being missing had been wired home.

Thursday brought in wires to the effect that several schooners had reported he had been detained in Henley Hr. (Labrador) for 5 days by weather & that he had been spoken at St. Anthony in north of N.F. Weather having been very rough the last ten days anxiety was allayed as it was realized he could not proceed & wd. not reach a telegraph station himself for some days.

On Thursday "Windsor Lake" brought in Dr. Bobardt & Sister Carwardine; very heavy weather.

Letter from Dr Bobardt to the MDSF

St. John's, November 4, 1893

After our work was done in Battle last Monday, October 30, Nurse Carwardine and self returned to St. John's in the ss *Windsor Lake*. We are now waiting Dr. Grenfell, who is safe and sound in his launch, on his way to St. John's, and will now be in telegraphic communication with us during the remainder of his cruise. All the parcels you sent arrived safely, and the clothing was very much appreciated by the residents round about Battle, enabling many to look forward to far greater happiness during the ensuing winter than they have ever experienced before. One old patriarch remarked that "we were the best friends he had yet met," and I can assure you they were all deeply grateful. I am staying with the

Governor, and shall remain at Government House until we sail. Everyone is much convinced that we have done good work.

Sincerely yours,
Albert Bobardt

Saturday, November 4th.	Still no news from Grenfell; if present rough weather continues he may be delayed a fortnight or more. Telegram arrived from G. at midday from Twillingate.
Sunday, November 5th.	Mr. Siddall, Congl. Ch. in morning; service in schoolroom till church is rebuilt. A bad day, rain & mud, wore long rubber N.Fd. banking boots all day in which to wade through the mud. In evening went to Mr. Morton's tabernacle (Methodist).
Monday, November 6th.	Polling day: much mud thrown about, & much underfoot, both very adhesive.[85] Very busy preparing for deerstalking expedition with Bobardt, buying, borrowing & telegraphing. Tried to catch G. with telegram asking him to join us. In evening called on Mr. & Mrs. Siddall & told them about Labrador; said Mr. S. to Mrs. S., "Oh, if only the Miss Rutts were here!" "Pray who are the Miss Rutts?" "Oh, two elderly ladies who live in the N.E. of London, &c., &c., my wife's best friends, &c." Odd; very. The chapel was burnt down in the fire of course, & I learnt incidentally that Mr. S's best helper in providing funds to rebuild was Mr. W. Wilson of Sheffield. Odd again; very.

Report of Dr Grenfell to the MDSF, 28 October to 7 November

Government House, St. John's,
November 1893

Dear Mr. Editor:

We waited at St. Anthony several days on the *Princess May* for the arrival of the *Albert*, being now safely across the Straits and being without coal or compass. But on Saturday, October 28, we heard she had met the same storm we had encountered in the Straits, had lost her boom and mainsail, and had run straight to St. John's. As we were unable to get coal we took in all the wood we dared carry on deck – dry birch cut in lengths about 3 ft. 6 in. long, to fit our fire – and intended to put stones in our coal bunker for ballast. However, at the last moment, we got from a schooner some slack [coal] with which we could eke out our wood supply, but which was itself useless for steaming purposes.

On the 31st we once more made a start, and crossing Hare Bay ran in the dark into Fichot Islands, a favourite station of the French fishermen. Next day, keeping close in shore, to get shelter from a north-east breeze, we reached Orange Harbour, and early on November 2 we crossed White Bay successfully. Our wood gave out on the journey, and we had to supplement our "slack" with everything combustible on board, and at night were still north of Cape John. In Harbour Round we passed that night, but had great difficulty in getting any fuel. Three men, however, consented to pull pieces out of their fishing stages for us, and as each contributed twenty-five poles, or "longas" [longers], as they are called here, we soon had as much as we could carry. I had here several patients – one poor fellow with severe and protracted asthma, and, of course, without any remedy. Many, too, were very poor, and we distributed among them the few remnants of our woollens.

Daylight on the 3rd saw us off Cape John, and once to the southward of that, I had no fear we could eventually reach St. John's. That great frowning perpendicular cape has no harbour with good shelter for ten miles on either side, and a perpetual seaway seems to heave up against it in winter. A fair wind one side of it becomes a foul wind the other, so we rejoiced that we had but a light air, and forgave the fog on that account. The port we wished to make (Toulinguet) was thirty-two miles across open sea, and of course, therefore, out of sight, so in case of accidents we lay into the bay, and made the south shore twenty miles to the inside of it, turning then out, and eventually, just at dark, dropping anchor in reach once more of civilisation and of coal.

Scarcely were we anchored when a telegram was brought off from His Excellency the Governor, which had been repeated to all the telegraph stations, stating anxiety existing about the *Princess May*, and the mail from the south coming in soon after, our old friend Captain Taylor was quickly aboard. He showed us his orders commissioning him to search all the islands and rocks on this coast, to ascertain our "fate," as it was considered certain we had foundered in the gale on the 21st. Most humiliating it was to have given such cause for trouble, but it was very cheering to feel so many people cared about us and thought of our safety. Moreover, it will have one good other effect, for it will demonstrate clearly what great need there is for communication with the north part of the island. Beyond being invaluable to Labrador vessels in summer, and all the fish planters, it might be very useful to the sealing vessels in spring; while if vessels were too late in the year, or were overdue and missing, such as we had been, much anxiety might be saved, and in case of loss, lives might quite possibly be saved. We had many friends calling at Toulinquet, but we left early next morning for Seldom-Come-By, the best place from which to make a passage round Cape Freels. Even so small a vessel as ours must lay five miles out to sea here, for innumerable shallows and reefs run off the shore. We arrived there about five o'clock, and found some thirty schooners from Labrador waiting to get a fair wind around Cape Freels. Our vessel was again soon so covered with friends from Labrador calling that she acquired considerable unsteadiness from the top ballast. Among these were two captains, who told me they had seen us from a distance, as we steamed along the French shore, and so they had most kindly telegraphed to St. John's news of our safety, when they heard the reports there. A Salvation Army captain had now joined our crew in the *Princess May*; I was giving him a working passage to St. John's. A most excellent addition he and his violin proved to be, and we were all convinced of his sterling worth.

At Seldom-Come-By we met another old friend of last year, the Rev. George Stoney, whose work had been marked by a great revival last winter. We had met several on the Labrador ascribing their conversion to his ministry. We at once organised a Saturday evening meeting, which our friend the Salvationist announced by rowing round among the schooners, and then "crying" it at intervals, like an old-fashioned bellman, at the top of his voice. The commodious chapel was crowded, gallery and all, and we commenced with my lantern views of Palestine and our Lord's life. Of all the many attractions of the *Albert*, I think, perhaps, the lantern has been the most striking in drawing audiences together. People seem willing to come any distance, and often to stop the night, at much inconvenience, to be present. We followed the lecture with a short service and prayer-meeting. So anxious were we to push on while we had a chance, that at daylight on Sunday [5 November] we decided to steam. Our friend Mr. Stoney came off to bid us good-bye, in the shivering cold preceding daylight, and we left with him the remnants of our tracts and literature for distribution. We had one trifling accident on this day, our pump giving out, and refusing to fill the boiler. However, after two hours under sail we again got under way. The delay was, however, costly, for the N.E. wind freshened very considerably till we reached Greenspond, and we had a wet time on the *Princess May*.

At Greenspond we fastened alongside the little coastal mailboat, the SS *Lance*, whose crew were really glad to see us back again, and then we were able at last to go ashore about 5 p.m., and really enjoy the rest of a Sunday evening ashore in a way that can only be appreciated by contrast. Daylight on Monday again saw us off. It was twenty-eight miles open sea to Cape Bonavista, and the SS *Lance* decided it would be too rough, with the north wind still holding, to land her mails. We should have followed her round the bay, but descried a small sail lying across, now some miles on the journey. This would prove company for us, and so we lay across. We made the passage in four and a quarter hours, a most creditable passage considering our damaged boiler tubes, and our not being able to keep up much steam, as we were afraid of our screw racing when it came out of water on the top of the seas. We ran into Catalina [6 November] at 1.30, it being now too late to venture across Trinity Bay. As we came in we were saluted by guns and flags from the sealing steamer *Nimrod*, which was here on electioneering purposes. Going aboard we found she would be leaving for St. John's at midnight, that would be after the polling. We arranged, therefore, for her to give the *Princess May* a line during the hours of darkness. True to time we left at midnight, the little *Princess May* for the first time with a leading line, in case anything should happen in the dark.

At daylight we had crossed both Trinity and Conception Bays, and were once again off Cape St. Francis. Here we let go our line, and racing the *Nimrod* into the Narrows, beat her by about a quarter of a mile. Soon we were alongside the *Albert*, and our mission to Labrador for 1893 was safely accomplished, except for the ocean passage to Yarmouth … [*continued, p. 210*]

CARIBOU HUNT

Tuesday, November 7th.   At station at 9 a.m. with rifle, fowling piece, tent, sleeping bag, box of grub, kettle, frying pan, change of clothes & "Strand Magazine"[86] & after having been introduced to all the local gentry – conductor &c. – went off with Bobardt on a week's shooting expedition. Destination was Terra Nova, 167 miles to the north along the line which is being built; the journey lasted 14 hours – 9 a.m. to 11 p.m. – and was accomplished in a long American car in which was a stove; it was interesting travelling as we wandered about from car to car talking & listening, even venturing into the post wagon, & looking out on the wild wooded country & down upon the little harbours & coves of Conception Bay. We had a certain feeling of freedom too, for did we not travel with free passes from Mr. [R.G.] Reid, the contractor of the line[87] – & so save $8 each – and did we not receive telegrams from the Governor every few hours telling us now of Grenfell's arrival in St. John's, & now of progress of elections.

At 11 p.m. we were met at the station by [R.B.] Stroud – a noted hunter & trapper in these parts who had been released from his work as foreman on the road by Mr. Reid, that he might take us into the country; he took us to the tilt of one Wiggens, a young man who ran away from his ship a few yrs. ago & has since risen to be master sawyer in the sawmills. Unfortunately his young children were none of the quietest, but they put themselves out & made up a bed & made us comfortable too, although some of the wooden laths did give way under our combined weight of 25 stone, 5 lbs.

Wednesday, November 8th. Up early & at 8 start for boathouse ¾ mile off; take out a dory & borrow extra axe & frying pan. Row 10 miles upstream and along the Terra Nova Pond; being very cold in boat B., Stroud & I walk last part of the way along the beach and in one part where there was sand found track of deer [caribou], lynx (or mountain cat), fox & rabbit.

Reach camping ground about noon & put on kettle; spot chosen was clump of firs & spruce & silver birch at edge of a wood which had been burnt. Take hurried meal of fried bacon, bread, butter & tea, & while our two packers – Dan Burton & John Dohey – pitch tent & build a lean-to for themselves we go for an 8-mile walk over the barrens looking for deer. Recent tracks very numerous, but we saw no animals; the deer have definite courses in travelling the country & follow one another like cattle walking home in the evening, one behind the other, so that they wear definite paths. Stroud is a man of *great* observation & although unable to read or write, of great intelligence; he has been a trapper all his life & knows much about the habits of the animals found here; all the deer of the island go to the bearberry hill district for the winter, & there they may be seen in companies of 200–300 at a time; all the tracks we saw were in the direction of this country, which we could see in the distance. We saw where the stags had been rubbing the fur off their horns to harden them for October, which is the great fighting month; they choose any young tree except the spruce & not uncommonly destroy the tree by stripping all the bark off; often in so rubbing they break off a branch, which becoming entangled in the horns is carried some distance, & in one place we saw a branch of an "elder" tree on the ground very far from any "elder" trees, evidently having been carried in the horns of a stag.[88]

The stag sheds his antlers every year, so we were not surprised to find several on the ground; after lying some years – 2 or 3 – the outer parts get softish & are then well gnawed by the deer; a horn will in time be quite consumed by deer, but the time will be long, for the antlers soften (by some of the calcareous salt being dissolved out) very slowly. We were shown where the deer had been feeding recently, throwing the soft, white moss on which they live about, & by examining the footprints Stroud was able to tell us that some were caused by deer passing during the night or early morning: i.e. after the ground froze over. In returning we passed the single foot of a rabbit – all that was left after a meal a fox had enjoyed. We had had a good walk over soft & wet country & again proved how useful the Esquimaux sealskin boot is, & when we returned to camp about 5, when it was getting dark, we were glad of a supper of pork, spuds & tea.

The kettle was supported over the fire by a long, springy birch stick stuck obliquely into the ground. We lay under shelter of a tarpaulin supported on a rough frame, consisting of two Y–shaped sticks &c., &c., driven obliquely into the ground & supporting a horizontal pole against which leaned several smaller sticks, over which again the tarpaulin was stretched; after supper we lay under this shelter protected from the wind on one side & warmed by the fire on the other & told yarns and learnt much about the habits of beasts & birds – Dan too is a good hunter & can tell some good deerstalking stories.

At 8 I went to the tent & "turned in," that is, got into a bag made of swanskin sewn down the bottom & two sides & with a bag as a pillow was soon asleep. Our candlestick was interesting, consisting of a stick split at one end to take a doubled piece of birch bark, the candle slipped into the loop thus formed by the bark and drawn home.

Thursday, November 9th. Woken at 6.15 in the grey dawn after a good night by John's voice, "breakfast's ready, boss," to find salt herring & potatoes ready. As we eat the sun rose, & after the morning pipe were ready for the day. Just before starting we saw an otter in the water fishing, & by imitating the sound it makes Stroud drew it within 10 yds. of the bank behind which we were hidden; he had his "Brown Sally" or gun, six-foot-long (muzzle loader) handy but ours were in our cases, so that when his cap missed fire we had not a second shot at an animal that was fairly ours (skin worth $10).

We rowed across river & started on the day's walk after arranging with Dan & John to take the boat six miles up river & camp in a clump of birches. We followed deer's tracks all day & noted the animals had all gone in towds. the bearberry [or partridgeberry, a variety of cranberry] hill country; at about 11 we saw a fine red fox ½ mile away & nearly to leeward of us, so we crouched & tolled him up to 200 yds., but then he got our scent & was off like the wind without once looking back, though we all squeaked like rabbits; we did not fire at that distance as the chances of hitting were not great & if we had hit our explosive bullet would have destroyed the skin, so we should have got no good & disturbed the country for nothing. A quarter mile further on we came round [the] edge of a wood & saw [a] stag, doe & fawn immediately to leeward of us; this was unfortunate, but we doubled back to come round "skirt of wood" to leeward of them & hoped they would not have got our wind, but when we were round the wood the deer had already moved off, having smelt us; I fired two shots at 330 yds. but too high, & it was not long before we saw the last of them.

We saw no more deer that day, but the crisp, fresh air & exercise were first class and we were on the constant lookout for game. Besides deer there were many other things to look at & for; in one place we found trace of a wolf, now a very rare animal (bounty on each head of $10 (Govt.) & skin worth $10); of the black bear there were many traces of where he had turned up stones to look for the pismire ant or broken up dead wood in which the ant is often found, or dragged down the mountain ash (rowan) – called dogberry here – for the berries; & in two places we saw where he had been clawing the earth; the black bear is not often shot here as he is about only in summer, the closed season for deer, & when the men are busy fishing; in winter he is asleep in his den, so we had no chance of meeting one; he must have fine teeth, for he often leaves big marks in the wood he splits to look for his food. We found two or three pismire or emmet nests & opened one; the ant is a large & busy one, & did not care for being disturbed; the nest seemed to be made entirely of vegetable matter & spread over with the leaves of the Indian tea. In Cape Breton the hunter will often eat them when he finds them asleep in wood – where they live in winter – but Stroud had never tried them.

A little rain mid-day & weather looked like snow; lunch by side of a brook. Stroud *very* surprised to see no deer; reason of absence seen when on returning in evening we found a track across the barrens & woods marked by marks in the trees showing someone who did not know the country had been in recently & disturbed the country.

Shot two partridge – really willow grouse – on way to camp. Right glad of supper at 6 – soup (of peameal, barley & pork), fried bacon and tea. Yarns of course.

Friday, November 10th.	Absence of game serious, so determine to leave camp & strike inland towds. bearberry hills for a couple of days. Packed up two sleeping bags, blankets & grub. Dull, cold day, freezing all day & ground hard to walk on, being lumpy as in the wet weather it had been broken up by 1000s of deer – all passing in. At 10 saw a deer feeding ¾ mile away to leeward, circled him, but he had moved on & before we saw him again he saw us & so we cd. not get near; Bobardt had a long shot at about 200 yds. & missed.

Walked all day – 18 miles in 7 hrs. over marshes partly frozen, moss-covered barrens & through woods. On going up a hill we saw a *large* silver grey fox (skin £15–20) & tolled him towds. us, but he sighted us & got suspicious, and a pond being between us he decided not to go after the sweet, squeaking morsel but make for the woods. By 4 we were very tired & a bit disappointed at seeing no deer as we knew they ought to be about, & we were already further in the country than any sportsmen had ever been before; the presence of so many recent tracks only made disappointment worse; so Stroud went off with my rifle & said he would not return without deer, while we went to the wood to prepare camp. A N.E. cold wind was blowing so we cut down trees & let them fall across one another, making a barricade 4 ft. high to windward & made it more windproof by interlacing spruce boughs. We made a great fire & after tea of bacon & cheese knocked the ice from the knees of our knickerbockers, which had got wet, lit our pipes & turned into our sleeping bags to keep warm.

At 7 Stroud shouts & we direct him through the wood by sending up sparks from the fire; on his shoulders he carried the hind quarters & skin of a fine fawn; after leaving us he walked 5 miles till he saw 7 deer in a marsh; he got within 200 yds. & fired at the stag, although it was too dark for him to see the sight on the gun; the stag was wounded but he got off, so s. fired at & killed a fawn as it was making away.

This put us all in far better spirits, so after cutting more wood for the night we turned in & slept well under a cold, clear, starlight sky. During the day we had seen more bear tracks, & I had caught a moth.

Saturday, November 11th. Night cold, but in blankets I slept well; breakfast at 5.20 in the dark; found skin boots frozen & had to toast them before getting them on; Stroud's beard too was full of ice. Start at 7.15 when there was sufficient light to see the country well. Went to see remains of fawn Stroud had shot & try to track the wounded stag; we had not been looking for the track long before on looking back the way we had come we saw a fine stag walk out of the woods ½ mile back; he crossed our track & got very suspicious, but came nearer cautiously; however, he was too cautious & when 300 yds. away turned round & was off. A quarter of a mile further on we came to some rising ground & from there saw a large barren doe 300 yds.

off behind a clump of trees; Bobardt kept her covered & ran down to the bushes while we stood still on the high ground – a deer cannot see clearly over 300 yds. & is not suspicious of man unless it smells him or sees him move – and as she came round feeding had a good shot at about 40 yds. – a very fat animal weighing about 3 cwt., meat worth 8 cents a lb., therefore about £5.

He was content & so would not accompany Stroud & me further on – we walked 6 miles further to Clode Sound N.W. River to the very edge of the bearberry hills but did not get within ½ mile of a deer although we saw 9 in all but in the distance, too far for us to go as we had to be back in good time – 13 miles further in than any sportsman had been before & no deer for me! We walked back another way & still no deer – they had nearly all gone further in for the winter, knowing bad weather was at hand; a strong, cold N.E. wind was blowing & snow seemed imminent. We reached Bobardt at 12.45 & found he had shot 2 stags & Dan Burton another, all very fine beasts; they had been resting in the main lead, so it appeared, & during the morning two companies of 4 in each had come by; Dan shot one at 300 yds. out of the first company & Bobardt two out of the second, one at 60 yds. & one as he was running at 150 – a good shot. After lunch we prepared for return to camp; Stroud shouldered the two forequarters of his fawn, Bobardt two large pairs of antlers, Dan a skin with horns & hindquarters of the fat doe, John a similar load, while I contented myself with a forequarter of the same animal – a queer-looking party indeed as we returned towds. camp. It was with regret we left so much meat & two skins behind, but we could not carry more & having 15 miles to pack what we took, we were unable to make two journeys. A large eagle was hovering over the remains of the fawn's carcass; we fired at it with bullets but did not hit; we went sufficiently near to frighten it away, however, & it flapped its wings together with a clap as he shook himself.

Half a mile further on we saw a doe & fawn 300 yds. off. I did not want to shoot as we had more than we could carry, but the men persuaded me as I had not had a shot at a deer within range; I got within 120 yds. before they saw me, but my first shot missed; to be shot at was a new sensation & they did not know what to make of it & seemed stupified, so that I had another chance & made better use of it; the horns were very small. These barrens are now named the "Doctors' Commons."[89] We were soon back in camp & enjoyed a good supper of fried venison and felt we had earned it, having been out all day walking 20 miles over hard, frozen, uneven ground; skin boots cannot be beaten over soft country & wet, but small stones & uneven, frozen ground are severely felt through the soleless bottoms although two thick prs. [of] socks or stockings are much protection.

Sunday, November 12th.   Bitterly cold night; we were all night with Uhlan caps[90] & blankets but the men were cold enough & did not sleep much. Cold & strong N.E. wind & threatenings of snow. Odd place for Sunday morning – 10 miles from our camp & boat, & 25 from the nearest house.

Began the day with tea at 1 a.m.; next thing was venison roasted on a stick at 7.30. Weather looked bad so think it best to push on for camp & shelter & at 8.30 we start again single file; Stroud first with hindquarters [of] fawn sitting on his neck with a leg over each shoulder; then came B. with roll of blankets & 2 pr. heavy antlers; I followed with a sack containing blankets &c. & forequarter of doe in a sack which rested on top of shoulders & was kept in place by my belt passing across forehead, with gun thrust horizontal through the load, & then came Dan & John with a skin & horns apiece & hindquarters of doe – the three men carried 80 lbs. each & looked odd with frying pan & kettle &c. dangling from their waists. B. & I carried about 40 lbs. & found that quite heavy enough to pack over the 10 miles of rough country we had to traverse. It was hardest work going through the woods as the rifle projecting would catch in the trees & turn the head suddenly, now one side & now another. We had an easy [rest] every 1 or 1½ mile; the ground I did not find so trying as I had 3 pr. socks on.

We christened the hills where we had seen the silver grey fox "Doctors' Hills" and put up a suitable inscription with date &c. to mark the locality. At 12.30 we lunched on venison & the very little cheese & hard biscuit we had left, & nearby I noticed an old camping place of some Micmac Indian hunters – there are a few of these hunters settled in the Gambo district. Reach camp at 4 p.m. & glad to rest. The change of wind necessitated change of position of camp, but we were soon in shelter & slippers and hard at work on supper. Prayers at 8.20 & turn in at 9.30.

Monday, November 13th.	Good night, not so cold because in camp. Soup 6.30, breakfast 7.30. Pack up & off at 9; had to break ice to get boat out of side run into the river – ice 2 inches thick. Row 4 miles & walk two down to first camping ground. Strong wind straight up the lake so we walk the 10 miles while Dan & John row the dory; B. goes on and I have long talk with Stroud on many things. Find more traces of bears and wood bitten off by the beaver. Reach Terra Nova station at 3.30 after having walked 100 miles in six days; boat arrives ½ [hour] later; unpack, stow boat away and have a welcome & much needed wash. Dan & Sam Smart (a master lumberer) to go in with men to bring out the deer we shot for their own use, this being a considerable contribution towards their winter's diet.

Turn in 8.45.

ST JOHN'S

Tuesday, November 14th.	Up 1.30 a.m. Train arrives at 3 & it's not till 2.30 that we reach St. John's – a long, slow journey. We sent presents of venison to Governor, Mr. Job, Dr. Harvey, Mrs. Smith, Rev. [J.S.] Thompson & Capt. Dined at Govt. House and met Mr. Reid the contractor for this r[ailwa]y line, a Scotch Canadian.

Grenfell well & in good spirits.

Wednesday, November 15th – *Friday, November 17th.*	Spent wading through the mud of this city paying bills, attending comee. meeting, paying calls & visiting the museum. Mail arrived on Wed. with letters from Mother, Etta & Ellen. Friday evening spent at hospital seeing cases with Dr. Shea.

Saturday, November 18th.   Morning wrote to Storrs; bought P.O.P. [printing-out paper] & borrowed plates from Chapman; very bad weather for printing. Afternoon again at hospital.

Report of Dr Grenfell, 28 October to 7 November 1893 (continued)

... The record of the *Princess May* was: sixty services held, attended by about 5,000 people, counting only those when away from the *Albert*; eighty-seven ports visited, most of them twice over; 794 patients treated, about twenty lantern lectures, four Moravian stations visited – viz., Zoar, Hopedale, Nain, and Okkak. Literature was distributed all along the coast, and to numbers of schooner crews, but I was unable to keep a record of the quantity, or the numbers of the Word of God given away. Everywhere, by everyone, the literature seemed vastly appreciated. To distressed and poverty-stricken families we were able to give much good and useful clothing. In some cases it was indeed clothing – "Naked, and ye clothed me." I hope, dear Mr. Editor, you may find it possible to reproduce some of our photographs in the *Toilers* later on of one or two of these families as we found them preparing for an Arctic winter. In some cases, also, we felt obliged to leave what food we could spare, in the way of biscuits and flour.

Dr. Bobardt in the hospital at Battle Harbour treated thirty-three in-patients and 647 out-patients; only two patients actually died in Battle Hospital; one or two reached home in time to end their days among their friends, instead of on bleak Labrador.

Dr. Curwen treated 1,052 patients on the *Albert*, and had three in-patients. He found it almost impossible to take in patients, owing to the constant moving about of the vessel north and south. He sent most of his patients, therefore, to Battle Harbour, where, as at times it was overfilled, Dr. Bobardt found it necessary to engage rooms in cottages on the island.

Besides the usual daily service, the *Albert* had many meetings, attended by about 6,000 people, while twice lantern meetings were held by the captain. The *Albert* visited ten harbours – some twice over. We were on the coast of Labrador 109 days. At St. John's we have been treated with universal kindness, though, owing to the elections, it was found impossible to hold general meetings till this week (November 30). We shall deliver two lectures in this country on the work, at the suggestion of our local auxiliary committee – one in St. John's, at which his Excellency the Governor will preside, in a hall lent by the Government; and the other in the second chief town in the island, Harbour Grace. Both lectures will be illustrated by slides made from negatives, and with a limelight lantern lent by the Governor.[91] After this we shall sail direct for Yarmouth.

Yours sincerely,
Wilfred Grenfell

Letter from Eliot Curwen to MDSF

Westbridge, Hampstead, N.W., December 1893

Dear Mr. Editor:

You, in common with a large number of the readers of the *Toilers*, will be glad to hear of the quick and comfortable passage the *Albert* made on her return across the Atlantic. The taking appearance of the ship had attracted a good deal of attention during our stay in St. John's, so that when I arrived on board on Monday, November 27, I was not surprised to find a large number of friends, including the captains of most of the English vessels in the harbour, who had come to wish us God speed. As we towed out of the harbour the hand at the flag halyards was kept very busy answering the flag salutes we received on all hands, and at 10.45, after saluting the city with a couple of gun rockets, Drs. Grenfell and Bobardt, and Mr. Job, left us in the latter's steam launch, and we set canvas, glad to be homeward bound, yet finding it difficult to say good-bye to those from whom we had received so much kindness during the year.

As far as incident is concerned the voyage was uneventful, and most of the interest lay in the extraordinary readings of the barometer and thermometer, and in watching the enormous swell as the waves caught us up, lifting us up as onto mountain tops, and then passing on, dropping us into the trough.

We left Newfoundland with the beginning of a strong westerly wind – the same wind that had caused such havoc on the coasts of North Europe the last few days – and kept it the whole of the passage, so that with a good steady power behind us we were able to make some capital runs over the sea, which for the most part was not very rough, and were glad to be without the anxiety that fog and the presence of icebergs entail. The first day took us 190 knots from land; and the next day, with its 100 knots, took us clear of the Arctic current, which, flowing down the Labrador and Newfoundland coasts, keeps the temperature of both sea and air at a low level.

On the third day the thermometer was 54° in the shade, and we were sitting on deck in our shirt sleeves, enjoying a balmy south wind and finding it hard to realise it was the last day of November. During the next four days the glass rose steadily till it reached [30.7], and the wind holding from the s. or w. We made a course like a bee line, and covered 223, 224, 183, and 178 knots. On the 5th inst. the glass began to fall, but the wind held, and during the next few days, with a good spread of canvas, we made runs of 175, 207, 206, and 206 knots. On Thursday morning, 7th inst., we crossed the longitude of the Scilly Islands, and the same night saw the double light at the Lizard; and you will not find it difficult to believe that all hands turned out, including the two sisters and Dr. Bobardt's Labrador boy, to see the first bit of the old country again. The night was one of those preternaturally clear ones, forerunners of strong winds, in which lights are seen great distances, and the glow of these powerful lamps was seen by us when we were more than 40 miles off, and the lights themselves at a distance of 23. Though so far from the shore we began to feel "at home." The Atlantic was behind us, and we had crossed it in ten days, maintaining an average of 7.6 knots an hour, or 182 knots a day – a rate which we believe has rarely or ever been recorded by a sailing vessel before.

Labrador Odyssey

All Friday, 8th, the barometer was very low, the sea rough, and appearance of the sky very threatening; and at night, when off Beachy Head, there was so much lightning that, expecting a dirty time, our captain determined to "lay-to" and not risk the Straits of Dover in the dark. Fortunately for us we were not in the track of gales that night, and the next morning opened with a clear sky. The wind being off shore our flags could not be read at the signal station at Dungeness, so we passed on unnoticed, drawing close in to land as we passed Folkstone and Dover, an then rounding South Foreland steered outside the Goodwins. Saturday night we felt very much "at home," for we fell in with the Lowestoft Fleet, and it seemed quite like old times to be surrounded by trawlers again. [It] being dark, however, we gave them the "go-by," and next morning at daylight sailed within a few yards of the Corton Lightship, seven miles from Yarmouth. We had had to wait for the rising tide and for daylight, but by 8.30 we were behind the tugboat, and, decked out with flags, announced our arrival by gun-rocket.

Our friends at Yarmouth, as elsewhere, were greatly surprised to see us so soon, for we were only twelve and a half days out of St. John's, and it was not thought possible for a sailing vessel to accomplish the distance in so short a time; the fact that the *Albert* has made this record is sufficient proof of her excellent qualities as a sea-going boat and a sailer, and it is to the lasting credit of Captain Trezise, who, being alone responsible for the navigation of the ship, on several occasions spent night and day on deck, not coming below even for meals. Needless to say, our welcome at Yarmouth was a warm one, and our feelings of thanks at having been given a safe return, and been permitted to do much work in the Master's name, very great. Believe me, yours very truly,

Eliot Curwen

APPENDIX:
DR GRENFELL'S
FUND-RAISING
REPORT

We left Government House, St. John's, where His Excellency, Sir Terence O'Brien, had so kindly entertained us since our arrival from Labrador, on Friday, December 1, by ss *Assyrian*, of the Allan Line, for Halifax, in Nova Scotia. The steamer is a good sea boat, and after the *Princess May* she seemed to us as steady as a rock, in spite of the fact that two head gales made us twenty-four hours late. We landed on Monday night, and proceeded with several other passengers to the Halifax Hotel. The following morning the question that proposed itself for solution was how to attack Canada in the interests of the Labrador fisherfolk under the M.D.S.F. flag.

Commencing with our introductions, we went to two of the leading ministers and asked their help. These led us to the Hon. W. Fielding, Prime Minister of Nova Scotia. This gentleman proved most kind, and with him we called on Lieut.-General A. Montgomery Moore, who at once promised to preside at a meeting the following Friday evening. Next we obtained a hall, and, through Mr. Fielding's help, at a reduced rental, and then interviewed all the papers, getting in advertisements and items of information. Wednesday we endeavoured to obtain a lime-light lantern, but one was not to be had in the city anywhere. My search ended in my finding in the city an old East London worker with whom I had had many mutual friends, and he most kindly offered his splendid oil lantern and sheet, and sent them up to the hall for me. He next introduced us to the clergyman he is working with here, the Rev.

Dyson Hague, of St. Paul's Church. Mr. Hague at once invited us to speak for a few minutes at his Wednesday evening week-night service – a largely attended gathering – thus extending to us a most welcome right hand of friendship.

During the day a few other calls were made, and at night, after service, we joined a meeting of young men in connection with the church, called the Brotherhood of St. Andrew. Here we found true friends at once, who set about helping us in every way possible, and to whom I wish to tender my warmest thanks. I must here say a word about this brotherhood. Its special object is to band young members of the Church together as a brotherhood, with the definite object of helping each to do personal work for Christ. The organisation has been immensely blessed. Thousands of men through Canada and the States have joined it, an annual conference is held, a monthly paper called *The St. Andrew's Cross* issued, and a splendid total of actual work is accomplished. Hotels are visited to invite and welcome strangers. Wharves and vessels are also regularly visited, strangers to the city noted and looked up, and in a thousand ways, perhaps little in themselves, young men are brought gradually forward as definite workers, not afraid to show their colours, but in manly, straightforward attempts to live up to the professions they intend to die by, and to accomplish good work while 'tis yet day, rather than to repent when the night is at hand.

Next morning Bishop Courtenay, of Nova Scotia, who had only just returned from a visit to outlying parishes, was kind enough to call, and he readily offered to speak at and open our meeting. Surely his kindness was not thrown away on us, entire strangers in a new city. This night we took part in a meeting at a large evangelistic hall, where my friend from East London, Mr. Winfield, nightly carries on his excellent work. He is perhaps the most indefatigable worker and visitor I have ever met, and his efforts have been largely crowned with success, many having become new creatures, and joined the regular congregation afterwards as the fruit of his labours.

Friday likewise was spent in calls, and in the evening we held our meeting, of which I have already forwarded you an account. Saturday was occupied with forming a committee, and a meeting in the Commercial Rooms; while on Sunday we had a large meeting at Dalhousie University, and in the evening a still larger gathering in the Rev. Mr. Bond's large Methodist church.

On Monday morning [11 December] we left by c.p.r. for Montreal, leaving behind us a well established branch of the m.d.s.f. Among many things that struck me as of great interest in this first Canadian city, were the excellent liquor laws and the excellent effects they have produced. I may say, all the time we were in Halifax we never saw a drunken man, and from what we heard of the jails, hospitals, and asylums, it is evident the police also do not find many victims from England's national enemy. Comparing this city with London, the same contrast appears that obtains in Constantinople, where "Christians" appear to figure in the jails for drunkenness, and the Mahomedans, who are teetotallers, have to pay to keep them there ...

A heavy snowstorm prevailed, and a low temperature also, all the way to Montreal, and the thermometer was five degrees below zero when we disembarked on Tuesday evening. Here we found Mr. William Munn, of the famous firm Stewart Munn [commission merchants],[92] waiting to meet us, and he kindly escorted us to comfortable quarters at the Windsor Hotel. Next morning we commenced our calls, and everywhere met with the greatest kindness. Bishop Bond, of Montreal, Dean Carmichael, Rev. Dr. Hunter, Rev. Dr. MacVicar, Rev. Dr. James Barclay, and numbers of other ministers, promised to announce our meeting. Sir Donald Smith, so well known in Canada for his princely gifts to charities, promised to preside. Sir Donald and Lord Mount Stephen recently presented Montreal with a million dollars for the Royal Victoria Hospital. Sir Donald is an old Labrador man. Many years of his early life were spent in Labrador, in the service of the Hudson's Bay Company, and he has countless stories to tell of his adventures, which extend from Quebec to Ungava Bay. Sir Wm. Dawson, so well known for his scientific books and his splendid Christian Evidence work – as well as for his making of McGill University – also promised to attend. Many other meetings were held in Montreal the same night, unfortunately, as ours; worst of all, Mr. Woolley, the modern John B. Gough,[93] and, they say, the best temperance orator of the day, was down to address an annual Christian Endeavour gathering.

However, when the time arrived quite a number of friends arrived also, and my fears were soon allayed that a thermometer below zero, and the attractions of a Christmas fireside, would keep Canadians away. So representative was the gathering, that Dean Carmichael said it was the best mission gathering in that respect he had ever seen.

We have now, I am glad to say, not only a large representative committee here, but already 1,300 dollars have been given, 1,000 promised annually, and the Board of Trade resolution forwarded to Ottawa to assist our work there. We have also organised a ladies' committee, or rather, found one ready organised, with Mrs. Kohl, 84, Crescent-street, as secretary, who will work through the winter to prepare sheets and household necessaries for Indian Harbour Hospital. Sir Donald Smith is chairman of the Montreal branch; William Munn, Esq., Board of Trade Buildings, is secretary. Our committee includes most of the leading Montreal laymen and clergy, Sir William Dawson among the number. Our committee will hold their inaugural meeting next Thursday, December 28 …

Yours sincerely,
Wilfred Grenfell

NOTES

1 *Coper*: Dutch vessel selling spirits to fishermen in the North Sea.
2 See entry for 7 June. By selling tobacco at sea, the MDSF gave fishermen an alternative to boarding the copers.
3 James Stalker, *The Life of St. Paul* (Edinburgh: T. & T. Clark 1885). See entries for 10 and 11 June.
4 Howard Saunders, *An Illustrated Manual of British Birds* (London: Gurney and Jackson 1889).
5 SS *Naronic*, a steel-hulled, four-masted schooner with twin screws, launched at Belfast in 1892, had been missing since February. In fact, a champagne bottle from the *Naronic* floated ashore in Virginia containing a letter stating that the vessel had struck an iceberg and was sinking. See *Shipping and Mercantile Gazette and Lloyd's List*, 30 March 1893.
6 The Rev. Dr Moses Harvey (1820–1901), Presbyterian minister, naturalist, and writer. Harvey had been instrumental in drawing attention to fishing conditions in Labrador and in bringing the MDSF to investigate the year before.
7 Vice-Admiral Sir George Tryon (1832–93) had been lost as a result of his own error when HMS *Victoria* collided with HMS *Camperdown* off Tripoli.
8 John Terence Nicholls O'Brien (1830–1903), former British army officer in India, governor of Newfoundland 1889–95. The observations on local affairs that follow appear to be given from his point of view.
9 Capt. W.S. Melville of the Leicester Regiment, ADC and private secretary.
10 Sir Robert Thorburn (1836–1900), businessman. In 1893 he helped form the Conservative Party in opposition to Whiteway but failed to win a seat that year.
11 Sir William Vallance Whiteway (1828–1908), promoter of the Newfoundland railway and of economic diversification. Prime minister 1878–85, he returned to public life to defeat Prime Minister Sir Robert Thorburn in 1889 and successfully negotiated a railway contract with R.G. Reid in 1890. He won the election of 1893 but was disqualified a year later.
12 Dr Henry Shea (1835–1918), medical superintendent of the General Hospital.
13 Hon. Augustus W. Harvey (1839–1903), St John's businessman and supporter of Sir William Whiteway. In 1889 he had been appointed chairman

of the fisheries commission, which became a department of government in 1893.

14 Moses Monroe (1842–95), businessman and co-leader with W.B. Grieve of the Conservative Party, a coalition of Water Street merchants opposing the policy of diversification pursued by Whiteway.

15 William Carson Job (1864–1943), joint manager of Job Bros and Co., fish exporters.

16 Walter Baine Grieve (1850–1921), manager of Baine Johnson & Co., fish merchants, and co-leader of the Conservative Party.

17 John Steer (1824–1918), St John's merchant, lived at Hope Cottage, formerly Arundel Cottage, south of the hatchery at Long Pond.

18 Newfoundland's game fish hatchery was provided for under the Crown Lands Act of 1884–85. Under this act, the Game Fish Protection Society was established, and the first importation of eggs took place in 1886. The society subsequently began work at Long Pond, then obtained rights to Murray's Pond and Butler's Pond. It paid an annual rental of 10,000 fish fry and was required to liberate these in public waters. After 1890, its main efforts were directed towards the encouragement of the rainbow trout. See Curwen's notebook, 118; W.B. Scott and E.J. Crossman, *Fishes Occurring in the Fresh Waters of Insular Newfoundland* (Toronto: University of Toronto Press 1964); and Tor Fosnaes, *In on the Pond: A Trouting Excursion in Victorian Newfoundland* (St John's: Harry Cuff 1994).

19 Amelia Ayre, sister of Charles Ayre of Devonshire, married John Steer in 1851.

20 The cornerstone was laid in 1843, and the building was consecrated in 1850. See C. Francis Rowe, *In Fields Afar: A Review of the Establishment of the Anglican Parish of St. John's and Its Cathedral* (St John's: Seawise Enterprise 1989).

21 The question concerning the continuance of French fishing rights on the west coast.

22 Thomas Raffles Job (1837–1917), senior partner of Job Bros & Co.

23 HMS *Blake*, completed in 1892, the largest cruiser built by the Admiralty. It was then serving as flagship on the North Atlantic–West Indies station.

24 HMS *Cleopatra*, a corvette of the Comus class, was less than a third the size of *Blake* and became obsolescent with the new ship construction of 1888 that brought *Blake* into being. From 1892, *Cleopatra* had functioned as the commodore's flagship for a squadron of three vessels tasked to monitor Anglo-French fishing rights in the North Atlantic. William Tait, the medical officer, reveals in *Cruise of HMS Cleopatra, 1892–1895* (Plymouth: C. Mansfield n.d.) that Commodore Curzon-Howe carried a large quantity of clothing on board, together with flour and biscuit, for distribution to the

destitute. The medical officers in the patrol vessels also rendered medical and surgical aid. In three years, he reckoned, they had treated 3,000 people.

25 Edwin J. Duder, Jr (1853–1918), St John's merchant.

26 David P. Patrick, foreman (later buyer) for Edwin Duder.

27 Wife of the Rev. John Curwen (1816–80), Congregationalist clergyman and developer of the Tonic-Sol-Fa system of music notation.

28 Probably *A Short History of Newfoundland: England's Oldest Colony* (London: William Collins Sons 1890). Curwen also seems to have been shown Harvey's "How I Discovered the Giant Devil-Fish," *Wide World* (1892): 732–9, and his "Narrow Escape of Two Fishermen from a Gigantic Cuttle-fish," *Rod and Gun and American Sportsman,* 6 December 1873.

29 Perhaps the Bible class primer by James Iverach.

30 Bordighera: a resort town on the Italian Riviera.

31 Perhaps the Sunday school text by Edward Augustus Horton, *Great Thoughts of Israel, for Intermediate Classes* (Boston 1895).

32 See also Robert E. Peary, *Northward over the "Great Ice": A Narrative of Life and Work along the Shores and upon the Interior Ice-Cap of Northern Greenland in the Years 1886 and 1891–1897* (London: Methuen 1898), 2: 3–17.

33 Capt. Henry B. Bartlett (1863–94), son of Abram Bartlett of Brigus, Newfoundland. The following year, having picked up Peary in Greenland and transported him to Philadelphia, he, with all hands, was lost at sea on the return trip.

34 Dr R.W. McAll (1821–93), promoter of the Independent Protestant Mission, Paris, had died on 11 May.

35 A two-masted, schooner-rigged vessel ranging from five to twenty tons, used for various fishing purposes.

36 Edward R. Burgess, Liberal member for Twillingate. See also 12 August.

37 Youngest son of Abram Bartlett.

38 Capt. Samuel Blandford (1840–1909), of Greenspond, Newfoundland, manager for Job Bros at Blanc Sablon. At the time, he represented Bonavista in the House of Assembly as one of Whiteway's Liberals but declined renomination in 1893. He was then appointed to the Legislative Council and remained a member until his death.

39 William Henry Whiteley (1834–1903), inventor of the cod trap, was born in Boston and came to Labrador in 1849. He ultimately became the agent for Job Bros until 1894. At the time of the journal, he was the MHA for Harbour Grace in Whiteway's Liberal party.

40 Bioluminescent dinoflagellates, a group of algae.

41 John Munn & Co., Harbour Grace, the largest supplier of the Labrador stationer fishery.

42 James Alva Wilson (1854–1920), clerk-in-charge of the Hudson's Bay Company dictrict of Esquimaux Bay, 1892–1901.

43 Hannah Michelin was the sister of diarist Lydia Campbell (see *Evening Telegram*, 3 December 1894.) Grenfell paid homage to Hannah Michelin thus during his visit to Rigolet: "An old woman of eighty-two years (guaranteed by Mr. Wilson) was showing me the trophies of her hunting last year. I photographed her shooting with her long double-barrelled gun. Even last winter she was chiselling holes through the thick ice and catching trout for the family; while she still continues to drive a dog team, though now, of course, three or four dogs are all she could manage. Certainly she is the most marvellous old lady I ever saw, as besides being a good seamstress and a tidy housewife, she is a good bootmaker and an excellent carpenter" (*Toilers* 8 [1893]: 309).

44 James J. Rogerson (1820–1907), philanthropist, temperance advocate, and political colleague of W.B. Grieve,

45 Johann Christian Louis Kästner (1837–1921), who had been in Labrador for over twenty years, reveals the separate trading and missionary functions of the Moravian enterprise at this time. Born at Altengesees, near Ebersdorf, Kästner apprenticed as a tailor at the Moravian establishment in Ebersdorf and later became a master tailor at Neudietendorf. In 1866–69, he was wholesaler with the firm of Just at Königsfeld, then was called as a "trade brother" to Labrador. Kästner travelled first to Malmesbury, England, to study English and left for Hopedale in June 1869, but he chose to leave trade in 1880 to enter missionary service. Returning to Germany in 1882, he was ordained a deacon the following year. At the request of the United Elder Conference, he received medical training in Stuttgart and Freiburg. He later served at both Hopedale and Nain as both missionary and trader. When Curwen arrived, he and his wife were "house parents" at Hopedale, but in 1895 he left Labrador because of illness.

46 Karl Erdmann Heinrich Simon (1862–1948) was born at Hammer-Vorwerk, Freistadt, and after an apprenticeship as a metalworker in Neusalz on the Oder worked in Zittau, Bautzen, and Niesky. He was received into the Moravian Church in 1884 and attended the missionary school at Niesky in 1888 before being called to Labrador. After ordination as an acolyte, Simon received a short training course in midwifery and arrived in Labrador in August 1889, serving at Hopedale and Ramah. Ordained a deacon at Nain, he worked at the mission store in Hopedale, 1891–96, and was there when Curwen arrived. Simon subsequently supervised the stations at Hebron, Okak, and Killinek before returning to Germany in 1920.

47 The Inuit farewell is also *aksunai* ("be strong").

48 Peter Mölgard Hansen (1859–1935), a gardener, was born at Lomborg, Jutland. He was received into the Moravian Church in 1879. Hansen attended missionary school at Niesky, 1884–87, and was called to serve in Labrador in 1887. Ordained an acolyte that same year, he arrived in Labrador in July 1887 and subsequently served at Hopedale and Nain. A year after he met Curwen, he returned to Europe for travel and medical treatment. He remained there as a Moravian church worker but declined ordination as a presbyter. Hansen retired in 1925.

49 Frank Jonadab Fry, an Englishman, had barely been in Labrador two months when Curwen arrived. Born in 1868 at Malmesbury, he studied for missionary work at Fairfield and was called to Labrador in 1892. Fry was ordained a deacon in June 1893 aboard the Mission ship *Harmony* in London, just before his departure. He served in Hopedale, 1893–96, then at Okak, but left for Europe in 1897.

50 See Jonathan Prince Cilley, Jr, *Bowdoin Boys in Labrador: An Account of the Bowdoin College Scientific Expedition to Labrador Led by Prof. Leslie A. Lee of the Biological Department* (Rockland: Rockland Publishing Co. [1894?].

51 *Kjoekkenmoeddinger*, or kitchen-middens. Curwen is aware of the interest in mounds of shells and artifacts begun by the Danes in the 1830s and an important part of the study of native American prehistory in the 1860s. It appears that Curwen had read Sir John Lubbock's imperialist synthesis *Pre-historic Times* (1865), wherein Lubbock ranged widely over archaeological subjects and drew parallels between Inuit stone tools and those of the European Upper Palaeolithic. See also Bruce G. Trigger, ed., *Native Shell Mounds of North America: Early Studies* (New York: Garland 1986).

52 Hymns of the evangelists Dwight L. Moody (1837–99) and Ira D. Sankey (1840–1908). Wilfred Grenfell claimed that his own renewal of Christian commitment occurred at a London revival meeting of Moody's while he was a medical student.

53 Capt. William J. Bartlett (1851–1931), a member of the committee formed in St John's the year before to build two hospitals in Labrador. He prosecuted the fishery at the station established by his father, Abram, at Turnavik and replaced his father at the seal fishery as captain of the ss *Panther*. His son was the explorer Capt. Robert A. Bartlett.

54 For the 1893 World's Fair in Chicago, the American businessman Charles Martin induced fifty-seven Inuit to come and live in an "Eskimo village" constructed for the occasion. Visitors at the exposition could observe the Labrador people in their native dress and ride on a komatik drawn along a narrow-gauge track by Labrador dogs. The Inuit were miserable from the start, some contracting typhoid fever. See William Forbush, *Pomiuk, A Prince of Labrador* (London: Marshall Brothers 1903), 49–58.

55 Alexander greens, or Scotch lovage (*Ligusticum scothicum*), a medicinal herb.

56 See *Evening Herald*, 11 and 14 September 1893.

57 Fridtjof Nansen, *The First Crossing of Greenland*, trans. H. M. Gepp (London: Longmans 1890).

58 Curwen writes in his notebook, "Dr. Hogan of Carbonear is on 'Windsor Lake,' a R.C., absolutely no good; gets £120 for his summer work in Labrador. Sick bay on board ghastly & lice infected; he says he has no means of washing patients & no clothes for them so when he takes anyone on board they are never washed or undressed but put in a bunk as they are" (17).

59 For archaeological descriptions of this area, see E.W. Hawkes, *The Labrador Eskimo*, Geological Survey of Canada, Anthropological Series no. 14 (Ottawa: Government Printing Bureau 1916). See also Junius B. Bird, *Archaeology of the Hopedale Area, Labrador*, Anthropological Papers of the American Museum of Natural History, vol. 39, part 2 (New York: American Museum of Natural History 1945); and T. Dale Stewart, *Anthropometric Observations on the Eskimos and Indians of Labrador*, material and data collected by William Duncan Strong, Anthropological Series, vol. 31, no. 1 (Chicago: Field Museum of Natural History 1939). A range of archaeological topics is also covered in the special issue of *Newfoundland Studies* 9 (1993): 155–329.

60 Gustav Renatus Schulze (1837–1914), born in Gramenz, near Bärwalde/Pomerania, and trained as a wheelwright, was received into the Moravian Church in 1859. He was called to missionary service in Labrador in 1867 and subsequently served in Hopedale and Okak before taking over the store at Hopedale in 1878. He next served at Hebron and Ramah and came to Zoar in 1891, where he was installed when Grenfell met him.

61 Carl Albert Martin (1861–1934), unlike most of his colleagues, was born into the Moravian Church, at Gnadenfrei, and he entered the theological seminary there in 1881. After a brief career as a teacher, he was ordained in 1888 and set out for Labrador. He served as acting superintendant in 1889, and he was made superintendent of the Labrador mission in 1890 at the age of twenty-nine. Martin was ordained a bishop at Herrnhut in 1899. In 1913, as German consul in Labrador, he received the Red Decoration of the Eagle (Fourth Class). Bishop Martin returned to Germany in 1923 and retired in Kleinwelka.

62 Carl Friedrich Kahle (1836–1907), born at Kühren, near Wurzen (Saxony), and trained as a joiner at Gnadenfrei, was received into the Moravian Church in 1858 and called to missionary service in Labrador in 1871. He was at Hopedale until 1879, then at Nain and Zoar as a trader. After a leave in Europe, 1885–86, he was at Okak, Hebron, and Nain, where he met Grenfell.

63 Siegmund Waldmann (1866–1948), a shoemaker, was born at Eutendorf, near Gaildorf/Württemberg, and called to missionary service in Labrador in 1891. When Grenfell arrived, he had been store helper at Okak, 1891–92. He later had a distinguished career in Labrador and did not retire until 1930.

64 Squire Joseph Townley (1865–1929), a cotton weaver, was born in Dukinfield, Cheshire, and called to missionary service in Labrador in 1890. He had served in Hopedale, 1891–92, then in Hebron and Ramah, 1892–93. He did not return to England until 1924.

65 Hermann Theodor Jannasch, a teacher, born 1849 in South Africa. Called to missionary service in Labrador in 1879, he subsequently served at Hopedale, Nain, and Okak, and in 1896 founded the new station in Makkovik. In 1903 he was recalled to Germany for service at Württemberg. He died at Bad Boll in 1931.

66 Curwen writes in his notebook, "An old heathen idea is that wife *cannot* live when husband dies. In Okkak a man died from a disease & his friends came to Mr. Keastner for *two* coffins saying that wife cd. not live without husband and had laid down & died; Mr. K. had seen her in good health the day before. Husbands occasionally died when the wife died. (Cf. Ossian's poems & easy-death habits of the women, pp. 35 & 53 in Ossian). Grief is sometimes excessive like this, but for a short time only; at other times no regret is shown. Tom Brown showed *no* sorrow, smoked pipe as he dug grave (this exceptional case); Benjamin really cut up, but his boy unconcerned at death of mother; Nathaniel's father-in-law much affected by his death" (20).

67 *Silapaaq*: a jacket drawn on over the head.

68 *Amaut*: jacket worn by nursing mother, with a large lined pouch over the back in which the child may be carried.

69 Robert Abram Bartlett (1875–1946), son of Capt. William Bartlett and later a distinguished fishing captain, sealer, and commander of Arctic explorations for Peary and Stefansson.

70 *Tasikqut*: a tool for stretching boots, skins, etc.

71 See *Evening Herald*, 14 August 1893.

72 Thrush: a children's disease of the mouth and throat.

73 Curwen declares in his notebook that women were maintained on site as a source of cheap labour: "Women on schooners & on shore: looked upon as necessary to cook & keep house clean & they as a rule split & head better than the men; they receive £7 or 8 whereas a man wants £20 to split fish. 'The girls have nothin' to do, just sat down and larkin' about: nothing to do but just mend the men's clothes.' It seems a matter of expense. Mr. Isaac Bartlett (Domino) and Mr. Percy (Salmon Bight) do not think them

absolutely necessary though doubt if N.Fders will ever do without them; they admit the serious moral risks. Nova Scotia schooners *never* carry women" (78–9).

74 Judge D.W. Prowse, in his *History of Newfoundland* (1895), writes of one such vessel arriving in Brigus in 1868: "With many others I went on board the *Hunter*, and as long as I live I shall never forget the scene – the women and children, goats, pigs, and dogs, crowded in her hold. After seeing and smelling, I believe I can now form an idea of the horrors of the middle passage, and the odours and sufferings of the chained negroes in the slaver's hold" (603).

75 Curwen wrote to the MDSF, "I was anxious to go to Domino again, as it was the most dead-alive place I had seen on the coast, the secret being that there is plenty of liquor in the harbour; there is no need to ask questions as to the presence or absence of liquor in the harbours on the coast, it is apparent at once" (*Toilers* 8 [1893]: 380).

76 *British Medical Journal* and *Chronicle of the London Missionary Society.*

77 See Curwen's entry for 19 October and Grenfell's reports, above, which were published in *Toilers of the Deep.*

78 The Rev. Arthur Charles Waghorne, for seventeen years a missionary of the Church of England, principally in the parish of New Harbour, and a relentless collector of plants. Ill health had forced him to retire, and having no means of subsistence he hoped to derive income from the sale of his collection of plants. He was spending the summer in Labrador collecting. See notice in *Banner of Faith* 4 (1885): 346–7; pamphlet [Arthur C. Waghorne], "To Botanists of Europe and North America: Newfoundland and Labrador Plants," [1893]; and Arthur C. Waghorne, "The Flora of Newfoundland, Labrador and St. Pierre et Miquelon," *Proc. and Trans. Nova Scotian Inst. Sci.* 8 (1890): 359–73, and 9 (1891): 83–100, 361–401.

Waghorne may have written a letter published in the *Harbour Grace Standard*, 10 March 1893, responding to Grenfell's reports of deficiencies on the Labrador coast the summer before. It reads in part, "It is remarkable how little Dr. Grenfell and the 'Toilers of the Deep' say about the moral and religious condition of our Labrador people. Probably this is because they have found that, though they be half-starved, they are not so outrageously wicked or indifferent to religion as the English North Sea fishermen. Morally and religiously our people, though perhaps nothing to boast about, may safely be claimed as being far ahead of the English working classes. They have had some to look after their welfare long before the MDSF ventured in the field." The debate over whether the mission had exaggerated conditions on the coast continued for decades, and the following spring there was another exchange of letters between Labrador missionaries of the local churches (see *Daily News*, 24 March, 25 April, 6 June, 25 June, 17 July, and 2 August 1894.)

79 For a description of the reopening of the hospital the following summer, see Dr F.W. Willway, "Twenty-six Years Ago," *Toilers* 35 (1920): 22–4, 35–9, and 50–2.

80 Bobardt writes of his visit to Caribou Island in *Toilers* 9 (1894): 42, "These people are by no means well off, and it was from this settlement that I obtained the young boy of nine years whom I have sent to England in the *Albert* this year. He is a bright little fellow, and has worked hard. With the consent of his father – he has no mother – I took him at first to the hospital and kept him there, sending him to school. As he turned out so well, I had him shipped on the *Albert* as assistant cook, &c."

81 Kate Douglas Wiggin, *Timothy's Quest: A Story for Anybody, Young or Old, Who Cares to Read It* (Boston and New York: Houghton Mifflin 1890).

82 Sir Edgar Rennie Bowring (1858–1943), then director of Bowring Bros, Ltd, a noted philanthropist and later Newfoundland high commissioner in the United Kingdom.

83 Michael Patrick Cashin (1864–1926), elected to the House of Assembly as Liberal member for Ferryland in 1893.

84 George Shea (1851–1932) had been Liberal MHA for Ferryland, 1885–93.

85 The campaign was even more vituperative than Curwen suggests. D.W. Prowse writes in *A History of Newfoundland* (London: Macmillan 1895) that "both the political parties vied with each other in keeping up this indecent carnival of scurrility. There was not even a stray gleam of coarse humour to palliate the nauseous dose" (531). The final standing was as follows: Liberal 23, Conservative 12, Independent 1. The Conservatives subseqently brought charges of bribery and corruption; as a result, sixteen members were found guilty of gaining votes with the promise of government work and were unseated. After a series of complex negotiations, twenty-one by-elections were held in 1894. Whiteway himself was defeated in the general election of 1897.

86 Illustrated British journal begun in 1891.

87 Robert Gillespie Reid (1842–1908), contracted by the Newfoundland government to build the Hall's Bay Railway in 1890 and the trans-island railway to Port aux Basques in 1893.

88 For a natural history of the Newfoundland caribou, heavily illustrated with photographs and map, see A.A. Radclyffe Dugmore, *The Romance of the Newfoundland Caribou* (Philadelphia: J.B. Lippincott; London: William Heinemann 1913).

89 Name borrowed from a site to the south of St Paul's Cathedral, London.

90 Style of cap with fur ears and front flap, worn by Uhlan cavalryman, or lancer.

91 Before leaving Newfoundland, Grenfell, Curwen, and Bobardt made a journey to Harbour Grace, where on 20 November Grenfell gave an illustrated lecture in St Paul's Hall, followed by short addresses by Curwen and Bobardt. A newspaper reported that Grenfell was "a lecturer of no mean order by his fluent, intelligent remarks, under which flowed a pleasing current of humour" (*Harbour Grace Standard*, 21 November 1893). On 23 November, another public lecture was given at the Star of the Sea Hall, St John's, in the presence of the governor (*Evening Telegram*, 24 November 1893).

92 Stewart Munn & Co. acted as receivers and shippers for Labrador and Newfoundland herring, cod, salmon, and trout. See Frederick William Terrill, comp., *A Chronology of Montreal and of Canada* (Montreal: John Lovell & Son 1893).

93 John Bartholemew Gough (1817–86), British-born temperance lecturer.

INDEX

Index

Whiteley, William, 65, 221n39
Whiteway, Sir William, xx, xxviii, 17, 18, 25, 219n11
Wilcox, Samuel (Batteau), 57

Wilcox, Walter (Batteau), 58, 59, 66
Williams, Sister Cecilia, xix, xx, xxx–xxxi, 35, 58, 92
Wilson, James A., 88–9, 222n42

Women in the fishery, xxii–xxiii, 117, 163, 225n73

Zoar, 125, 130